TALKING TO STRANGERS:

Mediated Therapeutic Communication

COMMUNICATION AND INFORMATION SCIENCE

Edited by
BRENDA DERVIN
The Ohio State University

Recent Titles

Laurien Alexandre • The Voice of America: From Detente to the Reagan Doctrine

Bruce Austin • Current Research in Film Volume 4

Barbara Bate & Anita Taylor • Women Communicating: Studies of Women's Talk

Donal Carbaugh • Talking American: Cultural Discourses on Donahue

Kathryn Carter and Carole Spitzack • Doing Research on Women's Communication: Perspectives on Theory and Method

Benjamin M. Compaine • Issues in New Information Technology

Gladys Ganley & Oswald Ganley • Global Political Fallout: The VCRs First Decade 1976–1985

Gladys Ganley & Oswald Ganley • To Inform or to Control Revised Edition

Gerald Goldhaber & George Barnett • The Handbook of Organizational Communication

Enrique Gonzalez-Manet • The Hidden War of Information

Gary Gumpert & Sandra Fish • Talking to Strangers: Mediated Therapeutic Communication

Cees Hamelink • The Technology Gamble: Informatics and Public Policy—A Study of Technological Change

Carrie Heeter & Bradley S. Greenberg • Cableviewing

Robert Jacobson • An "Open" Approach to Information Policymaking

Meheroo Jussawalla, Donald L. Lamberton & Neil D. Karunaratne • The Cost of Thinking: Information Economies in the Asian Pacific

Manfred Kochen • The Small World

John Lawrence and Bernard Timberg • Fair Use and Free Inquiry Second Edition

Robert Picard et al. • Press Concentration and Monopoly

Carl Erik Rosengren & Sven Windahl • Media Matter: TV Use in Childhood and Adolescence

Michael Rogers Rubin • Private Rights, Public Wrongs: The Computer and Personal Privacy

Ramona R. Rush & Donna Allen • Communications at the Crossroads: The Gender Gap Connection

Jorge Reina Schement & Leah Lievrouw • Competing Visions, Social Realities: Social Aspects of the Information Society

Jennifer Daryl Slack & Fred Fejes • The Ideology of the Information Age

Charles H. Tardy • A Handbook for the Study of Human Communication

Majid Tehranian • Technologies of Power: Information Machines and Democratic Prospects

Sari Thomas • Studies in Mass Media and Technology, Volumes 1–4

Carol Weinhaus & Anthony G. Oettinger • Behind the Telephone Debates

TALKING TO STRANGERS:

Mediated Therapeutic Communication

Gary Gumpert

and

Sandra L. Fish

Editors

ABLEX PUBLISHING CORPORATION
NORWOOD, NJ 07648

Library of Congress Cataloging-in-Publication Data

Talking to strangers : mediated therapeutic communication / Gary
   Gumpert and Sandra L. Fish, editors.
      p.   cm. — (Communication and information science)
   Includes bibliographical references.
   ISBN 0-89391-490-8 (cloth); 0-89391-626-9 (ppk)
   1. Mass media in counseling. I. Gumpert, Gary. II. Fish, Sandra
L. III. Series.
   RC466.3.T35 1989
   616.89'14—dc20   89-17817
                                           CIP

Ablex Publishing Corporation
355 Chestnut Street
Norwood, New Jersey 07648

Table of Contents

The Authors

Robert K. Avery (Ph.D., Pennsylvania State University) is professor of communication at the University of Utah in Salt Lake City. A former radio announcer and broadcast administrator, Professor Avery serves as academic advisor to KUER-FM and research consultant for KUED-TV. His principal areas of interest include public broadcasting, telecommunication policy, and the study of mediated encounters. He is founding editor of *Critical Studies in Mass Communication.*

Jane Banks (Ph.D., Ohio State University) is assistant professor of speech communication at Syracuse University, Syracuse, New York. Her interest in rhetoric, mass communication, and criticism began with her dissertation on editorial cartoons. She has written on the pornography debate, the image of technology on television, and Mary Kay cosmetics, as well as of Dr. Ruth. Her research interests include mediated interpersonal communication, cultural studies, feminist and Marxist criticism, and corporate cultures.

Dean C. Barnlund (Ph.D., Northwestern University) is professor of interpersonal and intercultural communication at San Francisco State University. He is the co-author with Stanley Jones and Franklyn Haiman of *Dynamics of Discussion,* and author of *Interpersonal Communication: Survey and Studies, Public and Private Self in Japan and United States* and *Communicative Styles of Japanese and Americans: Images and Realities.* His theoretical and research papers have been published in a variety of professional journals ranging from anthropology to communication to psychiatry.

Jacqueline C. Bouhoutsos (Ph.D.), founder and president of the Association for Media Psychology, is a clinical psychologist in independent practice in Santa Monica, California. Clinical professor of psychology at UCLA, she is a graduate of the University of California, Berkeley, and the University of Innsbruck, Austria. She currently chairs the Ethics Committee of the California State Psychological Association and the Committee on International Relations in Psychology of the American Psychological Association.

Robert Cathcart (Ph.D., Northwestern University) is professor of communication arts and sciences at Queens College of the City University of New York. He coedited, with Gary Gumpert, three editions of *Inter/Media: Interpersonal Communication in a Media World,* and is coauthor with Gary Gumpert of numerous articles, including ''Media Grammars, Generations, and Media Gaps'' which appeared in *Critical Studies in Mass Commu-*

nication and "I am a Camera: The Mediated Self" which appeared in *Communication Quarterly*.

Susan J. Drucker (J.D., St. John's University) is an attorney and assistant professor of communication arts at Hofstra University. Her primary areas of interest include media law and the effects of media upon the practice and concept of law. She is the author of "Cameras in the Courtroom: The Changing Legal System" published in *The New York State Bar Journal*. She is co-author, with Janice Platt, of "The Debating Game" which appeared in *Critical Studies in Mass Communication*.

Sandra L. Fish (Ph.D., Southern Illinois University) is Associate Professor of Communications at Ithaca College, Ithaca, New York. A former crisis counselor and president of the board of directors of Suicide Prevention and Crisis Service of Tompkins County, Inc., she is affiliated with Training for Change, Inc., Ithaca, New York. She is president of the Eastern Communication Association, 1989–90. Her principal areas of interest are therapeutic communication, gender and communication, multicultural communication, and bureaucracy. She has published in *Journal of Applied Communication Research* and in *The Bureaucratic Experience* by Ralph Hummel.

Patricia J. Fleming (Ph.D.) has a degree in English and has taught writing and communication and has done research on techniques used in story-telling that manifest the search for self-integration. In addition, she is the head of Personal Growth Technologies in Cambridge, MA, and the developer of the interactive computer program, the Software Listener. A licensed social worker in Massachusetts and author of *Beyond coping: How To Form a Vocational Achievement Support Group,* she consults on expressive psychomotor therapy at a treatment center for chronic pain and maintains a private practice.

Virginia H. Fry (Ph.D., Ohio State University) is visiting assistant professor of communication science at University of Connecticut, Storrs, Connecticut. Her research interests include the rhetorical use of language, semiotics, and media and contemporary culture. An active member of several professional associations including Semiotic Society of America, she has published in *Communication Yearbook, American Journal of Semiotics, Journalism Quarterly,* and *Journal of Communication Inquiry*.

Roger L. Gould (M.D., Northwestern University) is a diplomate of the American Board of Psychiatry and Neurology and president of Interactive Health Systems. The author of numerous publications including *Transformations: Growth and Change in the Adult Years,* he is associate clinical professor of psychiatry at the University of California, Los Angeles, where he directed the Neuropsychiatric Institute Outpatient Department 1965–70.

Gary Gumpert (Ph.D., Wayne State University) is professor of communication arts and sciences at Queens College, City University of New

York. He co-edited, with Robert Cathcart, three editions of *Inter/Media: Interpersonal Communication in the Media World,* and is coauthor, with Robert Cathcart, of numerous articles including "Mediated Interpersonal Communication: Toward a New Typology" which appeared in the *Quarterly Journal of Speech* and "Stereotyping: Images of the Foreigner" in *Intercultural Communication: A Reader.* He is the author of *Talking Tombstones and Other Tales of the Media Age.*

Laurel Hellerstein (Ph.D., University of Massachusetts) studied at the University of Arizona at Tucson before completing her BA and MA degrees in broadcast communication arts at San Francisco State University. Her area of interest is the work- and nonwork-related use of computer-mediated communication systems.

Stewart M. Hoover (Ph.D., University of Pennsylvania) is assistant professor of communication at Temple University, Philadelphia. He is the author of several articles and two books, *The Electronic Giant* (Elgin, IL: Brethren Press, 1982) and *Mass Media Religion: The Social Sources of the Electronic Church* (Beverly Hills: Sage, 1988), as well as co-editor with Robert Abelman of *Religious Television: Myths and Realities* (Norwood, NJ: Ablex, 1988). He conducts research on communication technology and traditionalist and religious cultures in the United States and in the developing world.

Gary L. Kreps (Ph.D., University of Southern California) is professor of communication studies, Northern Illinois University, where he is director of the corporate communication Resources Network. He is also a partner in Denton, Kreps & Weckerly Ltd. advertising agency. His research focuses on the role of communication in human organizations and the dissemination of health information in society. He is the author of numerous articles and books, including *Health Communication* with B. C. Thornton (New York: Longman, 1986); in 1985–86 he served as a senior research fellow at the National Cancer Institute, helping to direct formative evaluation of their Physicial Data Query on-line cancer information system.

Lindsy Van Gelder (B.A., Sarah Lawrence) is a free-lance writer and former newspaper reporter and columnist. She has written for *Omni, Town and Country, Rolling Stone, Vogue, Ms.,* and *Business Monthly* and has been contributing editor for *Ms.* and *PC Magazine.* She was one of the semifinalists in the NASA Journalist in Space Program and has been listed in Who's Who in American Women, Who's Who of Emerging Leaders of America, and Who's Who in the East.

Lawrence A. Wenner is Associate Dean of the College of Arts and Sciences and Professor of Communication Arts at the University of San Francisco where he holds the Louise M. Davies Chair of Contemporary Values in America for 1989–1990. He is formerly Director of the Media

Studies and Management Programs at Loyola Marymount University, a University Fellow at the University of Iowa (Ph.D., 1977), and a coeditor of *Media Gratifications Research* (Sage, 1985). He serves on the editorial board of a number of journals and his research has appeared in such journals as *Communication Research, Communication Monographs,* and the *Journal of Broadcasting and Electronic Media.* His current research combines media criticism and audience experience, with a special focus on media-based subcultures and interpretations of media texts in sport, rock and roll music, and other areas of popular culture.

Jody H. Wrightson (M.A., Kansas State University) is a doctoral student in communication at Ohio State University, Columbus, Ohio. Her interests are rhetoric and social change, and therapeutic communication.

Introduction

Gary Gumpert
Sandra L. Fish

We live in a complicated world, one in which we have access to distant places and times past. Contemporary life is served by a history of technological innovation and scientific development. It is a world in which technology, particularly communication technology, has been absorbed into the very fabric of everyday existence so that its presence is either expected or invisible. Automobiles, telephones, electricity, washing machines, radio, air-conditioning, computers, typewriters, satellites, airplanes—the list of inventions is endless. We are a part of an industrial society that has inherited the impact of several millennia of technological transformation. While it is patently clear that the world has been changed by the accelerated pace of technological innovation, it is less clear what the effects such drastic and both evolutionary and revolutionary changes have had on the nature of human relationships and needs.

Human beings are shaped by the past and they evolve in the present. The journey of change has been accompanied by determining forces that are not always understood. Societal fate is, in part, somewhat controlled by constraints other than those choreographed by the free will of individuals. Human beings have sought to transcend and extend the restrictions of their physical selves and have created communication technology to serve such purposes. While that technology was created to serve the needs and desires of society, it also continues to shape the needs that motivated its existence as well as to channel those needs into socially acceptable forms.

In all probability our needs and expectations for physical comfort have changed quite radically over the course of history. The demands for shelter, transportation, sanitation, nutrition, clothing, and even communication are quite different from the expectations of our distant ancestors. On the other hand, our psychological needs and expectations have remained relatively constant. We need love and we fear loneliness. We seek privacy but avoid isolation. We require spiritual support to answer the mystical questions of the soul that can never be answered definitively. We want support of our sexual identities and require approval for actions that are not always clear. We desire counsel and guidance when we are confused, weak, misled, or ill. But while the need for such satisfaction of the spirit remains a common quest for most people, the manner and fashion in which we satisfy these needs has been altered radically as the structure of society has changed.

The nature of our social relationships has changed with the reshaping of those places in which we work, play, and live. Industrialization and population have altered the social structure in which we exist and the way we connect with each other. The German sociologist Ferdinand Tonnies described and contrasted the traditional structure of "community" with the newer construct of "society." Tonnies called the former *Gemeinschaft*—an organization in which the constituents were bound together through tradition, friendship, and kinship. This refers to a community bound together by reciprocal sentiment. The community bound together by contract and division of labor and characterized by fluctuating dynamic relationships was referred to as a *Gesellschaft*:

> All intimate, private, and exclusive living together, so we discover, is understood as life in *Gemeinschaft* (community). *Gesellschaft* (society) is public life—it is the world itself. In *Gemeinschaft* with one's family, one lives from birth on, bound to it in weal and woe. One goes into *Gesellschaft* as one goes into a strange country. (Tonnies, 1963, pp. 33–34)

The traditional concept of community is linked to place and territory. It is intimately connected with relationships that radiate from contact and the cooperative awareness that individuals have in "labor, order, and management" (Tonnies, 1963). This model of community is essentially preindustrial and its primary focus is the family along with the obligations, values, and responsibilities that govern and preserve that body. Tradition, respect, ritual, deep bonds, and commitment characterize this construct. The shift from an agrarian to an industrial economy requires the development of a complex societal organization along with the development of new services, the relocation of workers, and the establishment of new patterns of housing.

Further, the increasing bureaucratization of modern life exacerbates feelings of alienation and meaninglessness. Ralph Hummel (1987) argues that bureaucracy is, in fact, replacing society as the primary form of interaction, reshaping and influencing people's ways of relating. In particular, he suggests that communication in bureacracy becomes one-way and ultimately ceases to exist because it no longer involves the *mutual* creation of meaning. The result is that people have decreased communal connections, responding and reacting to the command of organizational authority rather than the demands of community relationships.

The closely knit community is weakened—perhaps it even disappears—within the organizational structure of the *Gesellschaft*:

Gesellschaft, an aggregate by convention and laws of nature, is to be understood as a multitude of nature and artificial individuals, the wills and spheres
of whom are in many relations with and to one another, and remain nevertheless independent of one another and devoid of mutual familiar relationships. (Tonnies, p. 76)

The obligatory commitments, although perhaps not the functions and
needs, of community are dissipated in relationship patterns not bound by
the restrictions of geography.

Human beings have been emancipated from the boundaries of place
through transportation and communication technology. The train, plane,
and automobile create a potentially mobile population free to relocate with
time and opportunity. The newspaper and magazine capsulize the events
of the world and present them to the reader. The telegraph and telephone
transcend space and provide intimate and immediate connection. The
camera and photography preserve and retrieve memory. Community
which was linked to the sharp demarcation of territory dissolves. The identification between self and neighborhood, village, or town recedes into the
background as the contact and identification with myriad other points on
the globe becomes a reality. Community which was rooted in face-to-face
dialogue between two or more persons in the same place has been replaced
by the "media community." Contemporary dialogue is not restricted to *a*
place since the media of communication have dispersed or expanded the
possibilities through the reallocation of space.

In their analysis of urban structure, Melvin Webber and Carolyn Webber (1967) indicated the importance of media in the recognition of "community without propinquity" or "non-place" communities—association
where spatial proximity is not a necessary condition for community.

With few exceptions, the adult American is increasingly able to maintain
selected contacts with others on an interest basis, over increasingly great distances; and he is thus a member of an increasing number of interest-commu-
nities that are not territorially defined. (Webber, 1964, p. 111)

We inhabit spaces without the obligations that accompany community. In
the contemporary urban/suburban world most persons are potential members of a series of "non-place" communities. Such multiple membership
constitutes a person's "media community." These communities do not require the simultaneous physical presence of its members at one site, since
they are constituted by the connective facilities of print and electronic
media.

It could be said that the contemporary citizen has lost his or her community, but gained the world. That shift is characterized by an increasing emphasis placed on privacy and anonymity as values which guide lifestyles

and behavior. Neighbors are reduced to the nodding recognition of face and name, but without the obligations that accompany the more traditional concept of community. Family and relations are scattered and held together by occasional reunions and frequent telephone calls. However, not everyone has gained access to this new world; the means by which one becomes a member of a technological society depends in part on class and economics.

It is difficult to describe the loss of traditional community without some sense of judgement. The ledger of positive and negative attributes depends very much on point of view. Instead of responsibility without choice, freedom is gained. Instead of rigid moral codes, experimentation and pragmatics predominate. Instead of an expected support system, an ad hoc system of comfort is devised. There are a number of indications that the absence of *Gemeinschaft*, a lack of required connection with a community of propinquity, has left some sort of void not met by family or by media connections—the degree of mindless and passive media interaction in which we engage, the increasing need for mental health agencies and service to alleviate malaise, and the rise of media forms dedicated to therapy.

All human beings experience periodic depression, emotional barriers, disappointments; all require the love and understanding of others who listen and respond with encouragement and support.The opportunity for supportive interaction historically has been built into the structure of community of place. However, as the community of place recedes in the urban environment and is replaced by media connection, as the church and synagogue lose their functional identity, as public areas facilitating social intercourse such as pubs and cafes have either dwindled in number or are populated by strangers, as neighbors are replaced by newcomers, the natural and necessary cathartic interaction between two or more concerned persons is transformed into a therapeutic community dedicated to that specialized task. The function of therapy has probably always existed in some shape or form, although not always labeled and recognized as a separate and distinct human activity.

Therapy is a term which can be defined from a number of perspectives. For our purposes therapy can be defined as

> a prolonged series of contacts between a professionally trained person and someone seeking help; its focus is exclusively on the patient and his problems; it attempts to relieve or remove symptomatic behaviors that interfere with effective work or social relationships; its aim is to bring about a substantial change in perspective through interpretation or clarification; a variety of technical means be used to supplement verbal interaction. (Barnlund, 1968, p. 614)

Bellah et al. (1985) propose the existence of a "therapeutic attitude" premised on self-knowledge and self-realization which "emerges most fully in the ideology of many practitioners and clients of psychotherapy, but resounds much more broadly in the American middle class" (p. 98).

Over the past several decades there has been a rising demand for mental health services, particularly individual and group therapy. State, county, and private agencies provide psychiatrists, psychologists, and social workers for those in search of help. In addition, the increasing number of consciousness-raising, meditation, encounter, support, sensitivity, assertiveness training, and sexuality groups is nothing short of phenomenal. Small groups of individuals oftenguided by a trained leader meet regularly to discover and discuss the problems that plague their daily lives. These are therapeutic communities in which the participants interact in order to reveal, empathize, and discover how to cope with the intricacies of life.

It would be difficult to prove categorically a relationship between the proliferation of mental health services and the changing structure of society. However, it seems reasonable to assume that those functions which collectively constitute the mental health sector were originally integrated in the normal operations of community life, and with the transformation of community into the contemporary urban life structure, those services became recognized and operationally institutionalized. It is also probable that the nature of societal structure may indeed be linked to the creation of psychological and social problems. Communication media are a part of that societal structure and both contribute to and alleviate to the tensions of contemporary life in ways we are still discovering. Contemporary life is so complex and each component so intertwined with other factors that it is impossible to sort out a single factor as a cause of a psychosocial problem.

The need for psychological counseling and the transformation of societal response to that need does not end with the institutionalization of the process. It becomes absorbed into one of the forces that influenced and stimulated the reshaping or reorganization of social structures in the first place—communication technology. For example, in this century the telephone has fostered the restructuring of the family in that it facilitated separation but stressed contact. Today the telephone is an essential medium for psychological counseling which may, indeed, be linked to the need for a support system formerly provided in part by the family. The communication technology which responds to the social and psychological needs of human beings also alters those original needs and perhaps even creates a different set of problems. Indeed it can be argued that *mediated therapeutic communication,* if not therapy more generally, functions as a palliative, soothing the symptoms and masking the underlying problems of the distribution of power.

As the concepts of professional therapy, therapeutic interaction, and the treatment of psychological distress become central to the welfare and functioning of society, they also become the subject of film, television, novels, and news. In short, they become an important content of mass media. The result is not merely that entertainment and news feature the subject of therapy, but that in the long run the practitioners of the "therapeutic" are inevitably influenced by what they perceive in the media. How psychologists, social workers, and psychiatrists perceive themselves and their clients; what clients expect from the mental health profession; and our everyday attitudes toward the "therapeutic" are in all probability influenced by the presence of the therapeutic process in those media upon which we are dependent for news and entertainment. While we are aware of this influence, it is not the primary focus of this book. An analysis of media depictions of the therapeutic process would, however, be an interesting adjunct to *Talking to Strangers*.

Talking to Strangers seeks to explore the various ways in which media of communication serve the therapeutic needs of contemporary society. It grew out of our recognition that a growing and important phenomenon was emerging which was being reported on by few communication scholars. In this task we seek not to judge but to clarify and analyze; we have selected a group of authors who describe what we refer to as the phenomenon of *mediated therapeutic communication* and its many variations.

This volume does not take a critical stance, although such a perspective might add insight and suggest social or political solutions. In order to clarify the goals of *Talking to Strangers*, it might be helpful to articulate what it is not. It is not an endorsement of technological development or therapeutic means nor is it a social critique of a system which institutionalizes the mental health of its citizens. It is an explication and analysis of a current phenomenon in which media and "therapy" have become fused. It is not a historical account of how media developed to serve therapeutic needs, but it does seek to identify some of the ways in which the media function in the institutional sense of therapy. The case might be made that the bulk of mass media programming is therapeutic, in that violence may or may not be linked to purgation or that pornography may or may not be connected to the satisfaction of sexual desires, or that laughter is a requirement of a healthy society, but such a perspective is not within the scope of this book. This is not a survey of how the mass media do or do not serve the mental health of a nation. Instead, the position is taken the no medium was created as a "mass" medium, that no medium is inherently biased or linked to public policy. One must distinguish between the intrinsic properties of a medium and its institutionalization by the society in which it functions. Therefore, *Talking to Strangers* does not explain *why* media are used in a particular therapeutic fashion, but seeks instead to elucidate *how*.

As we began to explore the phenomenon and search for contributors to this volume, it became clear that there were many dimensions from which the concept of *mediated therapeutic communication* could be examined. Part of our problem was to clarify and describe the theme, scope, and audience of this volume to our potential authors. Another task was to create the whole concept by collecting the appropriate and insightful scholarly parts. Thirteen essays have been written expressly for *Talking to Strangers;* three have been previously published elsewhere. Each of the selected authors brings a unique background and point of view to bear on the problem. Seventeen participants have contributed to 16 essays. Four of our authors' orientations come from outside the communication field—a social worker, a journalist, a psychiatrist, and a clinical psychologist. The communication scholars represent a broad spectrum of the discipline of communication: interpersonal, organizational, rhetoric, semiotics, media and broadcasting, and law.

Collectively, a number of analytical paradigms are utilized and are explicit or implicit in most of the essays:

THE THERAPY–THERAPEUTIC PERSPECTIVE

What is the difference between "therapy" and "therapeutic"? When is "advice" transformed from a spontaneous recommendation or opinion into an institutional formula? Whether the current ambiguity in regard to the definition of "therapy" and "therapeutic" can ever be resolved and agreed upon is problematic. Often it is the context of therapy or the therapeutic which defines its function. Several authors in this volume attempt to clarify the problem.

THE MEDIATED–THERAPEUTIC PERSPECTIVE

The presence or absence of a medium in either the therapeutic or therapy situation alters that process. For example, the interposition of a medium into cases of psychological counseling becomes a variable which confounds the traditional evaluation of the process. A number of authors approach *mediated therapeutic communication* from the perspective of a specific medium—telephone, computer, radio, television, and print.

THE PUBLIC–PRIVATE CONTINUUM

Some forms of *mediated therapeutic communication* such as the crisis line, are private; others such as "Dr. Ruth's" sexual advice delivered on radio and television or "Dear Abby's" advice printed in the daily newspaper are addressed to an individual but intended for public consumption. *Mediated therapeutic communication* can be dyadic and private as well as dyadic and public. Talk radio, computer, telephone, and radio therapy can be group-oriented and either private or public. Thus the nature of such therapeutic situations involves different degrees of risk taking and disclosure since anonymity is often a requisitefor participation. A number of authors examine the private and public facets of *mediated therapeutic communication* and several articulate the legal and ethical implications involved.

INTENTIONAL–UNINTENTIONAL FUNCTIONS

In the case of commercially-oriented radio and television broadcasts, functional ambiguity of *mediated therapeutic communication* is built into programs. Such programs exist on several levels. Some of these mediated events are clearly intended as therapeutic while they simultaneously serve the function of entertainment. Radio psychologists advise troubled individuals who take advantage of the opportunity to talk to an expert. At the same time that advice is heard by a public which tunes in either vicariously or for the sake of entertainment. Indeed, the producers of such programs filter out those callers whose problems are not interesting, that is, potentially entertaining. The dualistic character of mass communication ventures is a central issue discussed in several of the essays.

INTERACTIVE–PASSIVE PARTICIPATION

Most of the manifestations of the *mediated therapeutic communication* are interactive, that is, they involve one individual with another or with computer software that serves as the proxy of another. Passive participation characterizes the ubiquitous listener to public mediated events. A major question regarding participation is the degree to which the changed nature of mediated interaction has created "spectator communities." The presence or absence of interaction as well as its quality becomes an important analytical factor through which *mediated therapeutic communication* is appraised by several of our authors.

We begin the volume with four chapters which lay the groundwork for the concept of *mediated therapeutic communication*. Dean Barnlund distinguishes therapy and therapeutic communication, and Gary Kreps extends the distinction into current institutionalized and mediated forms. Robert Cathcart and Gary Gumpert describe the various ways media may be used interpersonally; Jacqueline Bouhoutsos defines "media psychology" and the role of the media psychologist. Based on these frameworks, the remainder of the chapters address the plethora of media which in various ways facilitate therapeutic communication: Chapters 5 through 7 examine instances of advice/entertainment in the mass media. Chapters 8 through 10 describe interactions via computer networks. Chapters 11 through 13 identify ways in which a medium enables therapeutic caregivers to expand their services. Chapter 14 is a look at legal and ethical implications of mediated therapeutic communication. Chapters 15 and 16 deviate from the one-to-one interaction characterizing most of this volume and provide an adaptation of *mediated therapeutic communication* in a larger context—televised religious programming and mediated sports. In each chapter the author analyzes the therapeutic function of the medium, revealing the pervasiveness of new "media communities."

This volume directs attention to new ways of thinking regarding the interrelationships among media, interpersonal interaction, and therapeutic communication. We hope that it serves as a stimulus for continued creative exploration.

G.G.
S.L.F.

REFERENCES

Barnlund, D. C. (1968). Introduction to therapeutic communication. In D. C. Barnlund (Ed.), *Interpersonal communication: Survey and studies* (pp. 613–645). New York: Houghton Mifflin.

Bellah, R. N. et al. (1985). *Habits of the heart: Individualism and commitment in American life.* Berkeley: University of California Press.

Hummel, R. P. (1987). *The bureaucratic experience* (3rd ed.). New York: St. Martin's Press.

Tonnies, F. (1963). *Community and society* (C. P. Loomis, Trans. & Ed.). New York: Harper Torchbooks.

Webber, M. W. (1964). The urban place and the nonplace urban realm. *Explorations into urban structure.* Philadelphia: University of Pennsylvania Press.

Webber, M. W., & Webber, C. C. (1967). Culture, territoriality and the elastic mile. In H. W. Eldredge (Ed.), *Taming megalopolis: Vol. I. What is and what could be.* New York: Anchor Books.

1

Therapeutic Communication

Dean C. Barnlund

The distinction between "therapy" and "therapeutic communication," eloquently articulated in "Introduction to Therapeutic Communication" (Barnlund, 1968) foreshadowed the development of a major new conceptualization in communication. His characterization of the qualities of therapeutic communication serves as a primary organizing principle for the analyses in this volume.

Incomplete communication between people seems to be the rule rather than the exception. It is said that if, in a lifetime, one meets even two or three persons with whom one feels completely free and completely understood, one is fortunate. The list of complaints is endless: People do not take time, do not listen, do not try to understand, but interrupt, anticipate, criticize, or disregard what is said; in their own remarks they are frequently vague, inconsistent, verbose, insincere, or dogmatic. As a result, people often conclude conversations feeling more inadequate, more misunderstood, and more alienated than when they started them. Yet the partial success of most human exchanges and the dramatic impact of occasional moments of interpersonal rapport prompt people to seek more meaningful relationships with each other. Partial communication, though less than totally satisfying, seems infinitely better than no communication.

Advice on the conditions that promote healthy communication might be sought in the writings of novelists and playwrights or in the observations of prophets and philosophers, but the particular material to be examined here derives from scientific study of the therapeutic interview. The unifying theme is that in the interaction between patient and therapist one may obtain insight into principles of communication that facilitate interpersonal understanding and that might be applied more widely in the conduct of human affairs. This thesis is phrased succinctly by Rogers (1961, p. 330): "We may say then that psychotherapy is good communication within and between men. We may also turn that statement around and it will still be true. Good communication, free communication, within or between men, is always therapeutic."

The belief that communication and therapy are inextricably related is shared by therapists of many allegiances. Some describe psychotherapy as an intensified form of interpersonal communication; others refer to the therapist as an expert in handling disturbances of communication, and still others note that helping the client develop greater interpersonal competence is the aim of treatment. Despite many terminological and conceptual differences, there is common recognition that therapy is essentially an interpersonal and communicative process. Any research that clarifies the nature of interpersonal communication should be of interest to the therapist, and conversely, studies that demonstrate the nature of the therapeutic process should have a bearing on the ordinary, nonclinical interactions of people.

There are reasons for avoiding a new term like "therapeutic communication." It may sound presumptuous to some and be unclear to others. A number of substitutes are available—the terms "healthy," "facilitative," and "functional" have all been used to describe constructive communications—but there is little reason to shrink from this phrase if it will clarify the perspective adopted here. Interpersonal communications are destructive when they leave participants more vulnerable than before to the strains of future interactions; they are neutral when they add information but do not affect underlying values or attitudes; they are regarded as therapeutic when they provoke personal insight or reorientation and when they enable persons to participate in more satisfying ways in future social encounters.

It is useful, however, to distinguish between therapy and a therapeutic experience. Therapy usually involves a prolonged series of contacts between a professionally trained person and someone seeking help; its focus is exclusively on the patient and his problems; it attempts to relieve or remove symptomatic behaviors that interfere with effective work or social relationships; its aim is to bring about a substantial change in perspective through interpretation or clarification; a variety of technical means may be used to supplement verbal interaction. A therapeutic experience, on the other hand, may involve an interview with a professional therapist or spontaneous conversation with associates; talk may range over a variety of topics or focus on an issue that concerns only one of the participants; this process is carried on through ordinary discussion in which there is nearly equal participation; catharsis or insight may accompany such an encounter, but these are more often accidental than intended consequences. Greater awareness of self and one's effect upon others may result from such experiences, but dramatic changes of personality are less frequent. Our purpose in examining research on psychotherapy is to identify some of the principles of communication that govern interaction between therapist and patient, particularly those that may be applied more widely to ordinary encounters between teachers and students, supervisors and workers, and husbands and wives.

The vastness of the literature on therapy makes a complete summary impossible. Such a survey would have to include the writings of Freud, Jung, Adler, Rank, Rogers, Sullivan, Horney, and many others. It would have to describe existentialist, transactional, surgical, milieu, pharmacological, interactional, and group therapies, as well as religious revivals, thought control, and primitive healing. Even marriages, wars, lectures, depressions, and ordinary friendships have produced profound changes of personality. To limit consideration only to recognized forms of "talking cures" still leaves a formidable bibliography.

The object here is more modest: to provide a capsule description of several leading theories of personality disorder and the approach each adopts toward the treatment process, and then to concentrate on the actual conduct of the psychotherapeutic interview. The aim is simply to identify the principles that make it possible for one human being, through his or her presence and manner of communicating, to create conditions conducive to the effective functioning and personal growth of another. A closer integration of clinical and nonclinical psychological research, as Lennard and Bernstein (1960, p. 1) point out, may help to enrich both fields: "Our position is that the social sciences and the depth psychological fields (such as psychiatry and clinical psychology) have developed concepts of useful description and analysis of human interactions of all kinds, whether they occur in a therapeutic setting, a family setting, a political decision-making group, or a social work supervisory conference. In our view, many of the basic questions regarding the nature of interaction, communication, influence and change are the same for all the relationships listed."

APPROACHES TO THE THERAPEUTIC INTERVIEW

A brief description of three approaches to the therapeutic interview may provide an introduction to research on this topic. These therapies differ substantially in their philosophical and psychological assumption as well as in their communicative techniques. They are chosen from more than a dozen prominent therapies, partly because they hold a distinctive view of the treatment process and partly because there are research data on the manner in which their advocates actually conduct interviews.

PSYCHOANALYTIC APPROACH

The original, most widely known, and most extensively practiced form of therapy is that of psychoanalysis. Its theoretical rationale and methods of treatment derive mainly from the writings of Sigmund Freud. In the analytic view, the individual is driven by compelling aggressive and sexual drives which are brought under control through internalization of social standards. During infancy and childhood, through parental punishment, restriction, and encouragement, these primitive forces are channeled into socially acceptable forms of behavior. Each person works out different modes of accommodating the conflicting demands of self and society, expressing some impulses directly, repressing others, and displacing still others. The antecedents of adult behavior, both healthy and neurotic, must be sought in the habits of adjustment acquired in childhood, particularly through emotional attachment and interaction with powerful socializing agents such as parents.

Inevitably, many do not make the transition from child to socialized being successfully, and most persons appear to carry some psychic scars as a result of this transitional process. Such scars are revealed occasionally in dramatic antisocial acts, but they appear more often in subtler forms of neurotic and irrational behavior. The object of psychoanalytic treatment is to discover the pattern of these distortions in patients, probe their sources, and through insight help them to attain freedom to develop more satisfying modes of relating to others. The "fundamental rule" observed in the analytic interview is that the patient be encouraged to talk as freely as possible, with no attempt to censor his or her thoughts. The physical arrangement of the office and the analyst's uncritical acceptance combine to encourage the patient to verbalize repressed experience and thus make it accessible to treatment. This uninhibited flow of thought and feeling seems to serve a cathartic function and to be instrumental to diagnosis. The private symbolism of dream and fantasy provides further means of making the unconscious conscious and of identifying crippling inner conflicts. The therapist is active, listens attentively, maintains neutrality, and is particularly attuned to handling the patient's "resistances." Accurate identification of these psychic defenses and proper timing of interpretations of their functions are essential in dissipating them.

If free association and its accompanying interpretation is one axis of psychoanalytic treatment, the use of the therapist-patient relationship to change attitudes and behavior is the other. The authority, knowledge, insight, and parental concern of the therapist plus the patient's confidence in and dependence on him or her contribute to the development of "transference." Because of the patient's emotional attachment to the therapist, the patient tends to interact with the therapist along lines laid down in his early experiences with significant adult figures. The "working through" of this prototypic human relationship in its positive and negative aspects is a way of focusing on inappropriate and rigid patterns of interpersonal behavior. The tasks of the analyst are to encourage freer communication and to help patients obtain deeper insight into themselves.

CLIENT–CENTERED APPROACH

Among the most prominent and influential of the newer approaches is client-centered therapy. Its basic premises and procedures derive from the experience and writings of Carl Rogers, although he has often acknowledged the collaboration of his associates in developing and testing its methods. Rogers posits an innate drive to actualize the self in growth-promoting ways as the single motive behind human behavior. To guide this effort, the individual depends on his or her perception and symbolization of events, not on the events themselves. When a person is open to the inner and outer aspects of his experience, he will value and act in ways that are individually and socially constructive. This innate valuing process is not intellectual or mechanical but is imbued with feeling. During childhood, one develops a concept of the self along with a need for the positive regard of others. If the regard of others were unconditional, the child would continue to trust his own experience; but since others often evaluate him conditionally, he must choose between an external locus of evaluation (satisfying them) or an internal one (following his own impulses). To prevent the anxiety this dilemma creates, he or she defensively denies or distorts aspects of his own experience, thereby becoming estranged from himself. As Rogers has written (1959, p. 226), "He has not been true to himself, to his own natural organismic valuing of experience, but for the sake of preserving the positive regard of others has now come to falsify some of the values he experiences and to perceive them only in terms based upon their value to others." Without access to all relevant inner and outer facets of his perceptions, his valuing becomes self-defeating rather than self-enhancing. When denial or distortion are inadequate as defenses, or when these devices are forced beyond their capacity, disorganization of personality follows. The client-centered view of personality development has been extended to include a description of the fully-functioning person and of the improving or deteriorating interpersonal relationship.

The aim of client-centered therapy is to restore the client's lost capacity to trust his own impulses and feelings. In this process, the therapist's attitude is more crucial than his techniques, as Rogers has often emphasized. The client rather than the therapist is responsible for the goals of therapy, deciding within the interview what to talk about and when. The therapist's function is to create a permissive climate for communication and to convey his unqualified regard for the client. In his occasional responses, the therapist does not advise, diagnose, or evaluate positively or negatively; he or she conveys only a continuing interest, understanding, and respect for the feelings that are expressed. The principle means of communicating these attitudes is the "reflective response," in which the therapist verbalizes as carefully as possible what he understands to be the ongoing perceptions of the client, free of all interpretation or judgment. Since the interview is under the control of the client rather than the therapist, some have described this as a "following" rather than a "leading" therapy, although "accompanying" might be a more apt designation. Because the client is in a nonevaluative yet acceptant interpersonal relationship, his defensive distortions become unnecessary; he can admit all aspects of his experience, and he is free to make growth-promoting and socially constructive decisions.

LEARNING THEORY APPROACH

Unlike therapies which arose from the necessity of treating behavior problems, learning theory developed out of efforts to conceptualize a basic psychological process. No single theorist can be credited with its formulation; the influence of many scientists, including Pavlov, Hull, Miller, Dollard, Skinner, and Mowrer, is apparent. Learning theory includes much more than a method of treating maladjustment, but it has been provocatively applied to this problem. Since personality disorders and social inadequacy are themselves learned, the treatment process may also be seen as a learning or relearning experience. "Psychotherapy," according to Dollard and Miller (1950, p. 78), "establishes a set of conditions by which neurotic habits may be unlearned and nonneurotic habits learned." Perhaps because learning theory originated in an experimental rather than a healing context, it is the most rigorously stated of contemporary therapies and the most amenable to experimental verification.

Most learning manifests a common set of conditions. Innate or acquired drives prompt the individual to act, the specific form of his response being determined by situational cues. Particular reaction sequences are reinforced when their consequences effectively reduce the strength of the original drive. Reinforcers may include any object or event from a merit badge to an appreciative smile. Through reward or reinforcement certain behavior patterns become learned; through lack of reinforcement they are extinguished. Although situations are never identical, behavior tends to generalize beyond the circumstances in which it was first elicited. Behavior disorders occur as a result of the arousal of incompatible drives or incompatible responses. These conflicts are particularly intense when they are of the approach-avoidance type, and when they involve powerful emotions, especially fear. If caught persistently in this sort of dilemma, the individual ceases to attend to relevant internal or external factors, either suppressing (consciously) or repressing (unconsciously) relevant cues. Consequently, he or she behaves inappropriately, and the compromise solutions used to reduce discomfort often involve personally distressing symptoms, such as compulsions, phobias, delusions, rationalizations, and the like. These ineffective patterns become fixated and their sources remain hidden.

The aim of treatment is to reduce the paralyzing emotional bind of the patient, help him clarify and label underlying conflicts, and thus enable him to make a more flexible adjustment. The therapist accomplishes these aims through a number of measures: By encouraging free association in a permissive setting he helps extinguish the anxiety aroused by certain thoughts and situations; by helping the patient verbalize inner conflicts he makes them accessible to reason and promotes more discriminating behavior; through reinforcement he supports the patient's efforts to work out more adequate ways of satisfying basic needs. Learning theorists stress that the status, warmth, and empathic capacity of the therapists are important in producing constructive change.

Although theories of pathology and rehabilitation are not the major focus of this essay, the descriptions above provide a background and terminology for closer analysis of therapist-patient communication in the therapeutic interview.

THE THERAPEUTIC PROCESS

Since people spend the greater part of their lives interacting with each other, it is not surprising that a large part of what is called mental disorder or social inadequacy results from the way they communicate. A number of factors contributing to destructive patterns of behavior have already been suggested in previous sections. Psychological damage may result from social isolation, incompatible roles, ambiguous and conflicting message cues, status barriers and personal devaluation, and from critical or threatening remarks. Any of these may cause persons to become more anxious, insecure, or fearful about entering into full communication with other people,or may cause them, when required to interact, to rely on self-defeating maneuvers, such as selective inattention, verbal deception, stereotyping, over- or underverbalization, maintenance of facades, protective belligerence, or other forms of pseudocommunication.

It is the object of treatment, of course, to reverse this pattern—to increase the ease and accuracy of communication with self and others so that the individual may act more flexibly, more independently, and in growth-promoting rather than growth-inhibiting ways. This reversal is sought in most therapies through full and accurate communication between therapist and patient. Psychotherapy, at its best, according to Rothman and Sward (1958, p. 177), involves a "special sort of two-person relationship in which patient and therapist succeed in communicating with the least possible distortion and with a maximal degree of mutual understanding and responsiveness."

The purpose in reviewing research on the process of psychotherapy is to identify interactional principles which, if applied, might improve communication generally. But the attempt to derive such principles is subject to two limitations. The first one of vocabulary. Since each school has developed its own terminology, it is difficult to make precise comparisons of methods and outcomes. The second limitation is one of history. Because of the confidential nature of their contact with patients and their lack of training in experimental procedures, therapists have shown little interest until recently in the objective study of the treatment process. In 1935, Lasswell (1935) made an initial attempt to relate verbal and physiological changes during the therapeutic interview. But it was not until a decade later, through the encouragement of Rogers (1942), that serious analysis was undertaken. Accurate records were kept, categories of messages tested, and attempts made to relate process and outcome variables. Although scientific study of the therapeutic process now proceeds along a broader front, it is still far from balanced; nearly all the available findings relate to the three schools described above (plus that of group psychotherapy), and are not equally distributed even among these. Any conclusions, therefore, must be qualified because of limitations in the data.

PERSONAL RELATIONSHIPS OF THERAPIST AND PATIENT

The "therapeutic situation is not a place," according to Cameron (1947, p. 585), "but an interpersonal relationship." Nearly every prominent form of psychotherapy emphasizes the importance of the presence of another person and the creation of a particular kind of interpersonal rapport as prerequisite to constructive change. Rogers (1957), for example, states that the first of the necessary conditions for therapeutic changes is that two persons be in psychological contact with each other. But, since many interpersonal contacts are far from therapeutic, the specific character of the patient–therapist relationship must be described.

INTERPERSONAL CLIMATE

Most therapists feel that the general tone of the therapeutic encounter should be permissive. In negative terms, this means the absence of external threat, interference, or evaluation; in positive terms, it means the presence of a comfortable, trusting, and secure relationship. The disturbed person is usually in difficulty because critical aspects of his or her experience are unavailable to the person because of repression, denial, or distortion, and his or her relations with others are thereby crippled. In the therapeutic setting clients are "permitted" to express, to explore, to evaluate any impulse or response. While the therapies discussed here do not agree at every point on the characteristics of a desirable therapeutic relationship, they all emphasize the constructive value of permissiveness in reducing anxiety, in opening areas of unconscious experience, and in making repressed perceptions available to conscious examination.

Although social atmospheres are difficult to measure objectively, a number of investigators have explored the nature and consequences of an accepting interpersonal relationship. Asking college students to describe their expectations about persons highly motivated to help them, Thomas, Polansky, and Kounin (1955) found that they expected a person in a helping relationship to be easy to talk with, to maximize the areas open to discussion, to minimize embarrassment, and to be unlikely to disapprove. Coons (1957) compared the therapeutic value of participating in a permissive discussion group in which no reference was made to personal problems with participating in one which stressed diagnosis of individual difficulties. Patients in the permissive communicative setting made significantly better adjustment, suggesting that acceptance and interaction may have therapeutic value in the absence of any deliberate treatment.

Somewhat more precise appraisal of the effects of a nonevaluative setting is obtained from experiments within the framework of learning theory (Krasner, 1962; Bandura, 1961). Affective states such as fear or anxiety have been shown to decrease through lack of reinforcing responses by the therapist. Dittes (1957), for example, found that the permissive responses of a therapist produced progressive decline in fears associated with embarrassing sexual statements; Murray (1954), too, discovered that the accepting behavior of a therapist reduced defensiveness in a mental patient. "Atmosphere" effects in verbal conditioning studies show that emotional tension tends to dissipate in a nonevaluative climate. Apparently, as Dreikurs (1961, p. 82) has stated, the therapeutic interview is the first time for many to "experience an interpersonal relationship in which they don't have to be afraid, in which they feel understood, in which they encounter a certain amount of permissiveness, of acceptance, in which, for the first time in their lives they can reveal their deficiencies and their sins without losing status and worth which in itself is a therapeutic factor."

Permissiveness, of course, may have its limits. Scher(1960) has indicated that a moderately structured situation may be better for hospitalized patients than one that is very permissive or merely custodial. Rothman and Sward (1958) also warn that persons differ in their need for support, so that permissiveness may be perceived by some as a cold, uninterested, or even threatening attitude. Yet, by and large, there is consensus for the opinion expressed by Strupp (1960, p. 256): "The presence of a climate of warmth, love, and understanding would thus constitute a precondition for the exploration and living through of painful experiences, which is often necessary for emotional growth." An attitude of acceptance—in or out of the therapeutic context—would appear to encourage deeper awareness, more complete perception of self and others, and more flexible behavior.

CHARACTERISTICS OF THE THERAPIST

The therapist himself (or herself) may be a major agent of change. Though there are few studies linking specific attributes of the therapist to success in treatment, the impact of his or her status, interpersonal attitudes, and professional qualifications cannot be overlooked.

As with any agent of change, there is reason to expect that the therapist's position, age, authority, and reputation affect the patient's trust in him or her. In research on learning, experimenter prestige and attractiveness were found to influence the amount learned. Shapiro (1960) and Krasner (1962) have noted what the placebo effect contributes to therapeutic gains: The symbolic role of the physician rather than his medicine may account for the patient's recovery.

Credibility, which has been shown to be a potent force in persuasion, seems to operate in the treatment process, as suggested in Frank's recent book (1973), *Persuasion and Healing*. In an experimental analogue of the therapeutic situation, Bergin (1963) tested the role of credibility in affecting attitudes toward sexual identity. College students, after being given discrepant interpretations of their masculinity-femininity, were found to change their subsequent self-estimates on these dimensions only when the source of the interpretation was a highly credible one. The respect normally granted to those in the healing professions thus may enhance the potential of the therapist; reputation, education, and special training are likely to add to his or her persuasiveness. There is danger, however, of overrating the influence of such static factors. Credibility has usually been studied in settings involving a single contact with an unknown person rather than in the more intimate and prolonged relationship required by therapy.

More critical may be the personal characteristics the therapist displays within the therapeutic setting. Rogers (1957) has described six "necessary and sufficient" conditions for personal growth, most of which involve attitudes the therapist expresses within the interview itself. The first is that the therapist be congruent and genuine in his relations with the client, fully aware of his own experience. Denial or falsification of his reactions may only complicate the problems of a patient whose difficulties result from self-deception. Congruency on the part of the therapist may induce it in the patient, and thus it may become a therapeutic force. A second condition is that the therapist experience unconditional positive regard for the client, that he be able to accept the client as he is and may become. This respect frees the client from the necessity of continuing to deny any part of his feelings, positive or negative. A third attitude described by Rogers is that the therapist be capable of empathic understanding. He must be able to participate fully in the experience of the client, assuming the client's internal frame of reference without being threatened by it or confusing it with his own. Evidence that such involvement is more than merely verbal is provided by DiMascio, Boyd, Greenblatt, and Solomon (1955), who found that physiological changes in therapists accompanied changes in the emotional states of their patients.

Direct testing of the importance of these therapist attitudes has been carried out by Barrett-Lennard (1962). Inventories completed by clients at four different times during therapy demonstrated that empathic understanding, positive regard, and congruence contributed significantly to therapeutic gains, and that expert therapists scored higher on these qualities than nonexperts. None of these personal attributes is significant, of course, unless the therapist is able to communicate so that the client actually experiences his acceptance, warmth, interest, understanding, and congruence.

Many leading therapies would endorse these conditions, adding further prescriptions of their own. Dollard and Miller (1950), for example, characterize the ideal therapist as possessing mental freedom, empathy, restraint, and a positive outlook. It is not clear if the therapist must be an extremely well-adjusted person, although Bandura (1956) has concluded that the better adjusted and less anxious he is, the more effective his therapy.

Most schools of therapy prescribe the professional qualifications of the therapist explicitly and elaborately. Analytic approaches specify a rigorous medical or psychological background, extensive technical preparation, and personal analysis. Others stress the need for advanced psychological knowledge, training in the use of diagnostic tests, and internship. Specialized training is thought to equip the therapist with the necessary interpretive skills, provide him or her with a theoretical rationale for understanding the patient, and cultivate confidence in his or her methods. An opposing position is taken by Rogers (1957), who does not see psychotherapy as a special relationship different from all other constructive human relationships. Since the underlying values and personal attributes of the therapist are more critical factors than diagnostic skill, extensive technical preparation is not a prerequisite for facilitating growth in others. Advanced training is of value only if it increases the therapist's own congruence and empathic range. Although they disagree on professional requirements, nearly all therapies appear to emphasize the importance of communication, and to provide specific training in the interactive skills required in the therapeutic interview.

CHARACTERISTICS OF THE PATIENT

Most therapists place some restrictions on the persons they will accept for treatment. In "talking cures" there is a greater chance of success if the patient is of at least average intelligence and has minimal ability to communicate his experience. It is considered desirable, if not essential, that the client develop respect for the therapist and confidence in his or her ability to help. Anticipation and acceptance of the probability of change, along with willingness to become involved in the treatment process, is essential in effecting change. Most critical, however, is that the person be aware of his own anxiety, discomfort, incongruence, or inadequacy, and that this awareness prompt him to undergo a stressful communicative experience to achieve a higher degree of personal integration. Strong motivation for personal growth seems indispensable to all forms of therapy requiring participation.

THERAPIST–PATIENT COMPATIBILITY

No interpersonal relationship is sustained by a single participant, no matter how genuine or acceptant he or she may be. The specific needs, personal traits, and styles of communicating of both patient and therapist will necessarily limit the potential value of such encounters. The number of prematurely terminated and unsuccessful cases of therapy may reflect in part the limits of rapport. Carson and Heine (1962, p. 38) have hypothesized that "with very high similarity the therapist might be unable to maintain suitable distance and objectivity, whereas in the case of great dissimilarity he would not be able to empathize with or understand the patient's problems: In either case one might expect a decrement in therapeutic success." When 60 patient-therapist pairs were compared, it was found that both extreme similarity and extreme dissimilarity impeded progress—the former probably because of overidentification, the latter because of poor communication. In a study by Sapolsky (1960), patients in compatible patient-therapist pairs responded to verbal conditioning while those in incompatible pairs did not.

In several studies Fiedler (1951; Fiedler & Senior, 1952) found that better therapists tended to see more similarity between themselves and their patients, while patients of good therapists tended to idealize their therapists. A later study by Fiedler, Hutchins, and Dodge (1959) extended this principle beyond the formal therapy process. High assumed similarity in dormitory and military groups suggesting acceptant and close rather than distant and critical relationships was shown to have a therapeutic effect by contributing to reduced anxiety and increased self-acceptance.

The therapeutic relationship, despite its intensity, appears to possess many of the properties found in any healthy interpersonal setting. Shoben (1953, p. 126), for example, reflects the opinion of many when he writes: "If warmth, permissiveness, safety, and understanding seem to be prerequisites of any desirable human relationship rather than being peculiar properties of psycho-therapeutic interaction, this is precisely the case." Clinicians and patients, as well as teachers and students, were reported by Luft (1957) to agree in their rankings of statements describing the qualities of a helpful or harmful relationship. Parloff (1956), who arranged for experienced therapists to alternate in treating groups of patients, reported that the therapist who was able to establish the better social relationship also created the better therapeutic climate. Further evidence that interpersonal rapport may be most critical to therapeutic progress comes from studies by Whitehorn and Betz (1954). Comparing seven resident therapists whose patients had shown the greatest improvement with seven whose patients had shown the least, they found that the more successful therapists tended to view their patients as persons rather than as cases and to develop a close, trusting relationship with them.

Thus one of the dominant themes in both theoretical and experimental literature is that a healthy human relationship underlies much of the success of treatment. In the words of Wolstein (1954, p. 678), "For it is this direct and immediate contact with the analyst as a real person, based on the mutual understanding of both people in the interaction, which provides the patient with the secure knowledge that contact on an open and uncircuitous basis with another person is possible and necessary and perhaps even desirable." It is quite conceivable that the same basic attitudes manifested by a therapist in this special setting would create a solid basis for interpersonal communication in the wider social setting of the home, classroom, factory, and office. Rogers (1959, p. 188) has written: "At whatever times and in whatever relationships a person is free to be open and genuine about his own experience and sensitive to and acceptant of the experience of others, he may contribute to insight and growth in himself and another."

THERAPEUTIC INTERPERSONAL COMMUNICATION

In attempting to extract principles of therapeutic communication from research on psychotherapy, it is important to recall the differences between formal treatment and ordinary conversation. Therapy involves contact between a trained specialist, who provides the setting and who structures the relationship, and a second person, who initiates interaction exclusively to explore and obtain relief from his or her emotional problems. Such a relationship is aimed consciously at facilitating change in the person seeking help. Ordinary conversation involves an interaction between two or more persons playing a variety of roles, is initiated to satisfy a number of motives, covers a series of topics, and takes place in diverse settings. In a sense, everyday interpersonal engagements demand both more and less of participants in the way of communicative skills.

Yet the differences can easily be overemphasized and the underlying similarity obscured. The same processes operate in both, although the emphasis may differ. The object of interpersonal communication, as of therapy, is often to reduce alienation, to deepen awareness, to contribute to security of self and acceptance of others, and to increase the capacity to act independently and productively. What distinguishes "communication in therapy" and "therapeutic communication" is the element of intent: In the former the therapist deliberately creates a relationship which he or she believes will encourage growth in his patient; in the later, one person spontaneously responds in ways that permit constructive change in the other. The frequency of such instances of therapeutic interaction is suggested by Ruesch (1961, pp. 30–31):

> Therapeutic communication, therefore is not confined to an appointed hour in the doctor's office. On the contrary, it occurs almost anywhere—on the playfield, in battle, on the ward, at home, or at work. Neither is it bound to the use of certain props such as couch or chair, not does it run off according to a special formula. Generally therapeutic communication involves more than just the therapist and the patient. A child can be therapeutic for the mother and a boss can be therapeutic for his employee; therapy is done all day long by many people who do not know that they acts as therapists, and many people benefit from such experiences without knowing it. Therapeutic communication is not a method invented by physicians to combat illness; it is simply something that occurs spontaneously everywhere in daily life, and the physician is challenged to make these naturally occurring events happen more frequently.

Indeed, if society had to depend on a small guild of specialists to preserve its mental health, the human race would long ago have been destroyed by its own pathologies. But this has never been the case. There have always been people in all walks of life who have provided the silence or the words that brought insight or understanding. The aim here is merely to describe in summary form—drawing on research in psychotherapy—the attributes of a communicative relationship that are likely to contribute to personal growth in others.

1. A constructive communicative relationship is likely when there is willingness to become involved with the other person. This means willingness to take time, to avoid distraction, to be communicatively accessible, to risk attachment to others. The act of establishing communication may itself be therapeutic. A high level of verbal participation is unnecessary; the person need only be willing to concentrate on this situation, this person, and this message. Excommunication is a more common interpersonal event than a religious one; the act of cutting off persons who need to communicate is among the more destructive of human acts. It may take the form of disregarding those who are trying to establish interpersonal contact, but it also includes the rejection conveyed by posture or voice during a conversation. Involvement implies neither that one should be available to everyone regardless of circumstances, or that he aggressively turn every salutation into a serious conversation. It is important only that he be interested in others, and open to the meanings they express.

2. A constructive communicative relationship is likely when one or both persons convey positive regard for the other. The other is valued as a human being, not as an object to be coerced, manipulated, or used. He is prized for what he is and what he may become. Respect for his integrity is not affected by the specific things he may say, or feel, or do; positive acts do not increase his fundamental worth nor do negative acts diminish it. Such acceptance and concern are revealed by presence and attitude more often than by explicit statement.

3. A constructive communicative relationship is likely when a permissive psychological climate develops. Someone once observed that it is rare for anyone to get through a single day without being blamed for something, but it may be equally rare to get through a day without being praised. An atmosphere laden with positive or negative interpersonal judgments would seem to prevent a sensitive exchange of experience. The threat of disapproval forces communicants to distort what they think and feel; the possibility of approval encourages them to present facades that will create favorable images in the eyes of others. A permissive climate, one in which people seek to understand rather than to condemn or praise, allows communicants to express and explore their experience openly and honestly without the necessity of warping it to an external frame of reference.

4. A constructive communicative relationship is likely when there is the desire and the capacity to listen. Opportunity and encouragement to speak must be accompanied by motivation to attend to what is being said. This means listening without anticipating, without interfering, without competing, without refuting, and without forcing meanings into preconceived channels of interpretation. It involves a sensitive, total concentration on

what is explicitly stated as well as what is implied by nuances of inflection, phrasing, and movement.

In ordinary human relationships it is usually the teacher, the supervisor, the parent who is expected to do the talking, and the student, the worker, the child who is expected to listen. Research on communication in general, and on psychotherapy in particular, suggests that listening may be a more difficult communicative act than speaking. If so, it seems paradoxical that in so many interpersonal encounters it is the younger, the less informed, the less qualified, and the less secure participant who is given the heavier communicative responsibility.

5. A constructive communicative relationship is likely when empathic understanding is communicated. It is not enough to listen if one comprehends only in a detached or intellectual way. It appears to be more satisfying and helpful when the listener can participate fully in the experience of the speaker, sharing his or her assumptions, values, and motivation—seeing events as he or she sees them. Only through this kind of imaginative sharing in the phenomenological world of another person can one really sense how events appear to another and how another person feels about them. To do this requires some degree of personal security so that one is neither afraid to risk involvement nor likely to confound the experience with his or her own emotional reactions to it.

No matter how intently one listens to the meanings of another, it remains only a private experience until a reply is made that reflects the depth of this perception. Only when the originator of the message recognizes his or her intended meaning in the words of the receiver's response is the accuracy of that understanding clearly revealed. This is reassuring because it demonstrates that such experience can be shared successfully, and it encourages the speaker to continue to try to express even more elusive and complex personal meanings.

6. A constructive communicative relationship is likely when there is accurate reflection and clarification of feelings. Of all the verbal techniques of the therapist, this seems the most appropriate to apply more widely in the ordinary interactions of human beings. Argument, criticism, reassurance, sympathy, advice, even questions—all seem to interrupt or discourage the effort to communicate fully (though none of these responses may have as serious consequences for the secure person as they have for the seriously disturbed). But by rephrasing what has been heard, the listener encourages the other person to continue to explore his or her experience, and through his or her words provide a fresh perspective on these feelings. Moreover, probably no other form of response is so effective in conveying the positive regard, permissiveness, warm interest, or empathic understandings of the listener. Indeed, without these interpersonal attitudes, it

is doubtful that a listener could reflect feelings; with them, it is doubtful that any other response would come as easily or frequently.

7. A constructive communicative relationship is likely when the communicators are genuine and congruent. In stating a "tentative law of interpersonal relationships," Rogers (1959) stresses the factor of personal genuineness above all others. This suggests that the quality and depth of communication achieved interpersonally depends on the capacity of each person to be open to his own experience so that no feeling relevant to the relationship is denied awareness. It is the capacity to act spontaneously as a single, integrated organism rather than in a calculated and contrived way. With this intrapersonal sensitivity goes a willingness to express what is felt. Some have said it involves interpersonal transparency; others have described it as a full exposure of the self.

Clearly it is the opposite of presenting a facade, of consciously controlling what one feels or says or does in the interest of maintaining a particular image in the eyes of others. Deceit, given tangible form in inconsistent verbal and nonverbal cues, appears the major threat to the full exchange of views and feelings. Confrontation is converted from a genuine face-to-face encounter into a mask-to-mask interaction in which a communication of experience is replaced by a communication of clichés.

It should be repeated that interpersonal communication is dynamic rather than static; it tends to move either in destructive or therapeutic directions. Openness, acceptance, congruence, interest, and empathy in one person tend to permit these responses in others, contributing to an increasingly healthy atmosphere for the direct and sensitive exchange of experience. Similarly, the presence of a person who is defensive, indifferent, manipulative, hypercritical, and incapable of recognizing meanings in others contributes to an atmosphere that is competitive and alienating. A number of the attitudes manifest in the therapeutic setting seem directly applicable to the encounters of people in offices, classrooms, factories, in fact, in every context in which people are striving to understand the enigma of interaction.

CONCLUSION

Perhaps the deepest psychic need of humans is to symbolize experience within themselves and to communicate it meaningfully to others. "It is in interpersonal relations," wrote Foote and Cottrell (1955, p. v), "that man [sic] achieves the highest development of his humanity and gains the greatest satisfaction and happiness. It is also in interpersonal relations that men and women may be most thwarted and dehumanized and rendered most miserable."

So much publicity has been given to the ways people build barriers within and between themselves that some have surrendered to the view that the competitive, materialistic, depersonalized, and frenzied nature of modern life make close and creative contact between people impossible, or at best, infrequent and accidental. But in the therapeutic milieu, where communicative inadequacy and communicative sensitivity meet, one can observe some of the principles that foster personal development and social maturity. The research suggests that the more genuine, accepting, open, and empathic each person is, and the more each values the experience of the other, the more likely it is that their communication will contribute to the effective functioning and personal growth of each.

REFERENCES

Barnlund, D. C. (1968). *Interpersonal Communication: Survey and studies.* Boston: Houghton Mifflin.

Bandura, A. (1961). Psychotherapy as a learning process. *Psychology, 52,* 100–104.

Bandura, A. (1956). Psychotherapist's anxiety level, self-insight and psychotherapeutic competence. *Journal of Abnormal and Social Psychology, 52,* 333–337.

Barrett-Lennard, G. (1962). Dimensions of therapist response as causal factors in therapeutic change. *Psychological Monographs, 76* (562).

Bergin, A. (1963). The effect of dissonant persuasive communications upon changes in a self-referring attitude. *Journal of Personality, 30,* 423–438.

Cameron, N. (1947). *The psychology of behavior disorders: A biosocial interpretation.* Boston: Houghton Mifflin.

Carson, R., & Heine, R. (1962). Similarity and success in therapeutic dyads. *Journal of Consulting Psychology, 26,* 38–43.

Coons, W. (1957). Interaction and insight in group psychotherapy. *Canadian Journal of Psychology, 11,* 1–8.

DiMascio, A., Boyd, R., Greenblatt, M., & Solomon, H. (1955). The psychiatric interview, a sociophysiological study. *Diseases of the Nervous System, 16,* 4–9.

Dittes, J. (1957). Extinction during psychotherapy of GSR accompanying "embarrassing statements." *Journal of Abnormal and Social Psychology, 47,* 187–191.

Dollard, J., & Miller, N. (1950). *Personality and psychotherapy.* New York: McGraw-Hill.

Dreikurs, R. (1961). The Adlerian approach to therapy. In S. Stein (Ed.), *Contemporary psychotherapies* (pp. 68–87). New York: Free Press.

Fielder, F. (1950). The concept of an ideal therapeutic relationship. *Journal of Consulting Psychology, 14,* 239–245.

Fiedler, F. (1951). A method of objective quantification of certain countertransference attitudes. *Journal of Clinical Psychology, 7,* 101–107.

Fiedler, F., Hutchins, E., & Dodge, J. (1959). Quasi-therapeutic relations in small college and military groups. *Psychological Monographs, 73,* 1–28.

Fiedler, F., & Senior, K. (1952). An exploratory study of unconscious feeling reactions in fifteen patient-therapist pairs. *Journal of Abnormal and Social Psychology, 47,* 446–453.

Foote, N., & Cottrell, J., Jr. (1955). *Identity and personal competence.* Chicago: University of Chicago Press.

Krasner, L. (1962). The therapist as a social reinforcement machine. In H. Strupp & L. Luborsky (Eds.), *Research in psychotherapy* (Vol. 2). Washington, DC: American Psychological Association.

Lasswell, H. (1935). Verbal references and physiological changes during the psychoanalytic interview: A preliminary communication. *Psychoanalytic Review, 22,* 10–24.

Lennard, H., & Bernstein, A., with Hendin, H., & Palmore, E. (1960). *The anatomy of psychotherapy: Systems of communication and expectation.* New York: Columbia University Press.

Luft, J. (1957). Healthy interaction: A composite clinical picture. *Journal of General Psychology, 57,* 241–246.

Murray, E. (1954). A case study in behavioral analysis of psychotherapy. *Journal of Abnormal and Social Psychology, 49,* 305–310.

Parloff, M. (1956). Some factors affecting the quality of therapeutic relationships. *Journal of Abnormal and social Psychology, 52,* 5–10.

Rogers, C. (1961). *On becoming a person.* Boston: Houghton Mifflin.

Rogers, C. (1957). The necessary and sufficient conditions of psychotherapeutic change. *Journal of Consulting Psychology, 21,* 95–103.

Rogers, C. (1959). A theory of therapy, personality, and interpersonal relationships as developed in the client-centered framework. In S. Koch (Ed.), *Psychology: A study of a science* (Vol. 3, pp. 184–256). New York: McGraw-Hill.

Rogers, C. (1942a). *Counseling and psychotherapy.* Boston: Houghton Mifflin.

Rogers, C. (1942b). The use of electrically recorded interviews in improving psychotherapeutic techniques. *American Journal of Orthopsychiatry, 12,* 429–434.

Rothman, T., & Sward, K. (1958). Pharmacologic psychotherapy—verbal communication in psychoanalysis and psychotherapy. In P. Hoch & J. Zubin (Eds.), *Psychopathology of communication* (pp. 177–210). New York: Grune and Stratton.

Ruesch, J. (1961). *Therapeutic communication.* New York: W. W. Norton.

Sapolsky, A. (1960). Effect of interpersonal relationships upon verbal conditioning. *Journal of Abnormal and Social Psychology, 60,* 241–246.

Scher, J. (1960). The concept of the self in schizophrenia. *Journal of Existential Psychiatry, 1,* 64–88.

Shapiro, A. (1960). A contribution to a history of the placebo effect. *Behavioral Science, 5,* 109–135.

Shoben, E. (1953). Some observations on psychotherapy and the learning process. In O. Mowrer (Ed.), *Psychotherapy: Theory and research* (pp. 120–139). New York: Ronald.

Strupp, H. (1960). *Psychotherapists in action: Explorations of the therapist's contribution to the treatment process.* New York: Grune and Stratton.

Thomas, E., Polansky, N., & Kounin, J. (1955). The expected behavior of a potentially helpful person. *Human Relations, 8,* 165–174.

Whitehorn, J., & Betz, B. (1954). A study of psychotherapeutic relationships between physicians and schizophrenic patients. *American Journal of Psychiatry, 8,* 667–678.

Wolstein, B. (1954). The analysis of transference as an interpersonal process. *American Journal of Psychotherapy, 8,* 667–678.

2
The Nature of Therapeutic Communication

Gary L. Kreps

Elaborating on Barnlund's definitions, this article traces the development of therapeutic communication into its current institutionalized forms, such as the various mediated formats discussed by other authors in succeeding chapters. Kreps describes the characteristics of the therapeutic communicator as well as the role of therapeutic communication in interpersonal and organizational relationships.

THERAPEUTIC COMMUNICATION

Carole King vividly describes the value of therapeutic communication when she sings, "When you're down and troubled and need a helping hand/And nothing, no nothing is going right/Just close your eyes and think of me/And soon I will be there/To brighten up even your darkest night." She captures the supportive, nurturing nature of therapeutic interaction, as human communication that helps individuals come to grips with and overcome the personal traumas they face. Communicating therapeutically means being available to interact with people who are suffering. Such communication can enable troubled individuals to increase their understanding of their condition, relieve their pain, and identify strategies for improving their particular problematic situations.

Yet therapeutic communication, for all its human value, is a form of human interaction that is largely misunderstood. "Therapeutic communication" sounds like a formalized health care procedure that is used only in clinical settings, administered by professionally credentialed health care providers to troubled patients in dire need of psychological help. This is a limiting and misleading stereotype that confuses psychotherapy, a specific branch of clinical psychology, with the more general expression of helping in human interaction, therapeutic communication. Clinical psychotherapy accounts for a very small percentage of all the instances when helping interaction (therapeutic communication) occurs. In fact, the clinical connotations of therapeutic communication as psychotherapy obscure the fact that therapeutic communication is a pervasive and ubiquitous form of in-

29

teraction that can potentially be provided by any person to anyone in just about any social setting.

Therapeutic communication has been defined in many different ways by communication, psychology, social work, and health care scholars (Barnlund, 1968; Fuller & Quesada, 1973; Pettegrew, 1977; Rogers, 1957; Ruesch, 1957; Truax & Carkhuff, 1967). However, the perspective taken by Barnlund (1968) seems to be the most enlightening, encompassing, and liberating approach to the subject (Kreps & Thornton, 1984). Barnlund (see Chapter 1) explains that interpersonal communication is therapeutic when it helps facilitate communicators' development of personal insight or reorientation, and when it helps individuals enhance their effectiveness and satisfaction with their future communication activities.

Barnlund's approach to therapeutic communication implies that individuals have the potential for communicating therapeutically if they can help another person understand him- or herself more fully, thereby aiding that individual in deciding how to direct personal communication behaviors to best achieve individual needs and goals. Furthermore, according to this perspective, interpersonal feedback is a key element of therapeutic communication. Therapeutic interpersonal feedback informs people about how they are being perceived by relevant others, offering these individuals a clear picture of the reactions people have to their communication. The ability to gather information about the critical reactions relevant others have about our behavior enables us to evaluate the relative effectiveness of the interpersonal messages we have sent and to develop appropriate communication strategies for future interactions to best achieve our goals.

Certainly all human communication is not therapeutic. Human interaction can often have nontherapeutic effects by confusing and frustrating communicators rather than helping them achieve personal insight and reorientation. Watzlawick, Beavin, and Jackson (1967) have identified several situations where interpersonal relationships can become pathological due to nontherapeutic communication. Pathologies are disturbances that make human communication problematic and dissatisfying, while therapeutic communication functions to ameliorate pathologies. Similarly, Ruesch (1957, 1961) has differentiated between therapeutic communication and disturbed communication, suggesting that human communication can range on a continuum from highly therapeutic to highly disturbed (nontherapeutic). Effective communicators maximize their use of therapeutic communication with others and minimize their use of pathological communication strategies to enhance the quality of their interpersonal relationships. Therapeutic communication can be used by effective communicators in many different social situations to help people grow, adapt their behaviors to cope with difficult situations, improve their self-esteem, and increase their satisfaction with interpersonal relationships and their lives in general.

Interestingly, the intention to communicate therapeutically does not guarantee that therapeutic communication will occur. Therapeutic communication can occur during strategically planned therapeutic interchanges as well as in naturally occurring therapeutic interactions. Therapeutic communication can be provided by those who are unaware they are being therapeutic. For example, spontaneous acts of social support and sharing of relevant feedback often have a therapeutic impact on interactants. Many communication episodes that are not directly intended to be therapeutic but provide individuals with liberating opportunities to express themselves in unique ways (for example, venting frustrations through screaming, painting, or even mud wrestling) can be very therapeutic. Similarly, many interactions where people receive stimulating messages (such as seeing a theatrical performance, listening to music, or hearing a lecture) can also have therapeutic influences on individuals.

Sometimes those who intend to help others, perhaps by being overly sympathetic or too directive, can have minimal therapeutic influence. For example, demonstrations of sympathy for the problematic conditions of others can often be interpreted by troubled individuals as the expression of pity, causing them shame and hindering their ability to cope with their problems. Similarly, individuals who attempt to "help" troubled others by habitually making important decisions for these people can decrease the troubled persons' self-esteem and limit their ability to cope with difficult situations without guidance, short-circuiting their opportunities to be therapeutic. Another typical social situation where individuals intending to be therapeutic end up being nontherapeutic is when interpersonal communicators provide troubled relational partners with "quick and dirty" solutions to their problems without allowing their partners to explore their problems by engaging in meaningful dialogue. These "quick solution helpers" do not generally help solve their partner's problems and in fact can exacerbate these problems by not allowing the troubled individuals the freedom to examine key issues and identify their own problem-solving strategies. The key to therapeutic communication is certainly not in the intent to be therapeutic but in the ability to engage individuals in liberating and cathartic interaction that enhances individuals' personal insight, vigor, problem-solving resolve, and satisfaction with themselves.

THE INSTITUTIONALIZATION OF THERAPEUTIC
COMMUNICATION

The ever-increasing complexity of life in the modern world subjects human beings to a wide array of challenges and constraints (Toffler, 1970). The many stresses in everyday life increase public need for therapeutic communication. The multiple specters of AIDS, nuclear holocaust, and economic disaster, for example, in addition to the stresses of inexorable change, create intolerable levels of distress. Yet, as the need for therapeutic communication has increased, traditional informal interpersonal sources of therapeutic communication from friends, family, and co-workers have decreased. For example, the family, which has traditionally been a primary source of social support for members, is less able than in the past to serve as a major outlet for therapeutic communication in everyday life. The breakdown of the extended family, the increase of divorce, and the increase of single-parent families has decreased the number of familial opportunities for therapeutic communication by decreasing the size of the family. Moreover, as the world has grown more stressful, interpersonal relationships have become less satisfying in personal and professional life (Kreps, 1986; Kreps & Thornton, 1984; Rossiter & Pearce, 1975). The growing depersonalization and dehumanization of personal and professional relationships have decreased opportunities for therapeutic communication from those individuals we interact with at home, at work, or at play.

In response to increasing demand for therapeutic communication and decreasing traditional informal outlets available for satisfying this demand, specialized institutional sources for therapeutic communication have developed and prospered in modern society. Institutional sources are formally designed programs, organizations, and media used to provide therapeutic communication to different segments of the public. Some of these sources are business ventures that charge fees for providing their customers with therapeutic communication, other institutionalized programs provide therapeutic communication as a free public service, while still other institutional sources of therapeutic communication are presented through the media as a form of public entertainment.

Professional providers of therapeutic communication such as counselors, social workers, clinical psychologists, and psychiatrists perform an increasingly important therapeutic communication function for the public (Kreps & Thornton, 1984). Therapeutic communication is also being provided through a wide range of communication media in modern society. For example, newspaper advice columns, radio talk shows, television programs with call-in segments, computer networks, and telephone hotlines are sought as popular sources of mediated therapeutic communication, each of which is explored in subsequent chapters. Perhaps the anonymity provided by these mediated sources of therapeutic communication accounts for their popularity. Mediated sources of therapeutic communication are less risky and personally threatening for users than more traditional face-to-face channels of therapeutic communication because users are generally not personally known or identified by providers. Additionally, users exert more control over mediated therapeutic communication than in face-to-face interaction because they control the medium they are using. For example, if users feel threatened by or dissatisfied with the interaction they can easily terminate mediated therapeutic communications by hanging up, disconnecting, or discontinuing use of their communication medium. Not only do new forms of media as therapeutic communication need to be explored, but also the relative constructive and destructive uses of such media must be examined carefully. The authors in this volume address themselves to these questions in various ways.

THE THERAPEUTIC COMMUNICATOR

Several specific communication skills and competencies have been identified that enable individuals to communicate therapeutically. For example, Rossiter and Pearce (1975, pp. 193–194) have described honesty and validation as two key characteristics of therapeutic communication; they contend that "honesty accompanied by validation results in psychological growth for persons and that the lack of honesty and validation is likely to retard psychological growth and possibly bring about psychological deterioration." Truax and Carkhuff (1967) have identified three key characteristics demonstrated by therapeutic communicators that are similar to those offered by Rossiter and Pearce. These characteristics include (a) accurate empathy and understanding; (b) nonpossessive warmth and respect; (c) genuineness and authenticity. Rogers (1957) has described therapeutic communication characteristics similarly, identifying such attributes as genuineness and congruence, unconditional positive regard, and empathic understanding. Kreps and Thornton (1984) provide a combination and synthesis of these different key characteristics of therapeutic communicators identifying *empathy, trust, honesty, validation,* and *caring* as the primary elements of therapeutic communication.

Empathy refers to the ability to develop a full understanding of another person's condition and feelings and relate that understanding to the person. It requires the ability to imagine how one might feel if placed in another person's position. Communicators can demonstrate empathy nonverbally as well as verbally for one another by accurately communicating the other's feelings in interpersonal interaction.

Trust is a belief that another person will respect the needs and desires of another and will behave toward that person in a responsible and predictable manner. Trusting behaviors are those that "deliberately increase a person's vulnerability to another person" (Rossiter & Pearce, 1975, p. 123). It is risky to exhibit trusting behaviors to another because the person may not respond in a responsible way. In establishing a trusting relationship it may be necessary for relational partners to increase their vulnerabilty by disclosing personal information to one another. If relational partners respond responsibly to self-disclosures and reciprocate by communicating risky personal information of their own, the chances that trust will develop are good. If, however, an individual reacts irresponsibly or inappropriately to another's self-disclosure, trust will not develop. Due to the risk involved in establishing trusting relationships, trust is most often established gradually and incrementally over long periods of time. Trust is a key ingredient in therapeutic communication because it encourages interactants to disclose key information and accept feedback from one another. The anonymity afforded by many mediated communication channels can enhance development of trust, because the consumer can be relatively secure that the person on the other end of the mediated channel cannot harm them. This is similar to the "stranger on the train" phenomenon, where people are willing to divulge their innermost secrets to individuals they know they are unlikely ever to see again. The anonymity of mediated therapeutic communication can insulate consumers from providers, helping to reduce consumers' perceptions of vulnerability and increase their willingness to trust the person on the other end of the mediated channel.

Honesty refers to the ability to communicate truthfully, frankly, and sincerely. There is never total honesty in any situation, because there is never total truth. People perceive the world according to their own perceptions of reality, and often people perceive the world very differently from one another. Honest communication, however, does not imply objective truth, but subjective truth. It is not purposely deceptive, but is intended to be a truthful representation of subjective reality as the individual knows it. People communicate honestly to the extent that their messages accurately express their awareness of their experience and invite listeners to share in that experience (Rossiter & Pearce, 1975, p. 55). Honest self-disclosure in interpersonal relationships implicitly invites reciprocal honesty by relationship partners. Honesty facilitates therapeutic communication because it helps provide interactants with accurate information and encourages the development of trust.

Just as trust can be increased or decreased by the reputation of the organization represented in institutional therapeutic communication, perceptions of the honesty of providers are also dependent on the public image of the organization. However, the honesty of the consumer may be even more critical than the honesty of the provider in mediated therapeutic communication since it is the consumer who initiates the therapeutic process through self-disclosure. Mediated communication may encourage deception since it is so easy for people to disguise their true motives over the limited information channels. It is easier for people to mask their voices over the phone or misrepresent themselves in a letter than it is to deceive others in person. However, just as the anonymity of mediated therapeutic communication can decrease consumers' perceptions of vulnerability, so also can it increase their willingness to disclose information honestly because there is less risk involved in divulging their true feelings. This is probably one of the reasons that the anonymity of the confessional in the Catholic church helps confessors disclose their sins to their priests.

Validation occurs when a communicator feels that other communicators accept and respect what he or she has to say. Validating communication affirms the worth of the person and his or her experiences. To validate another person doesn't mean relational partners have to agree with everything the other says, but rather that they respect each other's right to express their opinions and take what they have to say seriously. Validating communication tends to humanize interaction. It tells communicators that what they say is important to their relational partners and their partners are willing to be influenced by the interpersonal messages that are exchanged. Communicators can validate one another in interpersonal communication by listening carefully to what is being said and responding to others' messages congruently. Validating the worth of others encourages communicators to express their opinions frankly and accept interpersonal feedback and suggestions. One of the primary reasons for the growing use of mediated and institutionalized channels for therapeutic communication undoubtedly is the loss of personal validation in everyday life.

Caring refers to the level of emotional involvement communicators express for one another. It is what Rogers (1957) calls "unconditional positive regard," the demonstration of interest and concern for the other person's well-being. Caring communication must be sincere and appropriate to be useful. Communicators can demonstrate caring for one another by expressing genuine concern over the other's problems and communicating a willingness to help the other person work through their hardships. Nonverbally, communicators can express caring for one another by paying attention to what the other person is saying, exhibiting emotionally congruent facial expressions, and by using vocal and tactile behaviors to show supportiveness. Caring messages facilitate therapeutic communication by increasing the intensity and sensitivity of human interaction.

Contrary to its positive influence on the expression of validation, the institutionalization and mediation of therapeutic communication seems to influence the expression of caring negatively. People can be trained to pay attention, but can they really be trained to care? Mediated therapeutic communication runs the serious risk of being superficial and contrived. What are the motivations of providers of institutionalized therapeutic communciation? Are radio talk show hosts really concerned about their callers, or are they trying to entertain the rest of their listeners at callers' expense? Genuine caring seems to encompass a sense of personal involvement and connectedness, yet the anonymity of mediated institutional communication contacts tends to negate that involvement. It takes very special, sincere, and sensitive individuals to express genuine caring for anonymous others as part of their job, especially when separated from those others by a mediated channel. Caring may be the weakest link in the provision of therapeutic communication via mediated channels.

Each of the five characteristics of therapeutic communication (empathy, trust, honesty, validation, and caring) are important skills for effective communication. In many communication situations the five characteristics overlap. For example, validation, honesty, and trust can be expressed through mutual self-disclosure. Empathy, trust, honesty, validation, and caring are also reciprocally occuring human communication behaviors. That is, the expression of empathic, trusting, honest, validating, or caring communications generally induces a reciprocal expression in return by those communicated with. Due to the norm of reciprocity, the use of therapeutic communication can encourage other communicators to interact similarly, evoking a spiraling or building effect in therapeutic communication.

How does the process of mediation affect the demonstration of these characteristics of mediated therapeutic communication, particularly in a society where the model of helping is formalized therapy? For example, the absence of visual stimuli during telephone interactions or the lack of vocal and visual cues when using online computer networks, along with the lack of reciprocity, indelibly alters the therapeutic characteristics of that medium. The authors in this volume attempt to explicate the relationship between the mediated and the therapeutic processes in the various instances under examination.

THERAPEUTIC COMMUNICATION AND INTERPERSONAL RELATIONSHIPS

Human relationships are developed to serve many different functions, with therapeutic communication being a common and extremely important relational outcome. Interpersonal relationships can provide communicators with excitement, support, friendship, love, financial gains, and intellectual stimulation, as well as help increase or decrease relational partners' overall health status. The more therapeutic human communication is, the more it helps individuals involved in relationships increase their satisfaction with themselves, increase their satisfaction with their interpersonal relationships, and enhance individual's perceptions of their psychological and physical health (Kreps & Thornton, 1984).

Therapeutic communication helps the development of effective interpersonal relationships by providing communicators with information about the expectations others have for them, as well as providing information about their level of success at meeting other peoples' expectations. Therapeutic communication facilitates the development of effective implicit contracts between communicators. Implicit contracts are the often unspoken agreements communicators make with one another in interpersonal relationships to attempt to mutually fulfill each others' interpersonal expectations. Implicit contracts are based on both recognition of the expectations of others and willingness to fulfill these expectations. The better relational partners are at establishing, updating, and living up to implicit contracts, the more satisfying and effective interpersonal relationships become. Ultimately, therapeutic communication enables individuals to interact more effectively with one another to achieve their personal and relational goals.

THERAPEUTIC COMMUNICATION AND ORGANIZATIONAL LIFE

Therapeutic communication is especially important in business and professional life due to the high levels of competition, uncertainty, and stress individuals face in organizational life. Yet, political pressures, high levels of competition, insensitive communication, dehumanization, job stress, burnout, ethical dilemmas, and other problems in modern organizations suggest that much organizational communication is nontherapeutic (Kreps, 1986). Nontherapeutic communication is counterproductive to the goals of organizations because it fosters dissatisfaction among communicators and undermines the spirit of cooperation that is essential to effective relationships and organization.

Ironically, therapeutic communication is largely unappreciated in organizational life. Very few managers recognize that therapeutic communication is a primary tool they can use in their organizations. Few business courses stress the importance of therapeutic communication in motivation, problem solving, orientation, performance review, or personnel development. Yet therapeutic communication can play an important role in accomplishing a wide range of organizational goals. The use of therapeutic communication in formal organizations can help organization members cope with the many stresses and ambiguities of organizational life through reorientation, adaptation, and personal growth.

SUMMARY

Therapeutic communication is an important, yet underutilized, form of interaction that provides people with key information about how well they are meeting their own and others' expectations and enables individuals to effectively adapt their message strategies to achieve their goals. Therapeutic communication is especially useful in developing and maintaining effective interpersonal relationships. It is a form of interaction that has great potential for improving the quality of personal and professional life. By developing the ability to express empathy, trust, honesty, validation, and caring, communicators can enhance their abilities to interact therapeutically, increase the quality of their communication, and help others cope with the problems that confront them. Mediated channels of communication have developed as provocative new institutionalized sources for therapeutic communication which require analysis and evaluation.

REFERENCES

Barnlund, D. C. (1968). Introduction to therapeutic communication. In D.C. Barnlund (Ed.), *Interpersonal communication: Survey and studies* (pp. 613–645). Boston: Houghton Mifflin.

Fuller, D., & Quesada, G. (1973). Communication in medical therapeutics. *Journal of Communication, 23,* 361–370.

Kreps, G. (1986). *Organizational communication: Theory and practice.* New York: Longman.

Kreps, G., & Thornton, B. C. (1984). *Health communication: Theory and practice.* New York: Longman.

Pettegrew, L. (1977). An investigation of therapeutic communicator style. In B. Ruben (Ed.), *Communication Yearbook 1* (pp. 593–604). New Brunswick, NJ: Transaction Press.

Rogers, C. (1957). The necessary and sufficient conditions of psychotherapeutic change. *Journal of Consulting Psychology, 21,* 95–103.

Rossiter, C. M., & Pearce, W. B. (1975). *Communicating personally: A theory of interpersonal communication and human relationships.* Indianapolis: Bobbs-Merrill.

Ruesch, J. (1961). *Therapeutic communication.* New York: Norton.

Ruesch, J. (1957). *Disturbed communication.* New York: Norton.

Toffler, A. (1970). *Future shock.* New York: Bantam Books.

Truax, C., & Carkhuff, R. (1967). *Toward effective counseling in psychotherapy: Training and practice.* Chicago: Aldine.

Watzlawick, P., Beavin, J., & Jackson, D. (1967). *Pragmatics of human communication.* New York: Norton.

3
Mediated Interpersonal Communication: Toward a New Typology*

Robert Cathcart
Gary Gumpert

Cathcart and Gumpert (1983) articulate the theoretical basis for this volume by delineating the concept of mediated interpersonal communication *as distinguished from mass media. The interposition of a medium between two people* mediates *the communication in subtle yet definable ways by altering both the process and the content. The authors outline the various ways interpersonal communication currently may be mediated and forecast a new typology to include (a) interpersonal mediated communication, (b) media-simulated interpersonal communication, (c) person-computer interpersonal communication, and (d) unicommunication. Each of these categories described in the article is exemplified and analyzed in one or more chapters in this volume.*

In 1962, Franklin Fearing offered four generalizations about situations in which human communication takes place:

1. They are situations in which human beings enter into certain strategic relationships with each other or with their environment.
2. They are situations the central characteristics of which is the production and utilization of signs, symbols, and symbolic acts.
3. They are situations which provide a maximal opportunity through the use of signs and symbols for the sharing of experience, achievement of goals, gaining of insights and, in general, mastering one's environment.
4. The sign or symbols material used in these situations is subject to the perceptual process of the individual involved.

We cite this not as the preferred way of looking at communication, but rather as descriptive of the research interests of communication scholars.

---

* From "Mediated Interpersonal Communication," by Robert Cathcart and Gary Gumpert, August 1983, *Quarterly Journal of Speech, 69,* pp. 267–277. Copyright 1983 by the Speech Communication Association. Reprinted by permission.

It is interesting and provocative that nowhere in this situational map can "media" be located as an important component of human communication. The same is true for accepted definitions of communication. For example, communication is "the process by which an individual (the communicator) transmits stimuli (usually verbal) to modify the behavior of other individuals (the audience)" (Hovland, Janis, & Kelly, 1953, p. 12). Or, "Communication: The transmission of information, ideas, emotions, skill, etc. by the use of symbol-words, figures, graphs, etc." (Berelson & Steiner, 1964, p. 527). Definitions, particularly those used in the study of speech communication, have minimized the role of media and channel in the communication process. The focus has been on the number of participants, source, and receiver relationships, and forms and functions of messages. The media of communication have been accepted, more or less, as fixed or neutral channels for the transmission of messages among participants.[1] It is difficult to find an interpersonal communication text or resource book that treats the subject of media as a significant factor.[2] The role of media in personal communication, has, by and large, been overlooked.

Mass communication scholars have exhibited a concern with the individual's interaction with the mass media. Robert K. Merton (1949), Joseph Klapper (1960), and Wilbur Schramm (1954) have analyzed the effects of mass media on the individual. In 1962, Elihu Katz and Paul Lazarsfeld wrote *Personal Influence: The Part Played by People in the Flow of Mass Communication*. The subtitle is significant for it indicated the authors' emphasis on the role of the individual in the mass communication process rather than on the role media plays in shaping interpersonal behavior. Despite this orientation, most definitions of "mass communication" fail to take into account the influential role of media in interpersonal communication. A definition which holds that mass communication connotes all mass media of communication in which a mechanism of interpersonal reproduction intervenes between the speaker and the audience make "medium" synonymous with "mass communication." Such a definition does not suffice because it overlooks the role of the media in interpersonal interaction. *All media are not mass media.* Any so called mass medium can be used for point-to-point transmission, for example, "ham radio," and any point-to-point medium can be used to reach a mass audience, for example, "junk mail." Mass communication refers to a specific utilization of medium—a circumstance of communication in which a medium replicates, duplicates,

---

[1] See, for example, D. K. Berlo (1960 p. 31), who states that "channel is a medium, a carrier of messages." (p. 31) Also, F. E. X. Dance & C. E. Larson (1976) who make no mention of media as channel or medium as a variable.

[2] In developing the first edition of *Inter/Media: Interpersonal communication in a media world* (1979), we were unable to find text books which treated media as a significant variable in interpersonal communication. See, for example, D. C. Barnlund (1968), G. M. Phillips and N. Metzger (1976), J. Stewart and G. D'Angelo (1975).

and disseminates identical content to a geographically widespread population. Therefore, the term "media" does not characterize a distinct type of communication because it does not account for or suggest its use. In the typology of human communication, "media" should not be relegated solely to the category "mass communication," nor should it be excluded from the other categories: interpersonal communication, group communication, and public communication.

To bridge the definitional gaps and reconcile the role of media in human communication, the following should be added to Fearing's generalizations:

1. There are interpersonal situations which require media for the purpose of communication.
2. The media are part of a complex of variables that influence behaviors and attitudes.
3. The content of media is both a reflection and projection of interpersonal behaviors.
4. An individual's self-image and its development is media-dependent.

If these claims accurately reflect the realities of media and human interaction then we would argue that what is needed is a new typology which will include media technology. The new typology should incorporate the traditional concepts of communication with the role of technological media.

Any typology which overlooks pervasive, potent media functions and connections ignores an increasingly significant and complex aspect of human communication. It must be recognized that even intrapersonal communication is media-involved. Intrapersonal communication refers to the internal dialogue that occurs between the "I" and the "me"—the dual processing system where information received from outside is processed through the ego to form a self-image.[3] It is generally accepted that there can be no sense of self without interaction with others, that is, without role taking and feedback which corrects or verifies the outcomes of internal dialogues.[4] Obviously television, radio, and film provide feedback which reinforce, negate and/or verify an individual's self-image (Novack, 1977). Portraits developed in novels, magazines, and newspapers have long served in the formulation and reinforcement of socially acceptable and unacceptable self-images (Kidd, 1975; Lull, 1980).

---

[3] For a discussion of the sense of self as the individual "I" and the "me" as social attitudes, see G. H. Mead (1934).

[4] Duncan (1962) claims that "The self and society originates and develops in communication." B. A. Fisher (1978) explains, "Dialogue implies the expression of self and the development of mutual understanding (that is, congruence) along with the development of self through social interaction . . . And the concept of role taking allows for the individual to discover and develop self through social interaction."

Of increased importance are photographs and recordings in the intrapersonal dialogue. The photograph creates and reflects socially desirable images. Voice and video recordings are being utilized to check self-image as well as improve one's projected image.[5] What makes this significant is the complete credulity with which persons accept photographs and recordings as unimpeachable portrayals of reality, often overriding interpersonal responses (Sontag, 1973).

Intrapersonal communication has traditionally been referred to as non-observable internalized dialogue which occurs in all humans. The medium of recording materializes that dialogue, bringing the internal more in line with the external, thereby altering the way the individual processes information during intrapersonal communication. There is a growing reliance upon media technology for self-assessment and image formation. This alone would call for research to determine the role media play in creating the "significant other."

Interpersonal communication refers to dyadic interaction which takes the form of verbal and nonverbal exchanges between two or more individuals, consciously aware of each other, usually interacting in the same time and space, performing interchangeable sender-receiver roles.[6] Through the interpersonal communication process people maintain and adjust their self-image, relate to others, cooperate in decision making, accomplish tasks, and make order of their environment. All acts of communication emerge from the need of two humans to connect symbolically. The dyad serves as the paradigm of human communication. Michael Schudson (1978), in an examination of the dyadic model, claims that "we have developed a notion that all communication *should* be like a certain model of conversation, whether that model really exists or not" (p. 323), and "the ideal not one concocted by social scientists. Rather it is a widely shared ideal in contemporary American culture which social science has uncritically adopted" (p. 323).

---

[5] The widespread use of audio and video recordings to improve the image of politicians, beauty contestants, salespersons, and so on is documented in newspaper and magazines articles. See, for example, "Rose Queen Prepares for the Pageant," *Los Angeles Times,* December 27, 1981, B-3; and "Cops go High Tech for Fiesta, Plan Second Year of Taping," *Santa Barbara Journal,* March 15, 1981, p. 14.

[6] We are using the term "interpersonal communication" in its generic sense, emphasizing function rather than relationship. Our approach is similar to that of D. P. Cushman and R. T. Craig (1976): "Interpersonal communication systems are distinguished from other general levels in terms of function, structure, and process, but primarily in terms of function. . . . A well-defined interpersonal system is necessarily a *small* system—paradigmatically a dyad. . . . Relationship issues like affection and openness, and process of development, presentation, and validation of self-conceptions seems necessary in view of the basic function of interpersonal system."

Humans have always sought mechanical means of extending and enhancing face-to-face communication to efficiently serve needs for security, socialization, collectivization, and fantasy. The result has been the permanentizing and electrifying of the channels of communication which make possible the reproduction of human communication over time and space. Each new technology not only extended the reach of human communication, it also altered the ways in which humans related to information and to each other.[7] If, however, it is maintained that mediated communication is synonymous with interpersonal communication, that is, adds only neutral channels of transmission, it will not be understood how media have altered interpersonal connections. It is time, therefore, to expand the traditional typology to include *"mediated interpersonal communication."* A number of scholars have recognized the need. Gerald R. Miller (1982) states:

> I will argue . . . that mass communication messages potentially affect interpersonal relationships in even more fundamental, pervasive ways which at this writing have received relatively little research attention. Specifically, I will propose that the media often: (1) exert a powerful impact on people's initial perceptions of other interpersonal transactions; (2) influence the manner in which information about other transactions is processed and interpreted; and in many cases (3) distract persons from gathering the kind of information they need to relate effectively in interpersonal settings. (p. 50)

Robert K. Avery and Thomas A. McCain (1982) point out that "the placement of intrapersonal communication and mass communication at opposite ends of a single continuum has resulted in masking the multifaceted nature of the differences among types of communicative encounters" (p. 30). They state that radio phone-in talk shows are a form of interpersonal communication with unique characteristics. They conclude that "the examination of interpersonal and media encounters must continue. Research on personal junctures with media and other needs careful description and understanding"(p. 39).

The term "mediated interpersonal communication" is a general category referring to any situation where a technological medium is introduced into face-to-face interaction. It includes:

1. *Interpersonal mediated communication:* telephone conversations, letters, CB radio, electronic mail, audio and video cassettes.
2. *Media-simulated interpersonal communication:* parasocial interactions, broadcast-teleparticipatory communication, etc.

---

[7] For a discussion of the symbiotic relationship between technology and communication from a historical perspective, see W. Ong (1961) and M. McLuhan (1962).

3. *Person-computer interpersonal communication:* computers utilized as interpersonal proxies.
4. *Uni-communication:* the utilization of such artifacts as T-shirts and bumper stickers for interpersonal interaction.[8]

Interpersonal mediated communication refers to any person-to-person interaction where a medium has been interposed to transcend the limitations of time and space. A technology is interposed between and is integral to the communicating parties. The interposed medium determines the quantity and quality of information and also shapes the relationships of the participants.[9] For example, a handwritten or typed letter can facilitate a personal relationship over distance, but the time it takes to transport the message along with the lack of immediate feedback alters the quality and quantity of information shared. The time factor also alters the relationship between the two participants. More significantly, interpersonal written communication differs from face-to-face communication because it requires mastery of a secondary coding system—written language—and a knowledge of the conventions of that medium. The fact that written communication can be stored and retrieved makes the exchange context-free and permanent. Consequently, there are things that can be said face-to-face that could never be put into writing.

Communication mediated by the personal letter is but one of several forms of interpersonal mediated communication. The telephone also transcends space—it allows us to carry on conversations in an essentially private and intimate manner far beyond the reach of the unmediated human voice.[10] Telephoning, however, utilizes only one sensory channel, and this limits the amount and quality of information transmitted. One has to compensate for the lack of nonverbal signals, which in turn, lowers predictability and makes for less control.

---

[8] While the categories listed under the concept of "mediated interpersonal communication" can be demonstrated, the classification labels should be considered "in progress."

[9] In comparing mediated interpersonal communication and interpersonal communication we will utilize the following basic characteristics of interpersonal communication: (a) It is transmitted through multiple channels. Sight, smell, touch, and taste operate as receiving channels. (b) It is spontaneous and evanescent. It cannot be recreated. (c) Feedback is immediate and continuous. (d) Interchangeable sender-receiver roles provide maximum control of content. (e) There is unlimited channel capacity and no production costs. (f) It utilizes implicit and restricted audio-verbal and audio-visual codes which make for privacy and intimacy. (g) Psychological as well as sociological and anthropological information is generated and processed. (h) Basic skills and conventions are learned informally at an early age, usually in noninstitutional settings.

[10] For an extensive analysis of the influence of the telephone, see I. Pool (1977). For a discussion of the significance of letter writing as verbal expression, see W. J. Ong (1967).

The widespread use of interposed interpersonal communication such as letter writing and telephoning has altered face-to-face relationships. For example, we do not have to leave the confines of our dwellings to maintain relationships over distance.[11] Face-to-face contact with the people in the street and marketplace can be avoided. The eyes, nose, and tongue can be protected from unwanted stimuli. Physical contact is eliminated even though telephone company ads suggest that we "reach out and touch someone." In addition, the telephone is altering proxemic norms. Edward Hall (1966) established that Americans maintain carefully proscribed interpersonal distances and that violation of spacial norms is risky. The telephone alters interpersonal spacial relationships. Telephonic conversation always takes place at a socially "intimate" distance. The other person's voice is literally next to our ear—the distance at which, according to Hall, the sense of sight is not nearly as important as touch, smell, and the feel of bodily warmth. Perhaps this is why, at times, the telephone can be so threatening. It invades intimate space, but denies us most of the sensory means of communication control and verification present in intimate situations.

Other interposed media such as "CB" and "ham radio," audio and video cassettes (utilized for one-to-one communication), computers (used to connect two or more people) can be categorized as interpersonal mediated communication.[12] They share with face-to-face communication the characteristics of interchangeability of sender-receiver roles, immediacy of feedback, and use of unrestricted codes. They differ from interpersonal communication in the lack of privacy and communication control—whatever message is sent is available to all receivers—making the information more *public* than private. This tends to transform the sender of a message into a *performer*, placing emphasis on messages which entertain or carry general public information. The association of audio and video tape with radio and television broadcasting further suggests public performance, deemphasizing verbal content, and, at the same time, limiting intimacy.

The ambiguity of private and public communication suggests another variation of mediated interpersonal communication: *media-simulated interpersonal communication*. This phenomenon was first explored by Horton and Wohl (1956) in their analysis of "para-social interaction."

In television, especially, the image which is presented makes available nuances of appearance and gesture to which ordinary social perception is atten-

---

[11] The electronic relationship and its implications for the future is one of the primary issues examined by A. Toffler (1980). M. M. Webber (1971) examines a related notion when he proposed "non-place communities."

[12] See Cowlan (1979) and Turkle (1980).

tive and to which interaction is cued. Sometimes the "actor"—whether he is playing himself or performing in a fictional role—is seen engaged with others; but often he faces the spectator, uses the mode of direct address, talks as if he were conversing personally and privately. The audience, for its part, responds with something more than mere running observation; it is, as it were, subtly insinuated into the program's action and internal social relationships and, by dint of this kind of staging, is ambiguously transformed into a group which observes and participates in the show by turns. The more the performer seems to adjust his performance to the supposed response of the audience, the more the audience tends to make the response anticipated. This simulacrum of conversational give and take may be called *para-social interaction*. (p. 215)

Parasocial interaction is a staple of mass media "personality" shows. The main ingredient is the illusion of intimacy created by the media personality through imitation of the gestures, conversational style, and the informal milieu of the face-to-face interaction. The audience members know the performer in the same way they know their friends; by observation and interpretation of gestures, voice, conversations, and actions. The celebrity program is designed to coach the audience into making personal judgments. Audience members report that they know these personalities better than their friends and neighbors. Though designed and controlled by media programmers and broadcast to a relatively undifferentiated audience, the parasocial interaction is not one-sided. The audience members are not passive observers of a skilled performance. Rather, they make appropriate responses to the personality's performance; they join into the joking, teasing, praising, admiring, gossiping, and telling of anecdotes. When they play this answering role, they are doing exactly the things that lead to friendship and intimacy. As Horton and Wohl (1956) point out, "the relationship of the devotee to the persona is . . . of the same order as, and related to, the network of actual social relations. . . . As a matter of fact, it seems profitable to consider the interaction with the persona as a phase of the role-enactments of the spectator's daily life" (p. 228). The broadcast audience's need for intimacy and the ability of performers to simulate face-to-face interaction explains in part the success of such personalities as Don MacNeil, Arthur Godfrey, Jack Paar, Phil Donahue, and Johnny Carson.

In the case of parasocial interaction, though, there can be only the illusion of intimacy and friendship. The sender and receiver roles are sharply separated and *never* interchange. This form of communication is highly institutionalized and control is not in the hands of either the sender or the receiver but is preplanned by media specialists who design and orchestrate the interaction. Though the audience member is aware that several million others are watching and interacting at the same time, the interaction seems intimate because the performer discloses personal information which is associated with intimacy. It seems private because the listener/viewer agrees to react as though the disclosure was made by a close friend in a face-to-face situation (Horton & Wohl, p. 219).

The importance of simulated mediated interpersonal communication is twofold. One, it functions as a substitute for face-to-face relationships. It is less demanding for some people to work out a close relationship with Johnny Carson than with their next-door neighbor. The "parasocial friend" is always predictable, never unpleasant, always sympathetic, never threatening. In other words, there are no challenges to the audience member's self-esteem, not limits on his or her ability to respond appropriately. Two, media producers of parasocial interaction set up unreal expectations which lead many people to feel that their own interpersonal relationships are inadequate because the parasocial relationship is based upon an ideal of face-to-face communication which is seldom achieved in practice. This leads to increased feelings of alienation and a greater reliance upon mass media for interpersonal satisfaction.

Closely related to parasocial interaction and an important part of media-simulated interpersonal communication is the radio talk show or what we call "broadcast teleparticipatory media." In a study of the talk radio phenomenon, Avery and Ellis (1979) point out that the exchange of messages between a call-in listener and talk radio host "creates a pattern of talk which defines a symbol system for the interactants. That is, social reality is uniquely defined by the interactants, and hence becomes significant to the communication process" (p. 116). A later study by Avery and McCain (1982) states:

> After reviewing the results of several talk radio shows, one might easily come to the conclusion that although the communication patterns between a call-in listener and a talk radio host reveal numerous similarities in the face to face encounter the unique characteristics imposed by this communication setting afford a special context that needs to be considered in order to develop a complete understanding of this particular media-person transaction.

It is significant that radio talk show conversation is more a public performance than a private and interrelational act. Despite its public aspect, the phone-in part of talk radio is carried on as though it were a private telephone conversation. The radio host is quite aware that the conversation is part of a public performance and one that must be handled and manipulated well if it is to be commercially viable. At the same time, the majority of the audience never call the talk show host but vicariously participate in the host-caller interaction much like neighbors who listen in on the telephone party line to learn what is going on and identify with one of the parties. For the non-caller the interaction serves an important nonthreatening function: coaching the listener for future media-personal and face-to-face conversations. The listener-caller selects a favorite radio host and interacts on a daily basis in much the same way that all of us select friends to interact with face-to-face. For the phone-in audience the radio talk show provides a relatively safe environment in which members can contact important public personalities, giving them status and a feeling of connection. The willingness of the "personality" to come into the home as a companion, listening to the caller and providing assurance that beliefs and values are shared, simulates interpersonal interaction.

Similar to parasocial interaction, broadcast teleparticipatory interaction represents a form of simulated interpersonal communication. Unlike telephone talk, sender-receiver roles are relatively fixed, there is little or no relational development, and the communicative code is restricted-implicit rather than unrestricted-implicit. Even on phone-in shows featuring psychologist hosts where callers often disclose intimate sexual information, both interactants follow carefully proscribed restricted language codes more suitable for public forums than the more unrestricted intimate codes of personal telephoning. Avery and Ellis report that callers never forget who is in control of the interaction (Avery & Ellis, 1979, p. 113). Callers know they can be cut off if they are boring, too bizarre, too emotional, too aggressive, and so on. If they do not please the host, who acts as interpreter and gatekeeper of what is interesting and acceptable to the audience, they will be stopped by disconnection.

Broadcast teleparticipatory media are viewed as entertainment by those in control of the program. They shape the public perception of an ideal interpersonal performance. The seven-second tape delay technology make source control absolute. Programmers can bleep out anything they think should not be heard, making the conversation "safe" for all participants. The exercise of this control teaches the audience the restricted code of "public" interpersonal communication; rewarding those who can perform the "ideal" intimate communication with the host. It is this public aspect, along with the placing of control in the hands of an unseen, unknown source, that establishes broadcast teleparticipatory interaction as a distinct type of mediated interpersonal communication. Research by Avery, Ellis, and McCain and others verifies that this is a firmly established and growing mode of interaction, one which many Americans are dependent upon for supplementing and/or substituting for daily face-to-face interaction.

The *person-computer interpersonal encounter* represents another facet of "mediated interpersonal communication." It includes any situation in which one party activates a computer which in turn responds appropriately in a graphic, alphanumeric, or vocal mode (or combinations thereof) thereby establishing a sender/receiver relationship.[13] In the computer-person interaction the computer is programmed by a person, but that person is not the sender or receiver of the message. The human partner interacts not with the computer programmer, but with the computer program. Ithiel de Sola Pool (1982) points out that prior to the introduction of the computer every communication device "took a message that had been composed by a human being and (with some occasional loss) delivered it unchanged to another human being. The computer for the first time provides a communication device by which a person may receive a message quite different from what any human sent. Indeed, machines may talk to each other" (pp. xi–xii).

Although person–computer transactions simulate dyadic communication, the process and the alternatives are predetermined. The human partner actives the computer, but once the encounter has begun the computer program controls the communication. To compensate for the loss of control we anthropomorphize the computer; that is, give it human qualities. The human partner can then "role-play" a face-to-face interaction because all the components of dyadic communication exist, except that one of the partners is a machine.

Not all human-computer contacts, however, are characterized by this particular interactive quality. The person-computer mediated encounter should be contrasted with the situation in which one communicates *through* a computer rather than *with* a computer. "Electronic mail," for example, represents a change of medium (paper to display screen) in which the computer is interposed. In this case the computer is a high-speed transmitter of what is essentially a written message. The person-computer mediated encounter, on the other hand, always involves direct dialogue between individual and computer.

Gumpert (1975) described "communication from one to many of values prescribed by associations in the environment through various non-electronic media. Uni-communication is a type of mediated interpersonal behavior" (p. 34).

Uni-communication is that communication mediated by objects of clothing, adornment, and personal possessions—houses, automobiles, furniture, and so on—which people select and display to communicate to others their status, affiliation, and self-esteem. It includes, also, more explicit messages like imprinted T-shirts, jackets, and caps, as well as bumper stickers, armbands, and buttons.

---

[13] For an overview of person-computer interactions, see Vail (1980, December). For a more general discussion of microcomputers, see Evans (1979).

Communicating something about one's status and role through clothing and personal possessions is, of course, an ancient and well established mode of communication.[14] Personal possessions—everything from the exterior and interior design of homes to a pair of Gucci loafers—can and do take on symbolic functions which impart implicit information to others and reinforce one's self-image. What has received little attention is how this attenuated, symbolic interaction operates as a form of mediated interpersonal communication. What makes it interpersonal is that it is self-disclosing and it produces sender-receiver relationships. The item displayed can serve one or more purposes and establish one or more relationships. For example, it can reveal group affiliation (wearing a Masonic ring), mark one's status (driving a white Mercedes Benz 450SL), identify a role (carrying a brief case), and express support for or rejection of established values and institutions (wearing a Star of David, displaying orange colored, spikey hair). The fact that a single item of attire can have multiple meanings makes it useful in establishing a variety of relationships. A studded black leather vest with "Hells Angels" inscribed can serve to identify, reject, boast, and so on, depending upon the context and the receiver's response. Uni-communication is extremely helpful for informing people of status, role, and affiliation in situations where face-to-face interaction is difficult and possibly risky.

What makes uni-communication important in an updated communication typology is an expanded function brought on by the mass media of communication and the mass distribution of "pop" symbols. Increasingly, individuals in all levels of society are making explicit messages out of these symbols and transmitting them to mass audiences. Wearing a T-shirt imprinted with "No Nukes" makes use of a utilitarian item of clothing to "broadcast" a message to any and all who come close enough to read the words and view the person displaying them. The bumper sticker, "Jesus Saves," makes use of an automobile, which is both a means of transportation and a symbol, to carry an additional and more explicit message to fellow drivers.

Such messages ordinarily do not originate with the person displaying them. Rather, they are mass-produced and distributed by groups who are campaigning for certain causes. The persons displaying these messages become part of the campaign as well as part of the transmission system. This makes uni-communication different from other forms of interpersonal interaction. It communicates affiliation with a group or suggests a social role rather than making an individual statement. Uni-communication facili-

---

[14] For an historical analysis of the symbolic nature of clothes, see Hollander (1976).

tates stimulus generalization rather than stimulus discrimination.[15] Receivers respond to the attached symbols and the individual as one entity; deriving different messages depending on the receiver's perceptions of the affiliate group or social role. Uni-communication discloses how the displayer views herself or himself in affiliation with others rather than in relationship to an individual receiver.

Receivers of uni-communication are confronted by the message in situations where face-to-face interaction is neither expected or desired. There is, however, a response and an interaction. The response is like the reaction to a billboard or a poster. We may not want to see it or read it, but the fact that it comes into our view draws our attention, makes us read, and we are forced to respond. The response is to the person as part of the message—with hostility, or anger, or admiration, or identification. It is an interpersonal interaction. Seldom is there any immediate, verbal feedback. Similar to the para-social and other mediated interactions, communication is carried on at a distance even though each person may be within social speaking range. The receiver decides what the message means and works out an appropriate verbal scenario. The sender has in mind a message, or maybe several messages, which may or may not coincide with the messages being formulated by receivers. Each is satisfied that something has been communicated. Each has been involved in a personal communicative interaction. Senders have made a statement—one which says something about who they are and how they feel. Receivers respond as though the message was directed at them as individuals. The fact that this same interaction is replicated thousand of times all over the nation (made possible by both mass distribution and mass media) creates a kind of national interpersonal dialogue about values, roles, and status.

We believe that uni-communication serves important interpersonal functions in our society. A study of it would tell us something about how we communicate and with whom in an increasingly impersonal environment where long-established institutions of social interaction are undergoing change. For example, we have created public places like "discos" and "singles" bars to serve courtship and match-pairing functions once exclusively the domain of the home and the church. These places exist to promote interpersonal relationships. In such places, the communication process is aided by the kind of clothing and jewelry worn which become explicit messages to others concerning one's status, one's availability, and one's feeling about the kinds of interactions one desires. We point this out

---

[15] For a discussion of generalization and discrimination responses in interpersonal communication, see Miller (1982).

as only one area of potential research into a type of mediated communication which has been ignored.

In summary, there may be other types of mediated interpersonal communication which we have not recognized. There are, of course, other forms of communication which need to be placed in an updated communication typology. The mediated political campaign is one example. The printed magazine or journal distributed to a select audience which is part of a specialized network, what Gumpert (1970) has called "mini-communication," is another example. We could go on, but the point is that a typology which compartmentalizes thought and research and prevents investigations of important types and forms of human communication cannot be tolerated. We are quite convinced that the traditional division of communication study into interpersonal, group and public, and mass communication is inadequate because it ignores the pervasiveness of media. We propose that media be incorporated in definitions of communication and that we begin to realign our research to account for the significant impact of media.

REFERENCES

Avery, R. K., & Ellis, D. G. (1979). Talk radio as an interpersonal phenomenon. In G. Gumpert & R. Cathcart(Eds.), *Inter/Media: Interpersonal communication in a media world* (pp. 110–118). New York: Oxford University Press.

Avery, R. K., & McCain, T. A. (1982). Interpersonal and mediated encounters: A reorientation to the communication process. In G. Gumpert & R. Cathcart (Eds.), *Inter/Media: Interpersonal communication in a media world, 2nd ed.* (pp. 25–35). New York: Oxford University Press.

Barnlund, D. C. (1968). *Interpersonal communication: Survey and studies.* New York: Houghton Mifflin.

Berlo, D. K. (1960). *The process of communication.* New York: Holt, Rinehart and Winston.

Cowlan, B. (1979). A revolution in personal communications: The explosive growth of citizens band radio. In G. Gumpert & R. Cathcart (Eds.), *Inter/Media: Interpersonal communication in a media world* (pp. 116–121). New York: Oxford University Press.

Cushman, D. P., & Craig, R. T. (1976). Communication systems: Interpersonal implications. In G. R. Miller (Ed.), *Explorations in interpersonal comunication* (pp. 37–58). Beverly Hills: Sage.

Dance, F. E. X., & Larson, C. E. (1976). *The functions of human communication.* New York: Holt, Rinehart and Winston.

DeVito, J. A. (1977). *The interpersonal communication book.* New York: Harper & Row.

Duncan, H. D. (1962). *Communication and social order.* New York: Bedminster Press.

Evans, C. (1979). *The micro millenium.* New York: Viking.

Fisher, B. A. (1978). *Perspectives on human communication.* New York: Macmillan.

Gumpert, G. (1975). The rise of uni-comm. *Today's Speech, 23,* 32–38.

Gumpert, G. (1970). The rise of mini-comm. *Journal of Communication, 20,* 280–290.

Hall, E. T. (1966). *The hidden dimension.* New York: Doubleday.

Hollander, A. (1976). *Seeing through clothes.* New York: Viking.

Horton, D., & Wohl, R. R. (1956). Mass communication and para-social interaction. *Psychiatry, 19,* 215–229.

Katz, E., & Lazarsfeld, L. (1962). *Personal influence: The part played by people in the flow of mass communication.* New York: The Free Press.

Kidd, V. (1975). Happily ever after and other relationship styles: Advice on interpersonal relations in popular magazines. *Quarterly Journal of Speech, 61,* 178–186.

Klapper, J. (1960). *The effects of mass communication.* New York: Free Press.

Lull, J. (1980). The social uses of television. *Human Communicaion Research, 6,* 58–68.

McLuhan, M. (1962). *The gutenberg galaxy.* Toronto: University of Toronto Press.

Mead, G. H. (1934). *Mind, self and society.* Chicago: University of Chicago Press.

Merton, R. K. (1949). Patterns of influence: A study of interpersonal influence and communication behavior. In P. F. Lazersfeld & F. N. Stanton (Eds.), *Communication Research* (pp. 45–161). New York: Harper.

Miller, G. R. (1982). A neglected connection: Mass media exposure and interpersonal communicative competency. In G. Gumpert & R. Cathcart (Eds.), *Inter/Media: Interpersonal communication in a media world, 2nd ed.* (pp. 42–51). New York: Oxford University Press.

Novack, M. (1977). Television shapes the soul. In L. L. Sellars & W. C. Rivers (Eds.), *Mass media issues* (pp. 218–225). New York: Prentice Hall.

Ong, W. (1977). *Interfaces of the word: Studies in the evolution of consciousness and culture.* Ithaca: Cornell University Press.

Ong, W. (1967). *The presence of the word.* New Haven, CT: Yale University Press.

Phillips, G. M., & Metzger, N. (1976). *Intimate communication.* Boston: Allyn & Bacon.

Pool, I. (1982). Forward. In W. P. Dizard, Jr. (Ed.), *The coming information age: An overview of technology, economics, and politics* (pp. xi–xii). New York: Longman.

Pool, I. (Ed.). (1977). *The social impact of the telephone.* Cambridge: M.I.T. Press.

Schramm, W. (1954). *The process and effects of mass communication.* Urbana: University of Illinois Press.

Schudson, M. (1978). The ideal of conversation in the study of mass media. *Communication Research, 5,* 320–325.

Sontag, S. (1973). *On photography.* New York: Farrar, Strauss & Giroux.

Stewart, J., & D'Angelo, G. (1975). *Together: Communicating interpersonally.* Reading, PA: Addison Wesley.

Toffler, A. (1980). *The third wave.* New York: William Morrow.

Turkle, S. (1980). Computer as rorschach. *Society, 17,* 25–34.

Vail, H. (1980, December). The home computer terminal: Transforming the households of tomorrow. *The Futurist,* 59–64.

Webber, M. M. et al. (Eds.). (1971). *Explorations into urban structure.* Philadelphia: University of Pennsylvania Press.

4
Media Psychology and Mediated Therapeutic Communication

Jacqueline C. Bouhoutsos

What is media psychology? What does a media psychologist do? Where is the line between "therapy" and "advice"? Bouhoutsos traces the changing professional guidelines regarding media psychologists and describes the various functions of such individuals, focusing on the educational and the therapeutic.

"Media psychology" is a term which has come into use only recently, and it is an unfamiliar concept to most psychologists and communication scholars. Some psychologists consider the appellation inaccurate and have suggested that a more appropriate descriptor would be "psychologists working with media." However, that would also be a misnomer, since mental health professionals involved with media come from a variety of disciplines. "Media psychology" might be better defined as a generic term meaning the study of individuals, and their consciousness and behavior in their physical and social environments, with particular emphasis on media as a part of that environment.

The term "media psychology" was adopted officially in February 1982 at a convention of psychologists that included many hosts of radio call-in psychology programs. Participants in that San Diego conference gathered together to share their experiences in hosting such programs and to discuss the ethics for the use of media by mental health professionals. They created an official framework within which to do so, and dubbed the new organization the Association for Media Psychology. Within a short period of time "media psychology" became known as a new specialty field within psychology, and in 1987 the Association became a division (46) of the American Psychological Association. The stated purpose of the Association is to transmit psychological information through media to the public, or to "give psychology away" (Miller, 1969). The original motivation, that of providing a forum for discussing radio call-in programs, has broadened considerably. Media psychologists are not only on radio, but working in other media as well. Many have written self-help books, produced, written, or directed films, and been in front of or behind television cameras in a variety of roles. Concerns on the part of organized psychology have surfaced about the impact of such books, programs, and films on the public. Calls for research have frequently appeared in the psychological literature (Bouhoutsos, 1983; Klonoff, 1983). Although some studies have been completed, we are only beginning to obtain data regarding the effects on the callers and listeners of psychological information provided through mediated communication.

Most of the radio call-in hosts are clinical psychologists. Historically, traditional training for clinical psychologists began with concentration on the dyad of therapist and patient. Couples or marital therapy enlarged the scope of the therapeutic focus, family therapy broadened it still more, and group therapy opened the therapeutic experience to include nonrelated individuals to share problems and concerns. But an extension of psychotherapy to include mass media audiences was anathema to most clinicians. In fact, working with media was considered to be unethical for psychologists. Principle 4J of the American Psychological Association Code of Ethics (1977–81) stated that

> psychological services and products for the purpose of diagnosis, treating, or giving personal advice to particular individuals are provided only in the context of a professional relationship and are not given by means of public lectures or demonstrations, newspaper or magazine articles, radio or television programs, mail, or similar media.

The APA Ethics Code stresses that the welfare of the consumer should be the primary focus of psychologists (Preamble and Principle 6); critics of psychology's involvement with media have been concerned about the taint of commercialism and fear that the ethical values of the mental health professions will be incompatible with the marketplace. It cannot be denied that concern for the "welfare of the consumer" is often in conflict with commercial goals. Principle 4 of the APA Code of Ethics warns psychologists not to participate for personal gain in commercial announcements and requires them to ensure that any professional announcements and advertisements are presented in a scientifically acceptable fashion; in addition, psychologists are told to "correct others" if they engage in activities which are contrary to the code. Such restrictions often do not fit well with industry requirements and often place media psychologists in conflict with their industry employers and with their professional colleagues.

Another concern of organized psychology has been the content of programs on which psychologists are hosts or guests. An entire chapter of a well-known text on ethics for psychologists (Keith-Spiegel & Koocher, 1985) is devoted to "Psychology for Mass-Media Audiences." The chapter is headed by an informative quotation (Weyand, 1980): "Cheap truth is like junk food. It comes in pretty packages, and you can place a take-out order, but it loses so much flavor by the time you get it home" (p. 200). The thrust of the chapter is that "what the public thinks it is learning about psychology is often distorted, trivialized, sensationalized, or inaccurate information. . . . Media are geared to sensationalism and exaggeration and, considering the quick-paced format, usually present information superficially" (p. 200). While these statements contain some truth, they are exaggerated, as generalizations are wont to be, and focus on the negative aspects of psychology and psychologists in the media. Other literature documents a number of ways in which media have been used to further the welfare of the consumer. Few if any concerns have been expressed concerning the use of mass media to change smoking, drinking, eating, exercise, and socialization patterns in the general population.

MEDIA PSYCHOLOGY AS EDUCATION OR PREVENTION

Media have been used extensively in recent years for purposes of education or prevention. Most of the programs have been designed and carried out by mental health experts who work with media. The Finnish studies on smoking (McAlister, Puska, Koskela, Pallonen, & Maccoby, 1980), the Stanford Heart Disease prevention program (Maccoby & Farquar, 1975), and the California Wellness effort with its emphasis on social networks (Klibanoff, Hersey, & Probst, 1983) have received recognition for their contribution to the prevention of mental and physical disorders. In all three instances mass media have been used to communicate materials designed to impact behavior of the general public: to stop smoking, alter dietary and exercise habits, and learn how to increase one's social network. Many extreme changes in our society may well be due to these types of media campaigns during the last five years. Yet it is unlikely that these efforts have been viewed as media psychology.

Similar interventions on smaller scales, however, have been recognized as media psychology. One dissertation addressed the frequent contention that television news is the cause of increased anxiety and stress on viewers. Miller (1979) studied the effects of television news on the stress level of the viewer and found that problems presented without resolution increased stress. However, the author found that if active interventive measures were suggested, the viewers could deal more easily with their own stress reactions. In a related study, Gardiner (1982) designed a mass media intervention for men going through the stress of a divorce. The study utilized local newspapers, radio stations, and public agencies to offer support. Positive results were documented and the model has been in use for several years.

We know from communication studies that programs which are committed to organizing the listening audience, such as the Gardiner project, are limited in their reach (Jamison & McAnany, 1978). In contrast, open broadcasts need only concentrate on getting out an interesting message. The more organized and limiting strategies clearly have advantages in promoting more complex and long-term behavior changes. Open radio is free to broadcast to a wider audience and get its messages across without organizing its audience. But it is more difficult to hold an audience with educational material presented in the traditional manner. Gunter and Theroux (1977) recommend "edvertising," that is, using advertising techniques to instruct. They point out that educational radio has assumed interest on the part of its audience and has failed frequently in its educational purpose because listeners simply turn off the program. Programs which "sell" knowledge and motivate the audience to change have been useful in formal education in a number of underdeveloped countries (Schramm, Coombs, Kahnert, & Lyle, 1967). Empirical studies in Nicaragua, Mexico, Kenya, and the Dominican Republic demonstrated that radio can be very effective in teaching basic educational precepts (Jamison & McAnany, 1978). Two-way radio has been shown to be particularly useful in providing instruction or directions for behavior change. In Alaska (Kreimer, 1977), Ecuador (Manoff International Inc., 1975), Kenya (Kinyanjui, 1974), Guatemala (Gomez, 1971), and Australia (Monoghan, Shun Wah, Steward, & Smith, 1978), such instruction-giving programs are among the most popular offerings via radio and have been shown to make an outstanding contribution to knowledge, attitude, and behavior change.

The literature on the uses of radio in formal education indicates that a number of different formats have been attempted. At the University of Massachussets an educational quiz show showed a superior learning gain for participants over those who learned by a lecture method (Gunter & Theroux, 1977). In one Latin American country a soap opera or "novella" was used as a device to enlist the populace in a learning project (Jamison & McAnany, 1978). The program got one of the highest ratings for viewership of all commercial programs. The commercial producers of that program made their money selling advertising while the Secretary of Public Education organized the listening audience. As a result of that particular program, 260,000 adults signed up for classes organized around the program. The authors pointed out that although cognitive elements are important in media messages, the primary thrust of effective content is affective material, the mainstay of soap operas or novellas.

SOAP OPERAS: VEHICLES FOR MEDIA PSYCHOLOGY

Soap operas with their high emotional content have been suggested as appropriate vehicles through which information about psychology might be taught in the United States (Cantor & Pingree, 1983). Approximately 20 million people watched such programs per day in 1970 (Nielson Television Index, 1981). Recent research indicates the number has been fairly constant. Soap operas are the most popular shows during daytime hours. Certainly soap operas present to national audiences views of social relationships and sexual intimacies (Cantor & Pingree, 1983). However, research shows that the majority of listeners or viewers of soap operas state that they do not listen to learn how to solve their problems or to apply what they learn to their lives, but that they listen for entertainment (Compesi, 1980). Despite their subjectively perceived reasons for watching, do watchers learn to deal with life problems better than nonwatchers?

It has been suggested periodically that soap operas would be a way to model better communication. Unfortunately, there have been few studies or even anecdotal material on the effects of soaps. An hypothesis has been suggested, but not yet researched, that soaps watchers may tend to approach problems in their lives as people-related while nonviewers might attribute difficulties to external causes—because soaps are so centered on relationships. For example, losing a job to a viewer might mean that he or she was personally to blame; to a nonviewer it might be viewed as due to the economy or to sex, race, or age discrimination. This dichotomy carried to extremes might lead to excessive guilt on the one hand or projection on the other. Although this hypothesis has not been researched, a related study showed that there was no difference between the way in which soaps viewers and nonviewers rated the frequency and severity of problems such as poor health, illicit love affairs, divorce, and unhappy marriages, despite the soaps' concentration on such problems.

Imparting specific knowledge rather than attitudes through soaps, however, might fare better. Cantor and Pingree (1983) have pointed out that viewers probably are more informed than nonviewers about battered women's refuges, about the procedures involved in abortion, and/or the risks and treatment options associated with breast cancer, all of which have figured prominently in soap operas.

Research on other types of television programs, particularly on educational television, has revealed positive benefits which accrue to frequent television viewers, not only in knowledge acquisition but in attitudinal change. For example, although criticized for promoting sex-role and racial stereotypes, television has been shown to combat stereotyping successfully (Johnston, 1983). It can educate children to utilize television more effectively and to develop critical viewing skills (Dorr, Graves, & Phelps, 1980). It can successfully transmit information about community resources and about the various life stages and problems (Sprafkin & Rubinstein, 1983). Unfortunately, in comparison to network television, and particularly to soap operas, viewers of these types of programs are limited in number. Public television, like public radio, plays to a select audience. Soap operas,

on the other hand, are seen by extremely large audiences but carry attendant dangers, such as the arousal of resentment of their own lives by frequent television viewers who compare their living conditions with those
of the opulent, dramatic, attractive figures on the tube (Cantor & Pingeree,
1983) or the data from a number of national surveys which suggest a positive relationship between television viewing and "unhealthy" beliefs, values, and lifestyles. For example, people who watch more television seem
to be relatively neglectful and complacent about their physical well-being,
are less informed about health and exercise less, despite Fonda, Hittleman,
and other hosts dedicated to improving physical well-being. Of course, the
very act of watching television may generate what is currently described
in the vernacular as "couch potatoes," the antithesis of physical well-being
in terms of smoking, drinking, eating, and lack of exercise.

Television psychology, however, has become increasingly prominent in
recent years as television news programs on major networks have taken on
an educative function. Experts in finance, law, consumer affairs, medicine,
dentistry, even veterinary medicine have been featured and have become
popular with mass audiences. Mental health professionals practicing media psychology also are in demand and are frequently seen offering crisis
intervention to disaster victims or their relatives, talking about child care,
or discussing other current problems such as treating AIDS victims or assisting victims of torture from Central America.

RESEARCH ON RADIO CALL-IN PSYCHOLOGY PROGRAMS

Research on the impact of radio on its listeners has been even more sparse
than studies on television, and those which have been done have been
mostly limited to studies designed to provide information to potential buy-
ers of air time: How many people of what ages and socioeconomic levels
listen to what kinds of programming and during what part of the day or
night? The effects of content on the listener have been of interest only if
the focus were on whether the audience will buy the advertised product.
Public concern about the effects of radio has been focused mainly on disc
jockeys and the lyrics of popular music with their emphasis on drugs and
sex, which are seen by many parents as a danger to children. But some
mental health professionals have become increasingly concerned that
damages might accrue to members of the listening public or callers of radio
call-in psychology programs. Public interest in media psychology has
grown phenomenally with an attendant willingness to discuss openly and
frankly the most intimate problems on television and radio. Although no
instance of damage has surfaced, despite the long history of call-in programs (the Institute of Family Relations which began in the 1950s, the

Private Line on KLAC in the 1960s, the Bill Ballance program on KABC in the 1970s), concerns continued to be voiced. Empirical evidence only became available in the mid-1980s, after the APA Ethics Code was changed to read, "When personal advice is given by means of . . . radio or television programs . . . the psychologist utilizes the most current relevant data and exercises the highest level of professional judgment" (APA, 1981). While this ethical principle did not clarify what constituted "relevant data" or establish criteria for "professional judgment," the change in the code was helpful in that it facilitated obtaining funding for research and opened discussion about such programs.

The first large-scale study (Bouhoutsos, Goodchilds, & Huddy, 1986) on radio call-in psychology programs laid many concerns to rest. However, findings pointed up other problems which had not been hypothesized. The research involved interviews with 368 individuals between 18 and 65 with equal number of males and females in two New York and two Los Angeles shopping malls. The locations were chosen as survey sites because they constitute the largest media markets and there are numerous radio psychology call-in programs aired in both cities. The mall survey was designed with the additional goal of finding sufficient numbers of listeners who would also have called such programs. The caller group was either absent from the malls or reluctant to so identify themselves. Subsequently a second study was designed specifically for callers.

An unexpected finding was that listening to such programs was such a ubiquitous phenomenon. Almost half (49 percent) of mall patrons surveyed on both coasts indicated that they had listened to such programs; of nonlisteners, 69 percent had heard of the programs and 42 percent of the respondents indicated they would listen if they had the opportunity. The large listening audience substantiated the hypothesis that hundreds of thousands or even millions of people would listen to these programs (Schwebel, 1982). As audiences increased, concern grew on the part of psychologists that people would listen more when they were upset, that they then might become even more depressed or anxious, and that they might attempt to substitute call-in psychology programs for needed psychotherapy. These concerns did not appear to be justified in that 78 percent of the respondents indicated that they listened no more frequently when things in their lives were worse, and 69 percent said that they never found the program disturbing. Also, 30 percent of listeners and 50 percent of callers had been or were currently in psychotherapy, hardly the psychologically unsophisticated population about whom the critics were concerned.

Another objection frequently voiced by critics of such programs was that listeners were trained to be voyeurs and that they used others' problems as entertainment. In response to a list of seven possible reasons for listening to such programs, educational values were the most frequently chosen (59 percent). These included wanting information to apply to their own lives (36 percent) and wanting to learn about psychology (23 percent). Listening in order to "hear about others' problems" (28 percent) and for amusement or entertainment (20 percent) were the only other reasons endorsed by any substantial number of listener respondents.

Despite the listeners' emphasis on educational values, however, they were no more knowledgeable than nonlisteners on a 7-item quiz about aspects of psychology. A retrospective review of those items suggested that perhaps symptoms of psychoses and knowledge about psychotherapy, which were the bases of some of the questions, may have not been subjects which held listeners' interest or even were covered on the programs. No questions about relationships were included, the most frequent topic which surfaced on the psychology call-in programs. Of greater concern is the finding that listeners were more confident about their psychological knowledge than were nonlisteners, a confidence which was decidedly misplaced, and which raises the old question of the dangers of a "little knowledge."

An interesting, but predictable, finding was that listeners watched more daytime television, listened more often to radio, and generally were a more frequent audience for electronic media across the board than nonlisteners. Most listened at home (72 percent), another 23 percent listened in their automobiles, and the remaining 5 percent listened at work.

As expected, 95 percent felt radio call-in psychology programs were definitely worth airing and 86 percent saw them as useful. Most (82 percent) thought that the programs were unlikely to create problems for people. Listeners were generally complimentary about the host of the program to which they listened, rating them as "intelligent" and "interested in the caller." Being "abrupt" was the most salient defect noted. Listeners did not appear to be worse off psychologically than nonlisteners; listeners stated that they listened to learn about themselves, about other people, and about psychology.

The concerns about radio call-in psychology programs expressed by the psychological community was absent from the public sphere. A small minority of nonlisteners expressed concern about the phenomenon, but listeners considered the programs helpful and informative and callers evaluated their on-air experience entirely positively. There did not appear to be any harm done to callers or listeners as measured on the study's "well-being" scales. In fact, there was a significant improvement in scale scores of callers in follow-up interviews done three months after the initial on-air contact. However, this finding may be an artifact caused either by callers initiating a call for help when they were feeling uncharacteristically stressed or by stress induced by the on-air experience itself.

The study found that most of the callers were given advice, that most followed that advice, and that the advice helped. Questions which were not answered by this study were the nature of the advice given and whether the advice resulted in actual behavioral change. Call-backs after several months yielded material which, while too limited to provide empirical data, nonetheless is interesting. Asked about what happened during the call to help or hurt, out of 38 codeable responses, 13 callers indicated that they had received emotional support or validation, 11 that they had received specific advice which had helped, eight that they increased their understanding of the situation, and six that they felt helped by "just talking to someone." Asked whether advice was given, 64 of the 88 (73 percent) interviewed replied in the affirmative, and 83 percent of those said that they had followed the advice. Serious doubt exists about the possibility of behavioral change having taken place, however, since about one-fourth of the callers stated that they were given referrals and less than 25 percent of these callers acted on the referrals.

On the other hand, personal anecdotes related to the author have substantiated that these programs are helpful in modeling and facilitating improved communication. One example involved a couple considering divorce after 20 years of marriage. Both made desultory attempts to discuss their difficulties, but the husband found these dialogues offensive and would become angry, breaking off communication. The wife began listening to radio psychology programs, turning them on in the small store which they operated jointly. Gradually, they began to discuss the calls at the dinner table and were surprised to find that they were able to talk about other people's relationships without becoming angry. Progressing to considering some of their own problems, they were able to see some similarities with those described by callers and to apply some of the advice they heard on the programs. It is not clear whether the advice as such was the assistance they used to repair their faulty relationship or whether it was the process which was modeled for them by the host of the radio call-in psychology program. It is possible that the content of most calls is less important than the accepting, understanding, problem-solving approach which is modeled.

MEDIA PSYCHOLOGY: SEARCH FOR A MODEL

The quest for a theoretical framework for radio call-in psychology has led to the consideration of a variety of models, including prevention, education, advice-giving, and psychotherapy. A model not previously considered is "mediated therapeutic communication." Kreps (see Chapter 2) and other communication scholars (Barnlund, 1968) have attempted to differentiate therapeutic communication from psychotherapy and to broaden its application to any individual who might wish to use such "interaction to help communicators cope with personal problems they face." Barnlund postulates that any individual can communicate therapeutically if he or she assists others to understand themselves and better achieve their needs and goals. This hypothesis raises a number of questions. How capable are the majority of people of assisting others to understand themselves? Is therapeutic communication learned behavior? Do people who are accepting of themselves and others communicate therapeutically without having to learn the skills? Can mediated therapeutic communication, such as that done on radio call-in psychology programs, assist individuals who are emotionally constricted, narcissistic, or otherwise impaired to communicate therapeutically? Unfortunately, we have more questions than answers, and the need for research is apparent. But clinically speaking, therapists see many individuals who are incapable of warmth, empathy, and sensitivity. Many have experienced deprivation and abuse as children, some are on drugs or alcohol, some are psychotic, still others have had life experiences which have embittered them and taught them not to trust others. It is unlikely that modeling empathic behavior or even teaching the behavioral components of comforting would be effective. Frequently such individuals are not only incapable of providing empathy, but also of accepting comforting behavior. These are the individuals who need psychotherapy and are best left to mental health professionals in the traditional treatment context.

"THERAPY" AND "THERAPEUTIC": WHERE IS THE BOUNDARY?

Is the process of radio call-in psychology sufficiently similar to what goes on in psychotherapy to confuse the public about the basic differences in the two phenomena? This is one of the concerns of organized psychology—that those individuals needing psychotherapy would substitute a palliative, ineffective short cut for necessary treatment. The ethical guidelines for radio psychologists (Association for Media Psychology, 1982) imply that substantive differences exist between radio psychology and psychotherapy. But do such differences exist and can we identify them?

A recent study by Henricks and Stiles (1987) compared samples of 58 radio psychology interviews recorded from three radio call-in psychology hosts' programs with samples of sessions from three psychotherapists, samples of informal conversations between students and professors, and also examples of doctors taking medical histories from their patients. Interchanges were coded in their entirety using a general purpose taxonomy for verbal response modes (Stiles, 1979). Findings indicated that the process of radio psychology differs from that of psychotherapy in most ways, is dissimilar to professor–student interchange, and is even more dissimilar to doctor–patient interviews, but that there are instances in which it is somewhat similar to cognitive/behavioral psychotherapy.

Caller behavior was also examined in this study. Although callers asked many questions, which may not be characteristic of psychotherapy (there has been little, if any, study of patient behavior), most of their process was reporting personal problems in a manner similar to clients in psychotherapy. The question then arises, if caller behavior is similar to patient behavior, can psychologist hosts avoid therapist responses?

Most radio call-in psychology hosts do not see themselves as providing psychotherapy via the media, nor, according to the listeners' study, do most of their listeners consider them typical psychotherapists. Both listeners and callers indicated that the greatest benefit to them was the hosts' advice, which they found helpful in coping with personal problems. On the other hand, in addition to describing the hosts as intelligent, listeners and callers commented favorably on the caring and warm behavior of most and negatively on the abruptness of some hosts. These findings suggest that both cognitive and affective components are important in the provision of radio psychology services. Similarly, therapeutic communication appears to require both aspects. Facilitating communicators' development of personal insight or reorientation (Barnlund, 1968) requires quite different functions from demonstrating empathy.

RESEARCH IN RELATED AREAS

The dual cognitive and emotional components of therapeutic communication have been given attention by both communication scholars and psychologists; two particular areas of study have been empathy and comforting strategies and behavior. The main body of research on empathy dates from the middle 1970s and was primarily done with children in the hope that empathy training might give rise to increased prosocial behavior and a diminution of aggressive behavior (Feshbach, 1983). Training activities included problem-solving games, story telling, listening to and making tape recordings, simple written exercises, acting out words, phrases, and stories, and role playing. The children's dramatizations were videotaped and shown to the group for discussion. The children were asked to identify the emotions portrayed, to imagine the preferences and behavior of different kinds of people, and finally, to take the roles of others in order to teach them to better appreciate the perspective of others. Although the Feshbach studies of empathy postulate the necessity for cognitive development as a precursor for development of empathy in the child, the affective component is also stressed. Empathy-like behaviors may emerge in the first few months of life, but some researchers maintain that only at three to four years of age are children sufficiently cognitively capable of empathizing so that there is genuine feeling for the distress of others. At the cognitive level, discriminative skills are necessary, that is, the ability to discriminate affective states of others. A second cognitive factor influencing empathy is the ability to assume the perspective and role of another. The emotional response is the third component, the ability of the child to experience the emotion that is being witnessed in order to share that emotion. Thus, empathy is viewed as a shared emotional response that the child experiences on perceiving another person's emotional reaction. Feshbach postulates that the observation of the "painful consequences of an aggressive act through the vicarious affective response of empathy, may be expected to function as inhibitors of the instigator's aggressive tendencies, thus contributing to an inverse relationship between empathy and aggression" (Feshbach, 1979). The activities used in this type of affective education—role playing, identifying emotional responses of others from the videotapes, acting out stories, identifying emotions in photographs or pantomimes of emotional situations—lend support to the importance of the use of media in modeling empathic responses.

Whether radio can be effective in modeling empathy, and if so, for what type of population, has not been studied. Although the hosts are perceived as warm and sensitive to callers, support has not been seen as a primary function of such programs. Radio call-in psychology programs have, in the main, been structured to provide advice to callers who have specific problems and who ask the hosts to solve the problems which they feel they cannot solve. The hosts respond in most instances by asking for more information, clarifying the information given and the problem as stated, then suggesting alternative ways of behaving or making referrals to sources of assistance. These are mainly cognitive functions. However, it is not unusual to have callers become extremely emotional during the discussion of their problems and for the hosts to exhibit comforting, supportive behavior. As mentioned above, most of the hosts are perceived by callers as sensitive, warm, and intelligent, and although the term *empathic* was not specifically used in the study, the term *warmth* might well be considered a synonym for empathic in this context.

Burleson (1984) differentiates between empathy and comforting behavior in that he sees empathy as a personality trait which influences the motivation to provide comfort while social perception skills are determinants of the competence to comfort others sensitively (p. 88). This position emphasizes the difficulty of separating the cognitive and affective components of empathy and the problems involved in clarifying the role of each. Significant are Burleson's findings that sensitive comforting activity is more likely to occur when the distressed individual has a close relationship with the comforter, exhibits salient signs of distress, and is perceived by the comforter as similar to himself or herself, suggesting that there are more affective than configitive bases for comforting behavior. Comforting behavior is viewed as a type of communication skill which enables communicators to assist distressed persons and has been shown by research (Aspy, 1975; Truax & Carkhuff, 1967) to result in fewer long-term emotional and psychosomatic problems. The antecedents of comforting skill have rarely been researched, but those studies which have been done appear to support the view that children who have been raised by non-power-assertive parents more frequently engaged in spontaneous acts of comforting (Zahn-Waxler, Radke-Yarrow, & King, 1979) and that person-centered maternal communication enhances the ability of children to focus spontaneously on the feelings and needs of others.

CONTRIBUTION TO MEDIATED THERAPEUTIC COMMUNICATION

Radio call-in psychology programs may be considered as modeling therapeutic communication on both cognitive and affective levels. Although most call-in psychology programs are hosted by psychologists, there are a number of shows which feature members of various other professions—psychiatry, social work, nursing, anthropology, biology—and some who have had no special training. However, almost half of the audience is unaware of the difference. The 1986 study revealed that 40 percent of the respondents incorrectly identified nonpsychologist hosts as psychologists. Even research psychologists (Stiles, 1979) have failed to differentiate between psychologists and other professionals.

In the 1960s the community mental health movement supported the training of paraprofessionals, and many outcome studies were done which compared the interventions of these workers with those of professionals. In one classic study (Rioch, 1962) little difference was found. The enthusiasm of the community mental health movement led to training bartenders, taxi drivers, hairdressers, and others in service occupations to provide "therapeutic" services, although care was taken not to label the interventions "therapy" (Bouhoutsos, 1970). Training in most instances consisted of teaching active listening. Advice-giving, confrontation, interpretations, and other such interventions were to be avoided because such activities were considered to demand the expertise of mental health professionals. Therapeutic communication as described in the communication literature also requires more than active listening. Facilitating communicators' development of personal insight or reorientation (Barnlund, 1968) suggests interventions similar to those used in some schools of psychotherapy.

From the perspective of most psychotherapists, especially those who are client-centered, the supportive function is important, but it is only a small part of therapy and the many varied techniques utilized in working with patients. A study (Hill, Thames, & Rardin, 1979) comparing verbal responses of therapists from various schools of therapy (Rogers, Perls, and Ellis) utilizing a verbal response category system found marked differences between these very distinguished therapists which were representative of their particular theoretical positions. For example, the analysis showed that Rogers avoids evaluation, interpretation, and criticism and provides encouragement, restating, and reflection. Perls, on the other hand, uses confrontation, direct guidance, and information while Ellis stresses re-education. Such studies of therapists' verbal responses have proliferated in the past three or four decades, and verbatim transcription has allowed careful analysis of the different schools of psychotherapy and a plethora of response category systems (Goodman & Dooley, 1976; Marsden, 1971; Kiesler, 1973; Stiles, 1979). Most of these systems have in common that they seek to provide empirical support for the relationships between the theory of each type of therapy and its application in the therapeutic process. For example, Stiles points out that client-centered therapy prescribes using only the client's frame of reference and favors reflection; Gestalt therapy advocates avoiding the patient's frame of reference in favor of the therapist's own existential frame of reference, thus calling forth advisement from the therapist about the "here and now," and psychoanalysis utilizes interpretation as the most important function for the therapist; advisement is unacceptable as well as confirmation, since the psychoanalytic viewpoint is that change comes from becoming aware of old meanings of experiences and recasting them in a new frame of referance provided by the therapist" (Stiles, 1979, p. 57). Thus, the process of therapy is dictated by the theoretical orientation of the therapist.

Radio call-in psychology program hosts also differ in their interventions, but it is not clear whether they do so because of their different theoretical orientations, a desire to please their audiences, or hypotheses about benefitting their callers and listeners. What little literature exists on media psychology contains differing opinions about the value of supportive interventions. For example, Mitchell, Billings, and Moos (1982) studies emphasize the importance of social support as primary prevention and Ricks (1983) states that:

> We should recognize that the measure of mental health efforts may be in the extent to which we generate successful social networks within families,

groups, and communities. To that end, we can ill afford to overlook electronic media as potential partners in our efforts to improve the human condition. In times where the economy restrains mental health professionals from increasing their numbers and programs and in localities where populations are remote from services, broadcast media, such as radio, literally and figuratively amplify our capability to change social awareness and increase supportive social behavior.

On the other hand, Levy (1989) enlisted 43 psychologists to judge 12 taped segments of four radio call-in psychology program hosts to assess the extent to which the calls provided social support for callers and for the listening audience. The judges' findings were that the conversations were marginally helpful to callers, and that they provided a moderate amount of social support. They assessed the interventive effectiveness of the hosts as quite varied. The quality of the advice and the accuracy in assessing callers' problems was rated below average. Viewed in terms of social support, the calls were rated by the judges as providing a moderate amount for the listening audience but less for the callers. The judges also concluded that although members of the listening audience might apply the offered advice to themselves, the effects would probably be inconsequential.

Quite different results were obtained in a Denver study (Bouhoutsos, 1989), which queried callers about why they called and whether they received what they wanted from their psychologist hosts. Originally designed to replicate the New York Study (Bouhoutsos, Goodchilds, & Huddy 1986), the same demographic questions were used, but additional information was sought regarding content. An important difference was the time of the Denver program, between 1 and 3 pm in comparison with New York's 9 pm to midnight schedule. Also, the areas reached by KOA, the Denver station, was heavily rural and 92 percent of the callers were white in contrast to the New York study where most of the callers were urban and of mixed ethnicity. Further differences noted were that over half of the Denver callers were employed, most of them full time. Sixty eight percent were married and living with their spouses and only 13 percent had never been married, a marked difference from the New York study where almost half of the callers had never been married and only a fourth were married and living with spouses. The average amount of schooling completed by the KOA callers was two years of college and 40 percent were college graduates or had professional training beyond the BA level in contrast to the New York study, in which over 50 percent had no more than a high school education.

Callers to both the New York and Denver programs were devoted listeners, almost three quarters of whom had been listening regularly for years. Asked whether they called with a specific problem and whether they had

had the problem for some time, three quarters responded positively, and well over half stated that they had had that problem for years.

Three quarters of the callers indicated that they called to get advice and 16 percent wanted information, but none of the callers revealed a need for support, sympathetic listening, or someone to talk to, needs which had surfaced in the New York study, suggesting that marked regional differences exist among callers as far as their needs and expectations for radio call-in psychology programs.

The Denver study (Bouhoutsos, 1988), in contrast to the New York study (Bouhoutsos, Goodchild, & Huddy, 1986), was taped off the air and it was thus possible to examine the content of the calls, adding other dimensions to the findings. The New York study was dependant on callers' responses for whatever content could be remembered by them in retrospect. Evaluation of the usefulness of the calls also rested solely on the judgment of the caller. The Denver study allowed for examination and rating of the content by judges. For example, the Denver callers were asked whether advice and/or referrals were given, whether specific language was modeled, and whether the call provided for them what they wanted. The callers' answers were compared with those of the judges who rated the tapes and analyzed the calls.

Of primary concern to the judges was the nature of the presenting problem as identified by the caller and whether the host focused on that identified problem or whether she reframed the problem. The judges identified the content initially designated by the caller as the problem area and assigned it to one of two categories: Inter- or Intrapersonal. Interpersonal problems were defined as external problems between callers and other individuals, systems or controls. Intrapersonal problems would include internal difficulties, such as self-esteem, depression, anxiety, anger, jealousy, and other feelings, or physical problems, difficulty in communication, conflicts dealing with sexuality, or other issues involving the individual's relationship with himself or herself.

The judges attempted to address the following questions: What was the problem initially presented by the caller and was that problem focused on by the host or was the focus changed? If it was changed, in what direction, inter- or intrapersonal?

Almost all problems (173) were originally presented as interpersonal. The Denver host expanded these (to 233) and changed 4/5 of them to intrapersonal, or internal focus. She also modeled specific language for callers in about half the calls. Neither support nor the provision of information were seen by the judges as the predominant mode used by the host, which findings supported the view of the callers and their expressed needs for advice rather than support. Referrals were given in almost 3/4 of the cases. Callers generally found the calls helpful, with over 90 percent rating them 6 or above on a 10-point scale. The mean rating of the helpfulness of the call as assessed by callers was 7.9, by the judges 7.8, a rather remarkable degree of agreement.

There was no relationship found between the rating the calls received and the amount of time allotted to that call, nor was there any significance found in the length of time the host spoke versus the time the caller spoke, so that the criticism expressed by both New York and Denver callers, that their time on air was too short, did not appear to affect the ratings. There was also no relationship between the ratings and whether or not calls were reframed. A very significant difference (at the .0001 level) was noted, however, in the focus by callers and host, with intrapersonal focus characterizing those of the host and interpersonal those of the callers. In other words, callers presented their problems in terms of external concerns and the host changed the focus to what was going on within the individual.

Despite the denial by callers of the need for support, callers given support by the host rated the calls significantly higher.

In conclusion, whether reframing is done or supportive intervention, radio call-in psychology programs and mediated therapeutic communication are clearly not psychotherapy, although similarities in process exist. Clearly more research is needed to explore boundaries and refine definitions. Communication scholars with an interest in psychology and psychologists interested in media might well find synergistic benefits from collaboration in these studies.

REFERENCES

American Psychological Association. (1977, 1981). *Ethical Standards of Psychologists*. Washington, DC: Author.

Aspy, D. (1975). Empathy: Let's get the hell on with it. *Counseling Psychology, 5,* 10–14.

Association for Media Psychology. (1982). *Guidelines*. Santa Monica, CA: Author.

Barnlund, D. (1968). Introduction to therapeutic communication. In D. C. Barnlund (Ed.), *Interpersonal communication: Survey and studies*. Boston: Houghton Mifflin.

Bouhoutsos, J. C. (1983). The mental health professions and the media. In P. A. Keller & L. G. Ritt (Eds.), *Innovations in clinical practice: A source book* (pp. 361–370). Sarasota, FL: Professional Resource Exchange, Inc.

Bouhoutsos, J. (1970). The non-traditionally trained mental health worker: Fad or future? *Professional Psychology, 1*(5), 455–459.

Bouhoutsos, J. Goodchilds, J., & Huddy, L. (1986). Media psychology: An empirical study of radio call-in psychology programs. *Professional Psychology: Research and Practice, 17*(5), 408–414.

Bouhoutsos, J. (1989). Unpublished manuscript.

Burleson, B. (1984). Comforting communication. In H. Sypher & J. Applegate (Eds.), *Communication by children and adults: Social cognitive and strategic processes* (pp. 63–104). Beverly Hills: Sage.

Cantor, G., & Pingree, S. (1983). *The soap opera.* Beverly Hills: Sage.

Compesi, R. (1980). Gratifications of daytime TV serial viewers. *Journalism Quarterly, 57,* 155–158.

Dorr, A., Graves, S. B., & Phelps, E. (1980). Television literacy for young children. *Journal of Communication, 30,* 71–83.

Feshbach, N. (1983). *Empathy in children.* Presentation at Beijing Normal University. Beijing, China.

Feshbach, N. (1979). Empathy training: A field study in affective education. In S. Feshbach & A. Fraczek (Eds.), *Aggression and behavior change: Journal of Clinical Child Biological and social processes* (pp. 234–249). New York: Praeger.

Gardiner, J. (1982). *A mass media campaign to promote divorce adjustment.* Unpublished doctoral dissertation, Utah State University, Provo.

Gomez, A. (1971). [Federation of Guatamalan Radio Transmission in the Schools]. Federacion Guattemalteca de escuelas radiofonicas. D. F. Friedrich Ebert Foundation Seminar on Rural Radio, Mexico.

Goodman, G., & Dooley, D. (1976). A framework for help-intended communication. *Psychotherapy, 13,* 106–117.

Gunter, J., & Theroux, J. (1977). Open-broadcast educational radio: Three paradigms. World Bank, Working Paper 266.

Henricks, W., & Stiles, W. (1987, May). *Radio psychology: "Advice" or "therapeutic service"?* Paper presented at Midwestern Psychological Association Convention, Chicago.

Hill, C., Thames, T., & Rardin, D. (1979). Comparison of Rogers, Perls, and Ellis on the Hill Counselor Verbal Response Category system. *Journal of Counseling Psychology, 26*(3), 198–203.

Jamison, D., & McAnany, E. (1978). *Radio for education and development.* Beverly Hills: Sage.

Johnston, J. (1983). Using television to change stereotypes. In J. Sprafkin, C. Swift, & R. Hess (Eds.), *RX television: Enhancing the preventive impact of TV* (pp. 67–82). New York: Haworth Press.

Keith-Spiegel, P., & Koocher, G. (1985). *Ethics in psychology: Professional standards and cases.* New York: Random House.

Kiesler, D. (1973). *The process of psychotherapy: Empirical foundations and systems of analysis.* Chicago: Aldine.

Kinyanjui, P. (1974). Training teachers by correspondence. *IEC Broadsheets on Distance Learning, 5.* Cambridge, England: International Extension College.

Klibanoff, L., Hersey, J., & Probst, J. (1983). An evaluation of FRIENDS CAN BE GOOD MEDICINE: Long term impacts of the pilot project and study of the statewide project Sacramento: California Department of Mental Health.

Klonoff, E. (1983). A star is born: Psychologists and the media. *Professional Psychology: Research and Practice, 14,* 847–854.

Kreimer, O. (1977). In P. Spain, D. Jamison, & E. McAnany (Eds.), *Radio for education and development: Case Studies.* Washington, DC: World Bank, Working Paper 266.

Levy, D. (1989). Social support and the media: Analysis of responses by radio talk show hosts. *Professional Psychology: Research and Practice, 20,* 73–78.

Maccoby, N., & Farquar, J. (1975). Communication for health: Unselling heart disease. *Journal of Communication, 25*(3), 114–126.

Manoff International Inc. (1975). *Mass Media and Nutrition Education* Progress Report. AID/TA-C-1133.

Marsden, G. (1971). Content-analysis studies of psychotherapy: 1954 through 1968. In A. Bergin & S. Garfield (Eds.), *Handbook of Psychotherapy and Behavior Change*. New York: Wiley.

McAlister, A., Puska, P., Koskela, K., Pallonen, U., & Maccoby, N. (1980). Mass communications and community organization for public health education. *American Psychologist, 35*(4), 375–379.

Miller, F. (1979). *Television news: Effect of content and presentation on viewer stress response*. Unpublished doctoral dissertation, United States International University, San Diego.

Miller, G. A. (1969). Psychology as a means of promoting human welfare. *American Psychologist, 24*, 1063–1075.

Mitchell, R., Billings, A., Andrews, G., & Moos, R. (1982). Social support and well-being. *Journal of Primary Prevention, 3*(2), 77–98.

Monaghan, J., Shun Wah, A., Steward, I., & Smith, L. (1978). The role of talkback radio: A study. *Journal of Commmunity Psychology, 6*, 351–356.

Nielson Television Index. (1981). *National audience demographics: Monday-Friday daytime estimates of individual network program audiences*. A. C. Nielsen: New York.

Ricks, J. (1983). *Radio, Social Support and Mental Health*. Presentation, World Congress of Mental Health, Washington, DC.

Rioch, M. (1962). *Pilot Project in Training Mental Health Counselors*. Report # 1254. Public Health Service, Washington, DC

Schramm, W., Coombs, P., Kahnert, & Lyle, J. (1967). *New educational media in action—case studies, I*. Unesco: Paris.

Schwebel, A. I. (1982). Radio psychologists: A community psychology/psycho-educational model. *Journal of Community Psychology, 10*, 181–184.

Sprafkin, J., & Rubinstein, E. (1983). Using television to improve the social behavior of institutionalized children. In J. Sprafkin, C. Swift, & R. Hess (Eds.), *Rx television: Enhancing the preventive impact of TV* (pp. 125–139). New York: Haworth Press.

Stiles, W. (1979). Verbal response modes and psychotherapeutic technique. *Psychiatry, 42*, 49–62.

Truax, C., & Carkhuff, R. (1967). *Toward effective counseling and psychotherapy: Training and practice*. Chicago: Aldine.

Weyand, C. (1980). *Surviving popular psychology*. Northridge, CA: Being Books. Cited in P. Keith-Spiegel & G. Koocher, (1985), *Ethics in psychology: Professional standards and cases*. New York: Random House.

Zahn-Waxler, C., Radke-Yarrow, M., & King, R. (1979). Child rearing and children's prosocial initiations toward victims of distress. *Child Development, 50*, 319–330.

5

Listening to Dr. Ruth: The New Sexual Primer

Jane Banks

One of the best-known media psychologists, Dr. Ruth Westheimer is a legitimate sex therapist as well. In this article the educational and therapeutic functions of the various "Dr. Ruth" programs are examined and positioned culturally. Banks' analysis of the paradoxical combination of public disclosure of the most intimate sexual issues illustrates Westheimer's curious success.

In 1980, Dr. Ruth Westheimer's call-in radio show, *Sexually Speaking,* debuted on the New York FM station, WYNY. Since then, Westheimer's many enterprises have enjoyed phenomenal commercial success. Her output includes two books, a board game, a sexually oriented "fantasy" tour of the Far East, appearances on the college lecture circuit and on network talk shows such as Carson and Letterman, television commercials, the radio show, and her cable television show on the *Lifetime* channel, now also in syndication. This commercial success and its attribution to Westheimer's unique television persona have dominated most of what has been written about her in the popular press. Descriptions of her radio and television programs have usually focused on how the shows rate as entertainment rather than how they function therapeutically or educationally.

Attention from the academic community to programs like Westheimer's has been scant; although there is a literature dealing with radio psychology, it focuses mostly on advice to practitioners unused to working with the media. An exception is a study conducted by Bouhoutsos, Goodchilds, and Huddy (1986) where callers to a radio program were questioned immediately before, immediately after, and three months after they discussed a problem on the air. The majority of their respondents felt that their calls had been helpful, but the researchers themselves could not reliably determine if this was so. In a study focusing specifically on Dr. Ruth, Brian Crow (1986) used conversational analysis rather than interview data to determine the extent to which interactions on Dr. Ruth's cable television show were adequate or valuable for the audience or the callers. Both studies are limited in scope. Crow's admitted "micro-level" analysis seeks answers about the effect of mediation on the interactions through an almost exclusive focus on transcriptions of the calls Dr. Ruth answers on the air. Not surprisingly, few observations about the effect of mediation resulted since written transcripts of the calls were not analyzed in their mediated context. An interesting picture of Westheimer as a skilled manager of interactions does emerge, however, and more research comparing face-to-face with mediated conversations would be valuable, although beyond the scope of this essay.

Like Crow's essay, this chapter examines Dr. Ruth's show, variously titled *Good Sex, The Dr. Ruth Show,* and currently, *Ask Dr. Ruth,* which appears nightly on the *Lifetime* network and is syndicated in some markets; and like Crow, this writer taped several shows for examination, specifically, 10 programs in March and April, 1987. This essay differs, however, in its approach. Rather than presenting the "micro-level" analysis that Crow offers, the purpose of this chapter is to present a "macro-level" look at Dr. Ruth's show as the site where a variety of functions intersect, some of which are common to many television discourses and some of which are unique to this program.

The first function to consider is the one that Dr. Ruth herself admits to—education. In *Health* magazine (1983), belying the article's own headline which referred to her as a sex therapist, she said, "There is no way one can do therapy over the air. All one can do is educate." Certainly much of what happens on the show can be seen as education, and for the purpose of this essay, education will be defined as the communication of information that is formulated for and relevant to a general audience of viewers rather than specific information and advice designed for and given to an individual, regardless of who is listening in. The difference between education and therapeutic communication is necessarily arbitrary, since it is obvious that education can be therapeutic and therapeutic communication can be educational. The distinction is nonetheless important and can be clarified by examining the difference between the following kinds of statements: To her general audience of viewers, Westheimer might say, "There is nothing wrong with occasional masturbation, even in the case where one also has a regular sex partner." This sort of remark is presented as a kind of sexual axiom, and to emphasize its general applicability, Westheimer addresses the camera directly. With an individual caller who is anxious about her husband's occasional masturbation, Westheimer might inquire about whether their sex life is otherwise satisfying and then tell the woman that this behavior most likely does not mean that her husband no longer finds her attractive. In this instance, although the general application of Westheimer's remarks is obvious, the response is designed specifically for the individual, and the general viewing audience is secondary. The individual, not the audience, is the object of Westheimer's remarks, and this is evidenced not only by the verbal design of the message, but also by the fact that, in such cases, Westheimer invariably looks past the camera rather than directly into it, making the distinction between the general viewer and the individual caller visually as well as verbally clear.

The show's format includes not only calls from viewers which Dr. Ruth answers on the air, but also questions for Dr. Ruth and for expert or celebrity guests from a studio audience, and simulated on-air therapy sessions between Dr. Ruth and actors playing the part of clients. Disease prevention, explosion of myths about sex, demystification of sexual concerns and problems, and the relentless promotion of contraception form an important part of each show. All of the show's segments work to fulfill this educational goal. At least once during each show Dr. Ruth will interrupt a caller who is talking about a specific problem to ask if he or she is using contraception. For instance, after a misunderstanding about whether a caller used contraception was cleared up, Dr. Ruth said: "I was just about to wish you very bad sex. Because if anybody wouldn't use contraception, that's what I would wish them." At this point, the interaction shifted from the interpersonal to the public realm, and what had been a message directed to a specific individual becomes a claim directed to the mass audience. Another instance of such a shift was noted in television critic Tom Shales' review in the *Washington Post* (May 10, 1985). After a call from a man who was concerned about his penis size, Westheimer said:

> Men, all of you are ignorant! You are constantly worried about the size of the penis. Let's shout it from the rooftops: The size of the penis has nothing to do with the sexual satisfaction of the woman. (p. C11)

Again, Westheimer moves from a therapeutic to an educational function in this sequence as she takes an individual concern to the level of public discourse for the purpose of exploding a sexual myth.

Dr. Ruth's co-host, Larry Angelo, also works with calls to promote the educational function of the show. Often, after a call that has been inconclusive or highly specfic such that the audience may not understand its relevance, Angelo will step in and refocus the content so that it makes a general kind of sense. For instance, during a call from a woman complaining that her lover was not as affectionate as she would like, Dr. Ruth advised her not to lecture him about it but rather to initiate affection with him and make him respond. After the caller was off the air, Angelo restated Dr. Ruth's answer more generally: "So sometimes action is better than words?" This statement opened the floor for a more generalized discussion of the value of nonverbal communication in sexual relationships, moving the discourse from the private level of individual counseling to the public level of sex education.

The role-play therapy sessions also reinforce this function. While these sessions sometimes deal with unusual problems, such as the case of a married man who discovers he has a child by a previous relationship, more often they are about problems that a great many viewers share, such as how to cope responsibly with teenage pregnancy or how a young man can find a way to tell his family that he is gay. After these therapy sessions, there are questions and comments from the studio audience, and the atmosphere of the show resembles a lively lecture-discussion in a college classroom.

Dr. Ruth's show may function for many viewers primarily as a source for information about sex. This function may be particularly important for younger viewers and for others who find that actively seeking information about sex is threatening. For these viewers, Dr. Ruth, her co-host Angelo, the callers, celebrity guests, and members of the studio audience take the risks of information seeking. Viewers who do not wish to admit ignorance of or interest in sexual matters can attribute their watching to a desire for entertainment or for laughs and obtain the information they want or need without seeming actually to look for it.

That the educational function of the show is paramount is evidenced by both the amount of effort made by Westheimer and Angelo to move back and forth from the interpersonal to the public level of discussion and by the amount of time on the show given over to Dr. Ruth's agenda of topics. The interpersonal discussions of specific problems with individual callers is generalized and moved to the level of public discourse, and, in case the callers' problems are not sufficiently congruent with subjects of general interest and concern for the mass audience, Westheimer reserves large segments of air time for her own agenda, taking most of the control of subjects out of the hands of her callers.

The second aspect of *Ask Dr. Ruth* to be examined in this essay is its function as simulated interpersonal communication. As early as 1956, psychologists Donald Horton and Richard Wohl identified what they referred to as "parasocial interaction" as an important function of television. Television, they argued—particularly the kind in which the performer directly addresses the camera—provides a sort of interpersonal relationship for viewers, a relationship with many of the advantages and few of the risks of face-to-face interaction: "Para-social relations may be governed by little or no sense of obligation, effort, or responsibility on the part of the spectator. He is free to withdraw at any moment" (p. 189). In their discussion of the research in this area, Cathcart and Gumpert (1983) also assert that mediated parasocial relationships may have advantages over "real" interactions because the television performer can approximate an ideal that is impossible in everyday life.

The notion that Dr. Ruth constitutes an ideal companion, sexual adviser, and educator is one aspect of the phenomenon that has been discussed at length by popular critics. Her popularity is attributed in these discussions almost entirely to her personal style. The *Washington Post* called her "The Pixie of Passion" (Shales, 1985), *Playboy* referred to her as "the pint-sized Pollyanna of passion" (1986), and *Time* talked about her as "The Munchkin of the Bedroom" (Lee, 1985). Numerous references to Westheimer's diminuitive size appear in popular discussions, as do mentions of her persona as the perfect relative (variously grandmother, mother, aunt) who is willing to answer viewers' questions about sex in detail, reassure them that they are normal, or even tell them that what they are doing is wrong. Westheimer's role as the ideal participant in a parasocial relationship is taken a step further by the aspect of the program that Cathcart and Gumpert (1983) refer to in their typology of mediated interpersonal communication as "broadcast telepaticipatory interaction" (p. 274). This interaction, they argue, works as a safer substitute for face-to-face relations, but in exchange for the relatively low risk of such encounters, the caller is faced with severe constraints on his or her communicative be-

> Unlike telephone talk, sender-receiver roles are relatively fixed, there is little or no relational development, and the communicative code is restricted-implicit rather than unrestricted-implicit. Even on phone-in shows featuring psychologist hosts where callers often disclose intimate sexual information, both interactants follow carefully proscribed restricted language codes more suitable for public forums . . . (p. 274)

That the commercial, mediated channel imposes constraints on attempts at interpersonal communication is obvious in the case of *Ask Dr. Ruth.* Even if callers were somehow unaware of the restricted symbolic range of television, the careful screening process would weed out those callers whose interaction seemed likely to violate acceptable rules. As Cathcart and Gumpert assert, "The exercise of this control teaches the audience the restricted code of 'public' interpersonal communication, rewarding those who can perform the 'ideal' intimate communication with the host" (p. 274). This "ideal" places restrictions on both participants, not solely the caller. If Dr. Ruth is to maintain the persona that has made her so successful, she must simultaneously fulfill the conflicting requirements for both public and interpersonal communication. Crow's analysis and examples from this author's sample programs indicate that she is largely successful. Crow (1966) describes two compliment sequences from Westheimer's show. One is brief, indicating an awareness of the rules of public interpersonal communication with regard to time constraints. The second is much longer than usual, requiring two promptings from Westheimer, and including two extra compliment sequences before the caller finally gets to the point (1986, p. 464–465). Crow argues that it is the sensitive nature of the problem (an ex-prostitute, now married, cannot enjoy sex) that has expanded the usual compliment sequence to such an extent, but an alternative explanation is that the caller is dissatisfied with the abridged nature of the relational development and seeks to expand it. This writer would argue that an almost parenthetical analysis by Crow is closer to the mark. Observing that the caller included a compliment to Westheimer's co-host Angelo about his looks, Crow attributes this behavior to her former calling as a prostitute. Another reading might indicate that the caller, like Dr. Ruth, has been a professional communicator and has standards for opening talk sequences necessary for putting clients at ease before the real work begins that outstrip the brevity required when one interacts with many people in an hour as Westheimer does. In spite of the differences between the interactants' requirements for meaningful communication, Westheimer prevails in both managing the time constraints and meeting at least some of the caller's needs.

Overall, Westheimer emerges as a skilled manager of interactions in her advice sequences with callers. Unlike most talk radio shows, there is no 7-second delay on *Ask Dr. Ruth*, so adhering to acceptable rules for public communication is the responsibility of the screening process and of Westheimer herself. Although the control room could cut off a caller who became obscene or abusive, Crow reports that this has never happened (p. 458). Westheimer herself manages those callers whose problems are presented in an incoherent or fragmented way by probing questions that lead the caller quickly to the point. In addition, callers to Dr. Ruth are never left hanging; Westheimer always effects a quick and optimistic closure even when she declines to give any advice other than a referral, thus minimizing any feeling of abandonment on the part of the callers.

Although Westheimer's interactions with callers are skillfully managed, the simulated interpersonal communication of *Ask Dr. Ruth* has disadvangages that are similar to those surrounding the show's educational function. Attempts are made in both cases to provide as much satisfaction to as many viewers as possible, but the publicness of the discourse precludes much attention to individual concerns. Westheimer, in taking over most of her show's agenda, tries to broaden its educational value to include as many viewers as possible, but a viewer seeking specific information must be one of the lucky few callers who gets through, or must wait until his or her concern arises on the air. Similarly, even though Westheimer's warm, unthreatening persona may approximate that of an ideal relative, the constraints of the medium preclude genuine interaction between her and viewers or even individual callers. And in both the case of education and the case of interaction, the gatekeeping and agenda-setting components of the show are almost entirely one-sided, with even the participation of the callers and members of the studio audience under the watchful and controlling eye of Westheimer and her staff. Thus, the relatively low risk of interaction and information seeking is counterbalanced by viewers' and callers' lack of genuine autonomy in relation to the show.

Closely related to the function of *Ask Dr. Ruth* as simulated interpersonal communication is its function as therapeutic communication. It is important to note here that both educational and interactional functions can also be described as therapeutic in the sense that any communication that helps people to function more effectively with others is therapeutic. But this section of the essay will focus specifically on two levels of interaction—two sets of "clients" in the therapeutic relationship. First are the callers, those people who call the toll-free number with questions for Westheimer, come up with a problem that suits the show's agenda for the day, survive the screening process, and get on the air to speak with the Doctor. The rewards for this vary, but most often the callers get a quick assessment of their problem through a set of probing questions that explore some of the alternative interpretations of the problem as initially stated by the caller, and then either a referral to a therapist for problems that require ongoing treatment, or some straightforward advice from Westheimer. The following sequence is a fairly typical example of an interaction with a caller. A 20-year-old woman called and told Westheimer that, although she was a virgin, she had visited a gynecologist and gotten on the pill because she and her boyfriend were planning to have intercourse. Her problem was her fear that intercourse would be painful. After congratulating the young woman on her responsible approach in ensuring good contraception, Westheimer began the questioning, advice-giving sequence:

R: Let me ask you a question, Dawn. When the two of you kiss, does it feel good?
C: Yes.
R: When he touches your breasts, does that feel good?
C: Yes.
R: Terrific. So when the two of you decide [to have intercourse], make sure you are in a place where you don't have to rush, all right?
C: All right.
R: Get a lubricant, a K-Y lubricant, even though you *are* getting moist, which means you *are* aroused and you *do* lubricate, and put a little bit of that lubricant inside your vagina—or, you know what? Let him do it. And then put your behind on a pillow and *you* actually hold his penis and you insert his penis into your vagina, so this way *you* have control, do you understand?
C: Yes.
R: And if you are very relaxed, and the two of you really love each other, and you are protected so that you don't have to worry about pregnancy, and you do it in a place where nobody can walk in, then you should be all right.

Here we see a typical pattern of interaction. The opening sequence, which was omitted from the transcript, was somewhat easier for Westheimer than usual because the participant omitted the compliment sequence that callers commonly begin with and simply stated her name and introduced her problem. After the problem was stated completely, Westheimer began her exploration with the three-question sequence inquiring how the young woman felt during kissing and petting and ending with its having been established that she was lubricating when she engaged in foreplay with her boyfriend. In this sequence we see an extremely efficient use of time by Westheimer. She does not inquire about the foreplay in detail, but asks just enough questions to ascertain that the woman is sexually interested in her young man. In this way Westheimer effectively eliminates alternative scenarios, such as the possibility that the woman's interest in having intercourse is solely because of pressure from her partner, and can then get down to an effective course of advice, being reasonably certain that she is on the right track. In the final advice sequences, we see a practicality that is typical of Westheimer's interactions, detailed even to the brand-name of the lubricant she advises the young woman to buy. The interaction has been brief, but effective. Westheimer does not explore the woman's fears with her or inquire into her feelings about becoming sexually active, but she does take the time to establish that the woman has some sexual interest in her partner before she gives her set of instructions. The instructions themselves are clear and explicit, although, like the opening interaction, brief. The caller seemed relieved at the end of the sequence, and thanked Westheimer in a way that suggested that she had gotten what she wanted.

In another example Westheimer's brevity seems inadequate. A housewife from Texas called complaining that she did not come to orgasm during intercourse. Probing questions from Westheimer revealed that she could bring herself to orgasm, but the woman is concerned about that, too:

C: I'm not sure if how I have an orgasm is the right way.
R: There's no such thing as the right way or wrong way. Does it feel good when you do it?
C: Yes.

Westheimer then returned to the woman's original question by instructing the woman to show her husband how to touch her and bring her to orgasm. She was quite explicit in doing this, telling the woman to move her husband's hand on or around the clitoris, and she reinforced this visually by demonstrating with her own hand. But the caller had been distracted from her original concern, and brought Westheimer back to the subject of how to orgasm.

C: To be very explicit, what I was concerned about is . . . you know . . . when you do reach an orgasm, your body moves in different ways, like your legs stiffen up, that type of thing. And that's why I was wondering . . . it's embarassing, you wonder, well—is that the right way?

Westheimer heard this woman's call for reassurance, and in her response we can see the conflict between wanting to comfort her caller and remaining mindful of the needs of her larger audience of viewers:

R: It certainly—*any* way that makes you feel good is the right way . . . and many women do report that their body gets a little bit tightened . . .

C: Yes?

R: And then they have an orgasm.

Westheimer's original response to her caller's concern about the "right way" to orgasm was clearly not sufficient. Instead of reassuring her caller that her orgasm was normal, she delivered a sexual axiom designed to keep all her viewers reassured. The caller was not satisfied that her description was normal and returned to the problem. Westheimer obviously recognized the concern the second time around and began to assure the caller that her specific type of orgasm was perfectly normal by saying "It certainly . . . ." At this point, Westheimer became mindful of her larger audience of viewers who might become concerned if she pronounced her caller's orgasm normal, implying that any different kind would be abnormal, and backed off the statement, returning to her axiom that there was no right or wrong way to orgasm. But sensing that this would not be enough for her caller to feel reassured, Westheimer points out that her reaction is common. Clearly, Westheimer was on the right track, as evidenced by the woman's anxious "Yes?" interrupting her description.

In this instance we see that there is clearly a conflict between the educational and therapeutic functions of the program. By moving her advice from the axiomatic to the specific, Westheimer could reassure her caller only at the expense of her viewers. To tell this woman that her orgasm is normal may have the effect of telling some viewers that theirs are abnormal, so what may be therapeutic to one viewer may be harmful to many others. Questions that callers raise on the air are controlled by Westheimer's gatekeepers who screen the calls, so it is difficult to say what the general trend of calls is, but calls what actually make it on the air generally fall into three categories: The first category centers around questions of normality, as in the call discussed above. The second group are those questions asking permission to engage in or to continue a certain kind of sexual behavior. Permission is sometimes given and sometimes withheld. For instance, when a teenage boy called asking if it was all right to masturbate more than once a day, Westheimer inquired about his social life. Upon hearing that it was nil, she suggested that he was using masturbation as a substitute for social interaction and that he limit it and put some of that energy into making friends of both sexes. The third category of questions are questions about relationship or sexual dysfunction. These range from questions that are not specifically about sex, such as how to deal with jealousy or how to tell someone that you don't want to see them anymore, to questions about specific sexual dysfunction such as premature ejaculation or failure to orgasm. It is in this third category of questions that Westheimer most often makes referrals to therapists. This may be why she sees what she does as educational rather than therapeutic. Westheimer has credentials as a bona fide sex therapist; she sees private clients three times a week and studied under Helen Singer Kaplan, probably the country's best-known sex therapist after Masters and Johnson. For problems that have standard treatment, such as premature ejaculation, Westheimer invariably recommends ongoing therapy and acknowledges the limitations of her on-air counsel. In response to a woman with a complicated problem involving her husband's current lack of interest in sex, his medication for high blood pressure, and his sexual affinity for pregnant women, she recommends therapy, saying "I could never solve that on the air"

Within the limitations imposed by the medium, Westheimer does a creditable job in helping her callers, and perhaps a better one in helping her second set of clients. These are the individual viewers who comprise that portion of the audience for whom at any given time the problem being discussed on the air is particularly relevant. For these people, whoever discusses "their" problem on the air serves as their surrogate, a bolder version of themselves who acts out their problems on the small screen. In this instance, the agenda-setting task performed by Westheimer and her staff supports the therapeutic function of the show. They can ensure that common problems that are not raised by callers get airplay anyway, and the segments in the show that do not include interactions with callers work to include more viewers in the therapeutic community. In addition to the callers, celebrity guests discuss sexual problems on the air, sometimes even their own. Comedian Richard Lewis, for instance, made jokes about his sexual anxieties on one segment. Some guests on *Ask Dr. Ruth* were experts in aspects of sexuality or relationships. A woman who writes a column on dating, for instance, shared stories about trying to meet eligible singles, and a journalist and a psychiatrist contributed their insights on cross-dressing, although not from the perspective of practitioners. On this particular topic, even co-host Angelo served as a surrogate for those viewers who might have more than a passing interest in transvestitism. In the opening moments of the show, after she introduced the topic, Westheimer said "I won't ask you what you have on under your suit, I won't even ask you, but today we're going to talk about men who wear women's clothes." Although the remark was obviously not meant seriously, Angelo's coy silence in response to Westheimer's teasing worked to demystify the topic for viewers.

Another important segment on the show that serves this second set of clients is the simulated therapy sessions where actors play the part of clients. The problems that these "clients" discuss with Westheimer are usually fairly common, and the audience is invited to identify with them as they serve as surrogates and literally "act out"some viewers' problems. After these therapy sessions, the viewing audience receives another invitation to participate when the studio audience is asked for questions and comments. On the show concerning how to meet prospective mates, two bartenders offered their first-hand observations of the singles scene, and a newly divorced man shared his experiences and made suggestions that he hoped would work for others in his situation, specifically, to another man in the audience who was struggling with the same problem:

> I'm just recently divorced, and this might help that fellow over there [points to another member of the studio audience] who was talking about what time period you go through before you start to date again. I went back to my friends. It worked for me—it might work for you, I don't know. I was shell-shocked just like you are, too, believe me. [cut to man who was talking about his divorce. Second man nods and smiles gratefully. To expert guest:] Is it friends that help us do it?

Here we see the establishment of what Westheimer herself called a "community of listeners" (*Playboy*, 1986). The two newly divorced men in the studio audience have formed a kind of support group, inviting those in similar situations to join with them for everyone's mutual benefit. Even viewers who would rather spend hours in the dentist's chair than 20 minutes in any kind of therapy can benefit from vicarious participation in this mediated alliance which provides them simultaneously with the comfort of closeness and the safety of distance. Viewers who engage with these temporary therapeutic communities can at any moment withdraw from the interaction and deny even to themselves that they have participated since these interactions are not "real" in the ordinary sense. This "intimate distance" offers a distinct advantage for many viewers who are unwilling to invest the requisite time, money, and emotional commitment involved in ongoing face-to-face therapy.

For both callers and viewers, the first and second set of clients, the disadvantages in the therapeutic relationships offered on *Ask Dr. Ruth* paradoxically work as advantages. As communication professionals, we tend to think that interactions work best when as many channels as possible are involved. The disembodiment and displacement of the interactions on Westheimer's show seem at first glance to be immense handicaps in the communication process. While this is certainly the case in some ways, as has been pointed out earlier in this essay, it is not the case in others. The anonymity offered callers, for instance, by the disembodied medium of the telephone hails back to the confessional where the priest was not only bound by a vow of silence but was also prevented from seeing the face of the penitent. This works effectively in two ways: First, the client-penitent does not have to "face up" to the sin, the priest does not see the individual, already laid bare by confession, in his or her full nakedness. It is obvious that anonymity makes it easier to confess, especially sexual sins, since the confessor may not see the body that comitted them. Secondly, although it is axiomatic in the field of communication that we receive extra information through the addition of channels in the communication process, there is some dissent regarding the accuracy of meanings derived from this additional information. Desmond Morris (1977) argues that people learn to control their visual affect displays quite effectively at an early age. He suggests that paralinguistic cues are more out of the individual's control, so that the most telling nonverbal "leakage" of feelings can be discerned over the telephone, where there are no contradictory visual cues to confuse the listener. This may be a way to account partially for Westheimer's often uncanny insight. Perhaps her ability to discern covered meanings so quickly and accurately is *because* of, not in spite of, the medium. The truncation that inheres in this version of mediated therapeutic communication, then, works as an enabler for both the client and the counselor while simultaneously restricting and abridging the therapeutic interaction.

Another advantage that may accrue from the disembodiment of the interactions on *Ask Dr. Ruth* is to mask or deny the sexual nature of the show. A therapeutic function of the program that can only be guessed at is its direct role in the sexual lives of some viewers. We have seen in this essay several examples of the explicitness of the sex talk on the program; this explicitness is unusual, even for cable, and *Ask Dr. Ruth* is syndicated on regular channels in some markets. In a study analyzing Westheimer's guest appearances on network talk shows, Rodney Buxton (1987) argues that it is Westheimer's professional credentials that allow her to talk so frankly on television. Certainly her privileged status as an expert with a diagnostic, clinical gaze contributes to the freedom that she has on the air; this, too, works to mask the sexual nature of the program. But it is the lack of a visual referent that may allow this talk most of all. While it is true that Westheimer herself is represented visually, as are her co-host Angelo, the studio audience members, and the celebrity guests, the sex itself is absent from the screen. The explicit sexual nature of the show is provided by the faceless callers and by Westheimer herself. And although the doctor is visually present, her image and voice work as an antisignifier of sex, given our cultural codes of what looks and sounds sexual. Even as the verbal content of the show titilates some viewers, the visual and aural content desexualize the program, allowing viewers to deny any sexual purpose in viewing. As *Time* critic John Lee (1985) noted,

When you listen to Dr. Ruth, you feel a surge of therapeutic uplift that many of us find to be missing from your average pornofilm. So you don't have to feel slimy at all when you hear what Yvonne of Tuscon does with the cool whip. (p. 52)

The multiple functions of the show allow viewers to attribute their viewing to any number of socially acceptable motives, and the contradictory visual, aural, and verbal cues further enable them to deny any prurient intent.

The interactions on *Ask Dr. Ruth* are not only disembodied, they are also displaced. When Westheimer refers to her "community of listeners," she is talking about a group of individuals whose unifying factor is something other than geographical location. Similarities of therapeutic method between Westheimer and a priest hearing confession were noted earlier in this essay. For some of her callers, Westheimer may have taken the place of an earlier confessor, even to the granting of absolution, and in some ways, shows like Westheimer's have replaced the function of institutions like the parish church. Gumpert (1987) notes that the community of place, characterized by the public square, the cafe, the local pub, and so on as primary sites of interaction, has been supplanted by the media community. As Gumpert points out, economic factors figure largely in this new "nonplace community" (p. 178). As we look to media communities to fulfill our interpersonal and therapeutic needs, our interactions that were both free and private are commodified and publicized. When therapeutic communication becomes the province of the professional, as it has in this century to a large extent, the relationship becomes economic as well in most cases. The therapeutic relationship is further commodified when it is mediated in the case of *Ask Dr. Ruth*. Callers and viewers do not write checks directly to Westheimer, Lifetime Network, or King Features Syndication, but a basic knowledge of media economics will tell us that the viewers are the commodity in the case of programs supported by advertising, and subscribers to the *Lifetime* network must pay fees.

In *Ask Dr. Ruth*, interactions are not only commodified, they are also publicized. Private acts and private talk are exposed to millions of viewers, quasisanitized for television by Westheimer's diagnostic, professional approach and by her antisexual visual and aural image. Mass exposure makes these interactions more public, and simultaneously disembodiment and displacement make them more private than face-to-face communication. Meyrowitz (1985) argues that one effect of media in general is the "blurring of public and private behaviors" (p. 93). What is true of media is truer of Westheimer's program since the behavior that is made public by the medium has always been considered particularly private.

In the last half-century, the community of place has been supplanted by a new environment where communication functions formerly fulfilled in libraries, kitchens, barbershops, cafes, and pubs have moved to a new location, although nobody can say precisely where that is. In the media community, interactions take place everywhere and nowhere. As education, interpersonal communication, therapeutic communication, and sexual behavior are publicized and commodified, they become anonymous, disembodied, displaced, and stripped of any risk at all. With *Ask Dr. Ruth*, needs for information, for interaction, for therapeutic communication, or for sex can at the same time be met and denied or effaced in a way that is impossible when they are fuliilled in a community of place. "Watching television" is the activity that subsumes and masks the show's other functions. In our new media environment, *Ask Dr. Ruth* is the ultimate in safe sex.

REFERENCES

Bouhoutsos, J. C., Goodchilds, J. D., & Huddy, L. (1986). Media psychology: An empirical study of radio call-in psychology programs. *Professional Psychology: Research and Practice, 17*(5), 408–414.

Buxton, R. A. (1987, May). *Dr. Ruth Westheimer: Upsetting the normalcy of the late-night talk show*. Paper presented at the meeting of the International Communication Association, Montreal, Canada.

Cathcart, R., & Gumpert, G. (1983). Mediated interpersonal communication: Toward a new typology. *Quarterly Journal of Speech, 69*, 267–277.

Crow, B. (1986). Conversational pragmatics in television talk: The discourse of *Good Sex. Media, Culture, and Society 8*, 457–484.

Gumpert, G. (1987). *Talking tombstones and other tales of the media age*. New York: Oxford University Press.

Horton, M., & Wohl, R. (1983). Mass communication and para-social interaction: Observations on intimacy at a distance. In G. Gumpert & R. Cathcart (Eds.), *Inter/Media: Interpersonal communication in a media world* (pp. 189–211). New York: Oxford University Press.

Lee, J. (1985, July 1). The munchkin of the bedroom. *Time*, p. 52.

Meyrowitz, J. (1985). *No sense of place*. New York: Oxford University Press.

Morris, D. (1977). *Manwatching*. New York: Harry N. Abrams, Inc.

Playboy interview: Dr. Ruth Westheimer. (1986, January). *Playboy*, pp. 61–76.

Shales, T. (1985, May 10). Dr. Ruth, TV's pixie of passion. *The Washington Post*, pp. Cl, Cll.

6
Talk Radio: The Private-Public Catharsis
Robert K. Avery

Tracing the development of talk radio to its current format, Avery identifies both the scope and functions of this form of mediated therapeutic communication. Both calling in and listening to talk radio appear to fulfill a need for interpersonal interaction. The fact that both the host and the listening audience are strangers to the caller may actually promote disclosure.

As this chapter was being written, the play *Talk Radio* was in performance at The Public Theatre in New York City; a U. S. district court jury had recently convicted two members of a neo-Nazi group for the machine gun slaying of Denver talk show host Alan Berg; and a white supremacist had inaugurated his weekly "Aryan Nations" talk radio program on KZZI in Salt Lake City, Utah. Talk radio was doing more than helping to generate news; it *was* news.

That talk or two-way radio has become a successful contemporary radio format is well established. As early as 1966, *Broadcasting* magazine published a special feature on this emerging genre and estimated that over 80 percent of all AM radio stations included some form of the talk format in their regular broadcast day. The annual radio state-of-the-art reports in the same publication that have appeared during the last two decades provide ample support for the continued viability of talk radio. True, some critics of the mid-1970s forecast the demise of the talk format as Americans tired of such controversial issues as Vietnam, political corruption, and domestic social reform, but the resourcefulness of talk hosts and program directors permitted the standard talk formats to endure the temporary drop in audience. President Carter took advantage of the unique qualities of talk radio when he exchanged viewpoints with callers nationwide in 1977; Governor Mario M. Cuomo used a call-in radio talk show to announce that he would not be a presidential candidate in 1988. Evidence of audience growth can be found in a 1984 study conducted by *Television/Radio Age*. Not only had local stations found new formulae for attracting loyal audiences, but talk show hosts were building national network ratings. The Mutual Broadcasting System, ABC, and NBC had all debuted talk formats with positive results. For example, NBC's *Talknet* grew from 24 affiliated stations in 1982 to 184 stations by 1984. Estimates place the total number of network and local talk shows at more than 3000.[1]

Much of the success of this program genre can be traced to the emergence of "sub formats" in which a particular talk host type attracts a corresponding segment of the total talk radio audience. By exploiting the personality and individual expertise of the talk host, audience members come to identify and expect a specific set of topics to be discussed and the interplay of the talk host's unique treatment. Such on-air personalities as Hilly Rose, Larry King, and Bruce Williams have carved out a special following due to their ability to focus on such specialties as Hollywood stars, sports figures, or the world of finance. But few talk hosts have achieved the popularity of that particular subset of communicasters who specialize in radio talk therapy. Known by such labels as "talk shrinks and "psych jockeys," these on-air psychologists have become a regular staple of the talk radio format. This chapter attempts to place this specialized form of mediated therapy within the historical and research context of talk radio, and suggests the important functions served by this successful interactive format.

EVOLUTION OF TALK RADIO

As with the case of most origins within the broadcast industry, there is little agreement as to precisely how the talk radio format began. Certainly some of radio's fledgling "toll" broadcasts of the early 1920s might be singled out as talk radio's birthplace, as individuals purchased time to express their own opinions or promote discussions of a particular point of view. The roots of contemporary talk radio programs might also be traced to the early telephone quiz shows of the 1930s when announcers telephoned members of the audience to ask questions. Later developments in radio technology permitted the broadcast of the respondents' end of the conversations. These programs of the late 1940s were often referred to as "beeper shows," as the Federal Communications Commission then required that all taped conversations broadcast over the air be accompanied by a periodic high-pitched tone. This familiar "beep" became synonymous with

---

[1] For discussions of the success of the talk format see "Talk Radio," *Broadcasting*, June 27, 1966, pp. 78–100; "Why AM Radio Stations Are Talking It Up," *Business Week*, June 15, 1981, pp. 99–100; "Talk's the Ticket in Spring Books," *Broadcasting*, July 4, 1983, p. 35; "News and Talk Radio," *Television/Radio Age*, June, 1984, pp. A1-A16.

talk shows, since audience participation programs were operated with a tape delay system in order to control callers' comments.

During the 1950s, radio yielded its role as the "family medium" to television. As radio was transformed from a network-dominated industry to a locally controlled medium, new formats evolved that would attempt to attract specific segments of the total listening audience. Aided by the development of the transistor, radio began promoting itself as the "go where you go, do what you do medium" and became the listener's constant companion. With this new portability came specialized program formats that were designed to deliver a targeted segment of the audience to commercial advertisers. The "Top-40," "Country," "Easy Listening," and "All News" formats, among others, emerged to serve their designated markets. According to McEachern (1970), the first "All Talk" radio format appeared on KABC, Los Angeles in 1963, though other stations that lay claim to that distinction include KCBS in San Francisco, WOR in New York City, and WBBM in Chicago. Talk show hosts ranged the entire spectrum of personality types and included such well-known media figures as antagonistic Joe Pyne and political satirist Mort Sahl.

By the late 1960s, the novelty of the talk format was beginning to fade as listeners tired of the seemingly endless rehash of political issues and social problems. The more loyal listeners were increasingly from the less commercially attractive 50-and-over age range. Costs associated with technical requirements and guest appearances were no longer justified in the face of dwindling audience figures, and some talk shows gave way to less expensive musical programming.

But just as the talk format appeared to be falling on hard times, the Storer Broadcasting station in Los Angeles, KGBS-AM, provided an innovation that revitalized the talk format. Responding to the need to reach women in the 18–34 age demographic during midday, station management moved their all-night disc jockey from KGBS-FM to host the newly created *Feminine Forum*. In the spring of 1971, Bill Ballance invited women 18 years of age and older to call the station and disclose their most intimate sexual experiences and fantasies. Initially he recorded the women's comments for playback between records, but when the results of the April/ May ratings sweep revealed that KGBS had doubled its midday audience, approval was given for the installation of a 7-second delay system, and *Feminine Forum* went live.

This management decision marked the beginning of the relatively short-lived, two-way talk format that has been referred to as "topless," "X-rated," or "sex-talk" radio. Bill Ballance encouraged women to discuss such tantalizing topics as their favorite sexual positions, how they went about turning on their lovers, the most outrageous places where they had made love, famous people with whom they wanted to have sex, actual secret affairs, and fantasies about sex with other women.[2] Ballance himself joined in the fantasy constructions and provided vicarious fulfillment for thousands of listeners.

The Bill Ballance Show was soon released through syndication, and its immediate success led to dozens of similar programs, most notably Don Chamberlain's *California Girls* (KNEW, San Francisco) and *The Dave Ambrose Show* (KLIF, Dallas). Critics of the broadcasts called them tasteless and disgusting voyeurism, while more appreciative observers suggested that this mediated interpersonal communication between the talk host and his female callers might be seen as having some "cathartic" or "therapeutic" benefits (Carlin, 1976). But those who considered the programs offensive far outnumbered those willing to speak out in support of the broadcasts. As the number of stations that adopted the sex-talk format increased, the number of complaints at the FCC's offices in Washington, DC grew porportionately. Finally, on April 11, 1973, the Commission adopted and issued a notice of apparent liability to the Sonderling Broadcasting Corporation, licensee of WGLD in Oak Park, Illinois. The FCC cited the station for violation of the federal statute prohibiting obscene, indecent, or profane language. The incidents in question were two broadcasts which involved discussions of oral sex by female callers that the Commission considered to be obscene by a five-to-one decision. Although a series of court cases by a citizens and a civil liberties group challenged the FCC decision for over two years, stations airing sex-talk shows quickly bowed to industry pressures and either removed or revised the programs.

TALK RADIO THERAPY

Regardless of one's assessment of Ballance's enterprising venture in terms of its social functioning for the listening audience, there can be no question that it had an enormous impact on the evolution of the talk radio format. Ballance had demonstrated radio's potential for providing public exhibitionism while affording private therapy. Although Ballance had no formal psychological training, he intuitively recognized the deep-seated need of women to talk about their sexuality, often as a means for them to deal with fears of inadequacy or the scars of adultery, incest, or rape. Women

---

[2] In addition to John Carlin's (1976) summary of the rise and fall of topless radio, descriptions of this talk genre can be found in "Touchiest Topic on Radio Now: Talk about Sex," *Broadcasting,* March 19, 1973, p. 118; "Sex on the Dial," *Newsweek,* September 4, 1972, p. 90; "And Now, Color Radio: You Can Color It Blue—For Plenty of Sex," *Wall Street Journal,* March 28, 1972, p. 1.

who were unable to reveal these experiences face-to-face with a professional therapist within the privacy of an office were willing to share their personal tragedy with a radio audience. Realizing that he was ill-prepared to provide the kind of counseling that many of his female callers really needed, Ballance requested the assistance of psychologist Norton Kristy who joined him on the air once each week. Kristy's appearances proved to be a valuable addition, and this success led to guest spots by other psychologists from the Los Angeles area.

The most significant guest appearance was that made by Dr. Toni Grant, the individual who today is most often associated with talk radio psychotherapy. Grant, a Vassar College graduate with a PhD in clinical psychology from Syracuse University, was given her own program on KABC, Los Angeles, in 1975. By 1980, her program had a regular audience of more than 115,000 listeners, the highest rating for her time period in a market of more than 70 stations. The four-hour *Dr. Toni Grant Program* was placed in an afternoon time slot to compete directly with television's daytime soap operas. In the words of KABC program director, Bruce Marr, "People are turning away from soap opera to listen to the radio shrinks because they can tune into the bedrooms of real people rather than just listen to actors" ("Dial Dr. Toni," 1980, p. 95). To what extent Marr's assessment explains the format's attraction is a matter for possible scholarly attention. However, there can be little question that the "talk shrink" has enormous popularity for caller and listener alike.

Virtually every major American city has at least one talk radio psychologist: Jay Browne in Boston; Karen Blaker and Judith Kuriansky in New York; Karen Shanor in Washington, DC; Sonja Friedman in Detroit; Sylvia Bagley in Salt Lake City; and Jennifer James in Seattle. Toni Grant's program is now distributed nationally on the Mutual Broadcasting System, and her principal competition, Sally Jessy Raphael, is heard nationally on NBC's *Talknet*. Unlike Grant, Sally Jessy Raphael has no formal credentials as a clinical psychologist, but her commitment to the self-actualization of the caller and her attempts to alleviate psychological and social struggles place her program within this same genre of talk radio offerings. Other talk hosts have backgrounds in such fields as social work, psychiatric nursing, and even anthropology. While not all successful psych jocks are women in their mid-30s or 40s, the vast majority fit that category. The early experience of Grant and the other guests of Ballance's *Feminine Forum* suggested that women project a warm reassuring voice for both female and male callers.

Although scholars have yet to investigate the success of talk psychotherapy from an audience perspective, there has been considerable speculation regarding its listener appeal. Some critics join Bruce Marr in arguing that the confessions of callers afford real-life soap opera that is better than what network writers can generate. That talk radio producers are sensitive to the entertainment value of each call-in listener is evident in the screening process employed on most programs, especially at the network level. Callers with obviously serious problems are immediately eliminated because they are not considered suitable listening for the typical audience member. By contrast, callers whose personal histories are unusual and who can articulate their problems concisely and in a lively manner stand the greatest chance of getting on the air. Grant believes that virtually everyone has problems coping with life's complexities and the callers selected for the program need to reflect the problems of the listener in a unique and personal way ("Dial Dr. Toni," 1980, p. 95). Sally Jessy Raphael speculates that "they're calling because they need a fix of hope. On my program, we traffic in hope" (Barthel, 1983, p. 128). The listener is attracted to the program because the callers reinforce the impression that personal problems are universal and despite our idiosyncratic trauma at any point in time, we are not alone in our struggle.

Despite the popular appeal of these programs, they have been the target of heated attacks by individuals within the community of clinical therapists. Opponents argue that the apparent "quick fix" offered by the talk host is a disservice to both caller and listener. Demands for professional censure led to a special inquiry by the American Psychological Association, but the eventual outcome was less than satisfying for the most vocal critics. The result has been a general "hands off" and an APA award for Dr. Toni Grant. The APA hopes that the visability of on-air psychologists will help increase the public's acceptance of psychotherapy as a common medical practice.

RESEARCH TRADITION

Given the proven success of talk radio, and specifically the talk psychologist formats, researchers have an important opportunity to investigate this particular form of mediated interpersonal communication. Among the questions which appear deserving of serious consideration are the following: What unique functions does this subset of talk radio serve? What are the potential dangers inherent in this form of mediated interaction? What advantages, if any, does this form of talk radio provide to the caller? To the listener? And what are the sociocultural implications of the popularity of this program genre?

These questions are by no means exhaustive and may ultimately be replaced by more substantive and theoretically supported inquiries that help explain our attraction to the public and private dimensions of mediated communication. However, such questions do afford guidance for a preliminary survey of existing literature and the suggestion of a possible research agenda.

Of the growing list of studies that have focused on two-way radio the largest portion have conceptualized the mediated encounter between talk host and call-in listener as a substitute for, or extension of, face-to-face communication. Turow (1974) found that the principal factor which motivates people to call a talk host is the strong need for interpersonal communication. Similar findings were reported by Bierig and Dimmick (1979) and Tramer and Jeffres (1983). These researchers added support to the position of Avery, Ellis, and Glover (1978) that call-in listeners are more likely to be motivated out of a need for support and reinforcement than to "speak out" or take an argumentative position. Also supported was the previous finding that callers to a radio talk show are more likely than the general population to be single and living alone, but less likely to be active as a member of social organizations or support groups. Results of these studies also suggest a positive relationship between the need for mediated companionship and the frequency of calls. To what extent the call-in listeners reflect the needs and interests of the noncaller is largely a matter of conjecture. One can speculate, however, that if talk radio serves to reinforce the beliefs, values, and opinions of the caller, the dialogue between host and caller affords entry points for the listener which are also reassuring and encourage continued listenership.

A recent study by Armstrong (1987) affords the preliminary empirical evidence that links the motives and listening behaviors of callers and noncallers. Findings revealed that while callers were more prone to be information-seekers than were noncallers, these two subsets of talk radio listeners did not differ significantly in their need for mediated companionship. Armstrong concluded: "Listening, rather than calling, may fulfill a desire for companionship, wherein companionship requires less active participation and involvement than information-seeking for its gratification" (p. 77). Callers did, however, report greater exposure to, and greater affinity with, talk radio, as well as less physical mobility and social accessibility than their noncaller counterparts.

To date, there has been an almost total absence of serious scholarly attention given to talk radio by health and psychological researchers, though Schwebel (1982) has outlined a psychoeducational model. One study by Grasha and Levi (1983) pointed to the pedagogical value of talk radio psychology for the training of mental health professionals. These writers recognized the ability of the talk psychologists to maintain enthusiasm and effective timing, reduce role conflict, and confront irrational beliefs expressed by callers. But other than recognizing positive professional traits among the talk hosts, no attempt was made to investigate the actual benefits provided to either caller or program listener.

If we can generalize from literature focusing on the sociology of the telephone (Aronson, 1971) and the role of the telephone in therapy sessions summarized by Lester (1977), there is evidence that talk radio may be providing an important communication function for the call-in listener. For example, Robertiello (1972) reported on two cases of psychoanalysis that employed telephone-mediated therapy sessions for patients who were unable to visit the psychoanalyst's office in person. In the one case the psychoanalyst reported no difference in patient response patterns, and in the second instance, the use of the telephone actually facilitated patient progress. In this second case, the patient was able to overcome emotional disruptions that had developed in face-to-face sessions, thus enabling her to experience her emotions in a more positive manner and to reflect upon the transference which had inhibited recent progress.

Chiles (1974) employed telephone sessions with a set of patients for the purpose of reinforcing behavior modification procedures. Daily telephone calls of a few minutes in duration enabled patients to report on aspects of their program, thus reinforcing the patient's self-image and facilitating the regular behavior modification regimen.

Williams and Douds (1973) were prompted to experiment with telephone therapy as a result of their experience with face-to-face counseling sessions which provoked humiliation and anxiety for their clients. Their findings indicate that in these problem cases, telephone contact gives patients a sense of greater control and greatly reduces fear of self-exposure because they can remain anonymous. Being unseen was reported as being an important factor in creating an open environment where some patients could self-disclose. Clearly, too, some patients found that it contributed to a sense of power equalization with the therapist, thus reducing tension and anger which interfered with the surfacing of relevant feelings.

MacKinnon and Michels (1970) also found positive benefits from engaging in telephone-mediated therapy sessions with a phobic housewife. These and other researchers underscore the importance of anonymity for patients who would often feel embarrassment and ridicule.

For individuals calling talk radio therapists, it seems reasonable to conclude that many of the same factors are operating in the willingness of callers to self-disclose. First, the talk host, though familiar to the caller in terms of his or her on-air presence, is a complete stranger. Those listening in to the conversation are also strangers from whom the caller can protect her or his identity. A longstanding sociological position is that it is easier to discuss one's problems with strangers than with personal acquaintances, professional colleagues, or even a trained clinician. Talk radio provides a relatively easily accessible stranger who will listen and offer advice. It can also be assumed that the caller's own feelings of loneliness and alienation are projected onto the listening audience, thus creating a sympathetic group of concerned listeners in the mind of the caller. The very fact that one caller often prompts another caller to phone in and self-disclose suggests that this sympathetic network in fact exists. On-air comments by callers in support or in appreciation of previous callers is a frequent occurrence.

Perhaps the greatest concern, cited earlier, is the matter of instant diagnosis and advice. In the short span of a listener's phone call, there is no opportunity for building a case history or developing the kind of counselor-patient relationship which enables the patient to recognize the complexity of his or her problems. However, that there is continuity across callers over time argues for the notion of radio audience as "community." The support system—whether imagined or real—does provide listeners with the confidence that they are not alone and that someone cares.

RESEARCH DIRECTIONS

Despite the studies reported in this brief overview, the literature relating to talk radio is at a very early stage of development. In addition to investigations employing interaction analysis and self-reporting techniques, early work by Ellis, Hawes, and Avery (1981), Higgins and Moss (1982), and Moss and Higgins (1986) point to the importance of textual analyses which help clarify the meanings embedded in the mediated interactions. Similarly, the need to build upon the work of Armstrong (1987) in order to further examine the motivations, experiences, and gratifications of the noncaller will enable us to better understand both the popularity and functioning of the two-way radio format.

There are also questions to be explored regarding the relationship between the type of information sought by callers and the relative success of talk radio in meeting listeners' expressed needs. According to a report released by the Association for Media Psychology, the topics on which callers most frequently request advice are "marriage, child care and discipline, phobias, depression, anxiety, sexual relations, sexual dysfunction, contraception, addiction, career change, and homosexuality" (Rice, 1983, p. 83). Correlates between host type, time of broadcast, listener demographics, and media consumption patterns could offer insights into the design and implementation of new mediated therapeutic services.

Whether one turns to the writings of mental health professionals, sociologists, media technologists, or the new breed of ecological futurists, one is left with the inescapable conclusion that we are growing older and that our life space will undergo dramatic changes in the decades ahead. With growing fragmentation within the traditionally defined family unit and loneliness and a sense of isolation becoming an increasingly endemic problem throughout our society, there is a growing need for surrogate or substitute relationships and the therapeutic guidance of well-informed individuals. The talk radio host can function as a friend to callers who are unable to initiate and sustain interpersonal relationships or who need help through a crisis period of depression or high anxiety. People of all ages and from every walk of life and ethnic origin need to be reminded that their existence has meaning, and that their problems and frustrations are shared by others.

As we begin to revise earlier conceptions of mediated interactions between call-in listeners and talk radio hosts, we will discover new research opportunities which will extend the growing literature on relational communication. As stated by Avery and McCain (1982, p. 39), "Research on personal junctures with media and others needs careful description and understanding." As these new pieces of the media-person mosiac fall into place, we can explain more fully the public and private roles of talk radio.

REFERENCES

Armstrong, C. (1987). *Communication differences between callers and noncallers of talk radio.* Unpublished masters thesis, Kent State University, Kent, OH.

Aronson, S. (1971). The sociology of the telephone. *International Journal of Comparative Sociology, 12,* 153–167.

Avery, R., Ellis, D., & Glover, T. (1978). Patterns of communication on talk radio. *Journal of Broadcasting, 22,* 5–17.

Avery, R., & McCain T. (1982). Interpersonal and mediated encounters: A reorientation to the mass communication process. In G. Gumpert & R. Cathcart (Eds.), *Inter/Media* (pp. 29–40). New York: Oxford University Press.

Barthel, J. (1983, April 26). Hi, you're on the air—what's your problem? *Woman's Day,* pp. 81ff.

Bierig, J., & Dimmick, J. (1979). The late night radio talk show as interpersonal communication. *Journalism Quarterly, 56*(1), 92–96.

Carlin, J. (1976). The rise and fall of topless radio. *Journal of Communication, 26*(1), 31–37.

Chiles, J. (1974). A practical therapeutic use of the telephone. *American Journal of Psychiatry, 131,* 1030–1031.

Ellis, D., Hawes, L., & Avery, R. (1981). Some pragmatics of talking on talk radio. *Urban Life, 10*(2), 155–177.

Dial Dr. Toni for therapy. (1980, May 26). *Time,* pp. 95.

Grasha, A., & Levi, L. (1983). *Radio talk-show psychology: Teaching-learning and professional issues.* Paper presented at the annual conference of the American Psychological Association, Anaheim, CA.

Higgins, C., & Moss, P. (1982). *Sounds real: Radio in everyday life.* St. Lucia: University of Queensland Press.

Lester, D. (1977). The use of the telephone in counseling and crisis intervention. In I. Pool (Ed.), *The social impact of the telephone* (pp. 454–472). Cambridge, MA: MIT Press.

MacKinnon, R., & Michels, R. (1970). The role of the telephone in the psychiatric interview. *Psychiatry, 33,* 82–93.

McEachern, M. (1970, July). The town meeting is not dead—it's alive and well on radio. *Today's Health, 48,* 32–33.

Moss, P., & Higgins, C. (1986). Radio voices. In G. Gumpert & R. Cathcart (Eds.), *Inter/Media* (pp. 282–299). New York: Oxford University Press.

Rice, B. (1983, August). Call-in therapy hits. *Psychology Today,* p. 83.

Robertiello, R. (1973). Telephone sessions. *Psychoanalytic Review, 59,* 633–634.

Schwebel, A. (1982). Radio psychologists: A community psychology/psycho-educational model. *Journal of Community Psychology, 10*(2), 181–184.

Tramer, H., & Jeffres, L. (1983). Talk radio—forum and companion. *Journal of Broadcasting, 27*(3), 297–300.

Turow, J. (1974). Talk show radio as interpersonal communication. *Journal of Broadcasting, 18*(2), 171–179.

Williams, T., & Douds, J. (1973). The unique contribution of telephone therapy. In D. Lester & G. Brockopp (Eds.), *Crisis intervention and counseling by telephone* (pp. 80–88). Springfield, IL: Thomas.

7

Ann Landers' Mediated Advice: The Intersection of Rhetorical and Interpersonal Forms

Virginia H. Fry
Jody H. Wrightson

An analysis of letters to Ann Landers reveals a preponderance of questions regarding interpersonal relationships, answered by a distanced third party who paradoxically reaffirms personal values and relationships. The authors conclude that Landers through her journalistic format reinforces the "cult of self" and the "ideology of intimacy," by emphasizing the message that our greatest personal fulfillment comes in intimate relations with others.

Any observer of life in contemporary America cannot escape noticing the tremendous importance Americans place on interpersonal relationships. Where once there was a gulf between private and public, now television programs, films, self-help books, popular music, and advertising all point to the willingness of Americans to shift discussion of their concerns with liking, loving, joining, and fitting in from the intimate to the public sphere. Concern with interpersonal relationships is so prevalent in American society that it has become responsible for the ebb and flow of the public careers of such men as Ted Kennedy, Jim Bakker, Gary Hart, Tom Eagleton, and most recently John Tower. Americans are willing to make judgments on the private as well as public lives of such figures. Often public careers are less dependent on relevant issues, on collegial relations, on one's stand on public issues, and on one's capabilities in public speaking and persuasion, than on the personal choices one makes in the conduct of one's intimate relationships.

Sennett (1974) coined the term "ideology of intimacy" to characterize this contemporary obsession with the self. In American society, this ideology undergirds private and public discourse concerning individual relational choices and behaviors. Because these discussions typically are mediated through our dominant communication forms such as newspapers, magazines, television, and film, it is no longer possible to draw distinct lines between private and public conduct. Though it now may be commonplace to state that what takes place in one realm impacts on the other, the precise relationship which exists between communication media and interpersonal conduct is less apparent.

The prevalence of mediated interpersonal communication in contemporary society (Cathcart & Gumpert, 1983) makes it imperative that we assess the extent to which mediated communication forms reflect and reify prevailing codes of interpersonal behavior and/or contribute to creating new socially desirable codes capable of guiding individuals to make different relational choices. This concern with the complicated symbiotic relationship between media and self is of particular importance in examining those mediated communication genres which may serve explicit therapeutic functions for individuals and society.

Nowhere is the American obsession with intimacy and interpersonal relationships seen more clearly than in the syndicated advice columns of Ann Landers and Abigail Van Buren. Subjects which were taboo a few decades ago easily find their way into the pages of our newspapers and magazines. The dilemmas confronting the self seem to be of unprecedented magnitude. Whereas individuals might have relied previously on neighbors, relatives, or local professionals for information, advice, and support, the syndicated advice column represents a particular historical moment in the detachment and elevation of self from community. In a predominantly mediated society, individuals capable of performing therapeutic functions for the self are more likely to emerge from a host of media personalities than from one's everyday face-to-face contacts. Our tendency to seek out mediated rather than nonmediated forms of therapeutic communication has contributed to the success of the syndicated advice column. In this genre, advice seekers, columnists, and faithful readers are united not only by their shared commitment to the supreme importance of the self and the dilemmas of the self but also by their reliance on the necessity of establishing a parasocial (Horton & Wohl, 1956) mediated therapeutic relationship.

Because this process has occurred within a cultural context dominated by mediated forms of communication, understanding the syndicated advice genre requires an exploration of the unique relationship which exists among the advice seeker, advice giver, and general reader. Horton and Wohl's (1956) parasocial perspective seems to explain one important aspect of this relationship which has special import for the therapeutic operation of the genre. Horton and Wohl argued that performers and spectators conspire together to ignore the fact that their relationship is mediated. Agreeing to view mediated interactions as if they were, in fact, not mediated allows media consumers to treat mediated personalities and to expect to be treated by them in ways which are most appropriate for face-to-face interactions. Though Horton and Wohl developed the parasocial model to explain the relationship between media performer and media consumer which characterizes television viewing in particular, this perspective equally accounts well for some dimensions of the therapeutic relationship which can form between advice columnist and reader.

Interpersonal communication, therapeutic communication, and the parasocial model of mediated interaction are predicated upon dyadic conversation as the most critical and most valued type of communication (Schudson, 1978). Although we shift discussions of our private lives into the public realm and although media personalities become our privileged confidants, we hold firm to the ideal of dyadic interaction. This ideal contributes to allowing both columnist and reader to view the syndicated column as a therapeutic form, for without it (and their shared willingness to bracket the fact that the relationship is mediated), it would be impossible for the genre to purport to function therapeutically. Taking therapeutic communication in its broadest sense as any communication which contributes to increased personal insight, individual reorientation, or learning which allows persons to enhance the satisfaction they glean from social interactions (Barnlund, 1968), it is only logical to assume that the therapeutic context within which this learning, insight, and reorientation are acquired be consistent with a highly valued model of communication. These assumptions also enable readers to expect the columnist to display essential characteristics of therapeutic communicators, such as empathy, trust, honesty, validation, and caring (Kreps & Thornton, 1984). Although the columnist may or may not possess these qualities in her nonmediated interactions, readers must assume that she actually possesses these characteristics in order for the syndicated column to function therapeutically. It is the adherence of columnist and reader to the dyadic conversational model and their respective willingness to conceive of the syndicated advice column as if it were predicated upon this model that allows this genre to perform any therapeutic function.

Given the mediated nature of the syndicated column, it is more useful to examine the characteristics of the message itself rather than the characteristics possessed by columnist or reader in assessing the therapeutic functioning of the genre. We cannot hope to have access to personal data for columnist and readers which would make it possible to identify the extent to which each as persons actually possessed desirable therapeutic attributes in their own interactions. The functioning of the form requires only that the columnist be assumed to possess these desirable characteristics, not that she actually do so in her own life.

Given our message focus, what mode of inquiry is appropriate for studying this mediated form of advice giving? We will argue that studying the syndicated advice columnist's messages should be of particular interest to rhetorical critics. Although all rhetorical critics do not agree on what constitutes an appropriate object of focus and method of investigation, there is general consensus that the job of the rhetorical critic is to describe, interpret, and/or evaluate various forms of public communication (see Brock & Scott, 1980, for their discussion of these three purposes of rhetorical criticism).

We believe that the syndicated advice column is a modern rhetorical communication genre which uniquely blends together the interpersonal, therapeutic, and mediated interests of some contemporary rhetorical critics. Although traditionally rhetorical critics have favored historical objects and methods of investigation, during the past two decades some critics have begun scrutinizing contemporary interpersonal and mass-mediated forms of communication for their implicit rhetorical dimensions. These studies provide a precedence for examining the syndicated advice column. Some researchers have linked together the study of rhetoric and interpersonal communication (Frentz, 1985; Glaser & Frank, 1982; Phillips, 1976; Scott, 1977; Sharf, 1979; Ward, Bluman, & Dauria, 1982). Though none have examined the syndicated advice column, Kidd (1975) studied the advice on interpersonal relationships contained in women's magazines between 1951 and 1973 and Bate and Self (1983) studied advice given to women in self-help books on career success. The 1980s has witnessed some interest in studying the rhetorical nature of psychotherapy (Makay, 1980) and therapeutic techniques and analytic systems (Vatz & Weinberg, 1983). Additionally, during the past two decades in particular numerous rhetorical scholars have become interested in the impact of media on communication practices.

Croft (1956) has argued that the goal of the rhetorical critic is to explain how message "propositions and audiences are *connected*" (p. 286). Describing, interpreting, and evaluating that connection and the way it is achieved rhetorically is particularly difficult with the syndicated advice column, in part because of its unique combination of the interpersonal, mediated, and therapeutic. The participants in this rhetorical form—the advice seeker or letter writer, the advice giver or columnist, and the general reader as rhetorical audience to the exchange between advice seeker and columnist— engage in a mediated rhetorical transaction which, as we noted already, relies on a set of parasocial assumptions for its functioning.

One of the unique features of the syndicated message (taking each letter and response as a communicative unit) is that it is a mediated interpersonal communication which takes nonmediated interpersonal communication as its content. Given the importance of self-discovery and enhanced self-knowledge in therapeutic communication, perhaps this metacommunication content is the essential distinguishing feature of all forms of mediated interpersonal communication which serve therapeutic functions.

Although it is not feasible to identify individual characteristics of the persons involved in the syndicated transaction, it is possible to examine specific message characteristics which indicate the actual language choices made by advice seekers and columnists as they engage in their metacommunication. Such an approach to content may provide clues for drawing inferences in the conclusion of this chapter about (a) the meanings which may be derived by advice seekers and other readers about the therapeutic success of the columnist's advice, and (b) the extent to which the columnist's advice serves to reinforce or alter societal standards and values of personal conduct. The overarching goal for the rhetorical critic of this genre is to explore, in Croft's (1956) terms, "how propositions and audiences are *connected*" to one another by examining the characteristics of the speaker's message (p. 286).

METHOD

Following the lead of other rhetorical critics (Redding, 1957; Bate & Self, 1983), our analysis will examine message content as a means of making inferences about the therapeutic functioning of the syndicated advice column in American society. Our focus is the syndicated advice column of Ann Landers. In this study we will (a) enumerate a typology of "Dear Ann" letters derived from actual letters which have been printed in the Ann Landers syndicated column, and (b) identify some of the particular features which characterize Landers' responses to certain types of letters. Our goal is to draw some inferences regarding the distinguishing characteristics of this mediated therapeutic genre as well as the social and cultural values which uphold and legitimize it.

First, it is important to classify the letters published in the Landers' column according to type. Although some letters appear which are addressed "Dear Reader" (these letters are from Ann and addressed to her readers), we are concerned with the letters written by readers and addressed to the columnist. After carefully studying the column, it is clear that readers write three kinds of letters to Ann Landers: pleas, requests, and testimonials. Typically, testimonials do not require a response from the columnist. Testimonials either support what Landers had advised, condemn her for her handling of other letters, or speak directly from their experience to other readers whose letters have been printed. By contrast, pleas and requests require a direct response from the columnist. Merely printing the letter will not suffice; the columnist must offer either advice or information. Pleas are "Dear Ann" letters which seek Ann's advice on how to deal with relational problems of personal significance. These usually involve a major role relationship with a spouse, child, in-law, parent, friend, or co-worker. Requests demand a response from the columnist, but the request is for a particular piece of information rather than a specific plea for advice on how to handle a sensitive interpersonal problem. Typical requests for information center on issues related to sex, health, communicable diseases, and state and federal laws.

We have decided to focus on pleas, the letters which specifically require the columnist to deal with interpersonal matters of significance to readers. Clearly, pleas are particular kinds of letters which perform special functions for letter writers and readers alike: direct requests for advice. We are particularly interested in examining the ways in which Landers responds to different kinds of pleas. For example, does Landers' language differ when she is responding to a plea for advice on how to discipline a child from when she is answering a letter asking for advice on how to handle a colleague at work? Our casual reading of the Landers' column suggested that such differences did exist, and that these differences could be identified and examined more systematically by establishing a range of possible responses and then coding the regular occurrences of those responses. This procedure, then, should allow us to accomplish our second goal, that of identifying some of the features which characterize Landers' responses to certain types of letters.

We believe Landers has three linguistic codes available to her in crafting her response to pleas. These three options are constatives, regulatives, and avowals. These categories are borrowed, with modification, from Habermas (1979).[1] Because constatives, regulatives, and avowals encompass the range of possibilities open to the columnist as she responds to a plea from a reader, they are methodologically sound as analytic categories (see Holsti's [1969] elaboration of the requirements for content analytic categories, particularly that they be both discrete and exclusive).

Before employing these categories to analyze pleas, it is necessary to explain the differences among them. Constatives, regulatives, and avowals differ in content and in their respective appeals to legitimacy. A constative is a type of speech act which makes assertions about truth; all constatives serve to make truth claims about some state, context, person, situation, and/or condition. Statements such as "It is raining" and "My car won't start" are claims which can be subjected to verification as being either truth or false. Both regulatives and avowals differ from constatives in that they cannot be proved to be either true or false. Instead, these types of speech acts typically appeal to shared assumptions about self, others, and the con-

---

[1] In borrowing these terms from Habermas, we do not mean to imply that the syndicated advice column comprises an ideal speech situation in Habermas' terms. Rather, with Habermas—who believed the ideal speech situation to be an ideal rather than a reality—we believe that, even though an ideal may not be realized, it is the fact that it could and may be realized which enables communication to take place. Additionally, the parasocial assumptions shared by columnist and readers seem quite similar to the basic features of Habermas' ideal speech situation.

text of interaction. Regulatives govern the relationship among communicative participants by promising, ordering, requesting, and so on. It is possible to make a promise to a child or parent, to order a spouse or subordinate to perform some task, or to request some favor, service, or advice from a friend or colleague without explicitly performing these speech acts linguistically. For example, when a wife and mother, without glancing at her daughter or husband, utters "The cat wants out," linguistically she is making a statement which could be either true or false. The fact that her daughter immediately lets out the cat indicates, however, that the family's shared knowledge of roles, responsibilities, and interactional history framed the statement as a request or order directed to the daughter. Thus, regulatives structure interpersonal relationships and ensure the smooth functioning of communication by appealing to generally accepted standards of appropriateness, propriety, and routinized behaviors. Unlike regulatives, avowals are speech acts which express feelings, sentiments, desires, and so forth. Although a speaker's sincerity and credibility could be judged as truth or false, avowals differ from constatives because a speaker's intention is being evaluated rather than a particular external state of affairs. To respond to the question "Do you love me?" by saying "Of course I do" is an illustration of an avowal. The questioner might attempt to determine the sincerity of the response but this is always a determination made in terms of feelings, intentions, and emotions rather than truth or falsity.

Constatives, regulatives, and avowals differ not only in their content but also in the forms of legitimation to which they must appeal. The manner in which a particular speech act is legitimized impacts directly on how the message is received and interpreted by an audience. To accept a message it is necessary to believe in the criteria which legitimize the message itself. This is of special importance in assessing the impact of mediated messages deemed to have potential therapeutic import because no therapeutic change will take place (that is, the advice will not be accepted) unless the reader also accepts the manner in which the advice is legitimized. Choosing a constative which appeals to verifiable states of truth or falsehood over a regulative or an avowal which require the audience to accept particular social and emotional codes of conduct may reflect the columnist's belief that her advice is more likely to be accepted if it is presented as true rather than merely right or appropriate. Given another plea, a very different choice might be made; Landers' might use a regulative or an avowal, which she believes has a better chance of legitimizing her advice on that particular topic or issue with her readers. The importance of the ways in which linguistic choices are legitimized will be explored more fully in the discussion section of this chapter.

The letters and responses in our sample were drawn from two sources.

The book, *Ann Landers Says Truth is Stranger . . .*, published in 1968, is a compilation of selected letters from the first 13 years of the column. The remaining letters/responses in our data were collected directly from the Landers' newspaper column during the summer of 1987. In both cases, every third letter was coded as letter type and type of speech act response. The possible responses of constatives, regulatives, and avowals were coded only in letters identified as pleas.

RESULTS

Pleas and testimonials comprised the vast majority of letter types. Of the 230 letters coded, 44.8 percent were pleas and 38.7 percent were testimonials. The remaining types, request and "Dear Reader," comprised 14.3 percent and 2.2 percent, respectively. Since only pleas were coded further, the following percentages pertain to pleas only. Of the 103 pleas, the vast majority (64.1 percent) engendered a regulative response from Landers. Avowals, the next largest percentage, comprised 22.3 percent of the responses. Constatives made up only 10.7 percent of the responses, and 2 percent of the responses were other.

The above totals represent a compilation of the letters drawn from the first 13 years of the column and those selected more recently from this year. Though these two samples were separated during the coding process in order to determine whether significant differences would arise between the two, only two differences appeared which may be potentially significant. First, of the earlier letters only 6.3 percent were categorized as requests whereas requests comprised 22 percent of the recent sample. Second, while in the dated sample none of the pleas brought a constative response, 10.7 percent of the recent letters used that form.

DISCUSSION

This study has been based upon the assumption, shared by Habermas and others (Austin, 1962; Searle, 1969), that language use is always a form of communicative action. As Austin (1962) has argued persuasively, to *say* something is to *do* something. Put another way, every communicative message not only contains particular propositional contents (truth claims) but also performs certain social actions because the message is produced according to the rules (grammatical, societal, and other) which guide the production and interpretation of messages of that type. Keeping this framework in mind, in this section, we will discuss the importance of the content of the syndicated advice messages we analyzed as well as identify the communicative actions performed for readers. In other words, in this section we are interested in what the syndicated advice column *does* for individuals and society, in addition to providing advice to readers, and how it performs those actions.

Bluntly put, the syndicated advice column appears to perform a regulative function for society. For the most part, the columnist elects to respond to pleas by appealing to standards of appropriateness and propriety. Emphasizing such standards suggests that it is important to avoid calling attention to oneself as someone who does not know how to act properly in a range of delicate situations. Although an individual may feel like acting inappropriately, the columnist urges readers to take others into consideration by reminding them that they should be sensitive to the various ways in which their behavior might be understood and interpeted by others. This suggests a propositional content, or claim, designed to increase each individual's awareness of and sensitivity to the needs and viewpoints of others. The columnist reminds readers that one is always a part of a society which imposes certain standards and restrictions on behavior, and at times, self-interest must be secondary to the needs and expectations of others.

In one sense, then, the propositional content of the Landers' syndicated advice column appears to be encouraging readers to become better therapeutic ommunicators. Based on Barnlund's (1968) view that therapeutic communication is a form of communication which enhances individual insight, allows for a reorientation of the individual, or teaches the individual how to become more satisfied in social interactions, it is possible to suggest that Landers' takes these goals as her own and tries to communicate them to her readers. Even though this ideal of the therapeutic self may not be realized in all individuals, it remains a basic goal for columnist and reader.

Thus, the syndicated advice column is a form of communication made possible because participants suppose others to share a commitment to a communicative ideal centered on self-improvement, increased sensitivity to others, gradual learning about the self, and a belief in equality and fairness in communication. Despite the fact that the syndicated advice column is a mediated form of communication, the communicative ideal which legitimizes it is the dyad, the interpersonal relationship, and the face-to-face encounter. The syndicated advice column serves to regulate these relationships for individuals and for society.

Given its emphasis on considering the viewpoint of others, it is possible to interpret this message as a subversion of the cult of the self which prevails in contemporary American society. However, although this subversion, on one level of analysis, is a proper interpretation of the columnist's message, we think the overarching message (propositional content) actually reinforces the cult of the self and the ideology of intimacy in some particularly interesting ways.

In her introduction to *Ann Landers Says Truth is Stranger . . .* (1968), Landers explains her view of her column:

> The success of the Ann Landers column underscores for me, at least, the central tragedy of our society—the loneliness, the insecurity, the fear that bedevils, cripples, and paralyzes so many of us. The column presents daily evidence that financial success and social and political status open no doors to peace of mind and contentment. (Preface)

The essential therapeutic learning which Landers' believes needs to take place, then, ultimately reinforces our cultural elevation of intimacy and self-exploration. The need for intimacy, in fact, is, according to Landers, the fundamental need for our society. Pursuing goals in the social and political world do not provide the self with its essential needs, and consequently cannot keep individuals from feeling lonely, fearful, and insecure.

Since Landers claims that social and political success do not result in individual happiness, one might expect her to rely more on avowals than on regulatives in her advice to her readers. Because avowals emphasize personal feelings, sentiments, and desires they would seem to be more consistent with Landers' explicit devaluation of public goals than advice which encourages readers to take seriously societal standards of propriety. This is not the case, however.

We believe Landers is able to maintain the cult of the self, and thus avoid paradox, by treating society dualistically. For Landers, the social world outside of the self has two dimensions: One is purely external to the self and cannot bring personal satisfaction, whereas the other is a direct extension of the self and directly impinges on the self's happiness. The external component we term "status" and relates to social and economic standing and position, to overall criteria for success and achievement. This category also pertains to class. These dimensions of the social world are meaningless when viewed using Sennett's (1974) phrase mentioned earlier, "the ideology of intimacy." The aspects of the social world which do have a significant impact on the self, however, are one's close personal relationships which demand that one act with empathy, understanding, and caring, that is, therapeutically. Individuals who do not come within this circle may deserve politeness, but encounters with them do not engage the self in significant ways. Thus, one's immediate circle is important; the rest of society is less so because these people are removed from one's world.

How and why does this message engage the self, the advice seeker, and the general reader of the Landers' column? In other words, how does Landers do what she does? We believe this question can be answered in several ways. It is perhaps somewhat ironic that the message which elevates one's immediate circle of relationships above the rest of society should come from a mediated therapeutic genre which by its nature encompasses those outside one's immediate circle. The message content would seem to be in conflict with the message form. On the other hand, the metacommunication content of the genre (its mediated interpersonal form coupled with its specific advice on interpersonal relationships content) enables the syndicated advice columnist to perform a regulative function for society. This function acquires some force as well from the willingness of the participants in the genre to treat their communication para-socially, a fact which allows them to forget that they are not actually communicating to persons within their own valued intimate sphere.

The standards which legitimize the message derive from one's dyadic relationships within one's immediate sphere and from the culture at large. The cultural ideal which values the dyad as the premier communication form allows Landers to use this communication ideal to perpetuate one aspect of the American mythology which masks the existence and importance of status and class in American society. What matters is what kind of person you are and how you conduct your affairs. Social and political achievement will not bring one contentment and peace. By directing attention to the self and one's intimate relationships, the columnist reinforces cultural codes which mask the existence of class and status in American society. By affirming intimacy over public achievement, we need never become concerned with the fact that all Americans do not have the same access to the avenues necessary for social and political activity and recognition.

Before concluding, it is necessary to comment on two results of our research which appeared to be anomalies: the larger percentage of requests in the more recent letters and the absence of constatives in the columnist's responses to the earlier letters. It is possible that these variations derived from the inherent differences in the two sources of data. As explained in the method section, letters from Landers' earlier years were selected from a book which compiled selected letters from the column whereas the recent letters were collected directly from the newspaper column printed during the summer of 1987. Perhaps the process of collecting the letters into book form accounts for the differences in numbers of requests and constatives. However, it is equally possible that these differences are, in fact, representative of social and cultural changes which impact on both readers and columnist. An increase in the number of direct requests for information from readers coupled with an increase in the columnist's use of constatives may point to a perception on the part of readers and columnist of the need for more and more expert information regarding health, sexuality, political, and legal matters. If today's world is perceived to be an increasingly complex and complicated place for the self to reside, one means of coping with this world is to focus on the need for specialized information derived from experts. Much of the information Landers utilizes in her constative speech acts comes from others with specialized technical knowledge of law, medicine, and family relations. Readers' willingness to turn to a columnist rather than to someone within their immediate realm and the columnist's willingness to see her role as information dispenser join together readers and columnist in a shared commitment to the American cultural mythology of expertise, specialization, and information. Perhaps it is paradoxical that those who preserve the ideology of the self cling so tenaciously to the belief that "others always know best."

Given the concerns expressed in the title of this article, it is important to conclude with a brief comment on rhetorical and interpersonal communication in a mass-mediated world. A contemporary theory of rhetoric must incorporate both the nature and function of mediated forms of communication and the rhetorical role public treatments of interpersonal communication may have in our lives. First, given the rhetorical critic's interest in understanding how speaker and audience are joined together as communicators, it is of special importance to consider the ways in which this relationship between speaker and audience may be altered in mediated communication forms. Are speaker and audience "connected" by fundamentally different means in mediated communication forms? Second, of equal importance is increasing our understanding of communication forms, particularly mediated interpersonal forms, which may function to perpetuate existing societal norms and values more than to effect change. Our tendency to treat rhetorical acts as if rhetoric always functions as an agency of change is not likely to be sensitive to rhetorical forms which may reinforce prevailing norms. Clearly, a contemporary theory of rhetoric and critical rhetorical practice should examine the normalizing potentiality of mediated interpersonal communication. Studies of communicative forms, like the syndicated advice column which regulate communicative practices by reinforcing cultural ideals of communication, provide useful data for any student of contemporary culture.

Finally, a study of the syndicated advice column should prove useful to specialists in other fields as well as to the general reader interested in mediated therapeutic communication of all types. Landers' assumption of the role of journalistic therapist, the ways she goes about enacting her role, and her success in this capacity can tell us much about the needs, desires, goals, and expectations of the society in which we live. Her syndicated advice is directed to a perceived public audience which is conceptualized in particular ways. Studying the column can tell us not only what she thinks of us but also, and perhaps more importantly, provide clues to our communicative ideals, those often taken-for-granted standards by which we evaluate our relationships and find them wanting.

REFERENCES

Austin, J. L. (1962). *How to do things with words.* Cambridge, MA: Harvard University Press.

Barnlund, D. C. (1968). Introduction to therapeutic communication. In D. C. Barnlund (Ed.), *Interpersonal communication: Survey and studies.* Boston: Houghton Mifflin.

Bate, B., & Self, L. S. (1983). The rhetoric of career success books for women. *Journal of Communication, 33,* 149–165.

Brock, B. L., & Scott, R. L. (1980). *Methods of rhetorical criticism: A twentieth-century perspective* (2nd ed., rev.). Detroit: Wayne State University Press.

Cathcart, R., & Gumpert, G. (1983). Mediated interpersonal communication: Toward a new typology. *Quarterly Journal of Speech, 69,* 267–277.

Croft, A. J. (1956). The functions of rhetorical criticism. *Quarterly Journal of Speech, 42,* 283–291.

Frentz, T. S. (1985). Rhetorical conversation, time, and moral action. *Quarterly Journal of Speech, 71,* 1–18.

Glaser, S. R., & Frank, D. (1982). Rhetorical criticism of interpersonal discourse: An exploratory study. *Communication Quarterly, 30,* 353–358.

Habermas, J. (1979). *Communication and the evolution of society.* (T. McCarthy, Trans.). Boston: Beacon Press.

Holsti, O. R. (1969). *Content analysis for the social sciences and humanities.* Reading, MA: Addison-Wesley.

Horton, D., & Wohl, R. R. (1956). Mass communication and para-social interaction. *Psychiatry, 19,* 215–229.

Kidd, V. (1975). Happily ever after and other relationship styles: Advice on interpersonal relations in popular magazines, 1951–1973. *Quarterly Journal of Speech. 61,* 31–39.

Kreps, G., & Thornton, B. C. (1984). *Health communications: Theory and practice.* New York: Longman.

Landers, A. (1968). *Ann Landers says truth is stranger . . .* Englewood Cliffs, NJ: Prentice-Hall.

Makay, J. J. (1980). Psychotherapy as a rhetoric for secular grace. *Central States Speech Journal, 31,* 184–196.

Phillips, G. M. (1976). Rhetoric and its alternative as bases for examination of intimate communication. *Communication Quarterly, 24,* 11–23.

Redding, C. (1957). Extrinsic and intrinsic criticism. *Western Journal of Speech Communication, 21,* 96–102.

Schudson, M. (1978). The ideal of conversation in the study of mass communication. *Communication Research, 3,* 258–268.

Scott, R. L. (1977). Communication as an intentional, social system. *Human Communication Research, 3,* 258–268.

Searle, J. R. (1969). *Speech acts: An essay in the philosophy of language.* London: Cambridge University Press.

Sennett, R. (1974). *The fall of public man.* New York: Random House.

Sharf, R. F. (1979). Rhetorical analysis of nonpublic discourse. *Communication Quarterly, 27,* 21–30.

Vatz, R. E., & Weinberg, L. S. (1983). *Thomas Szasz: Primary values and major contentions.* Buffalo: Prometheus Books.

Ward, S. A., Bluman, D. L., & Dauria, A. F. (1982). Rhetorical sensitivity recast: Theoretical assumptions of an informal interpersonal rhetoric. *Communication Quarterly, 30,* 189–195.

8
Electronic Advice Columns: Humanizing the Machine

Laurel Hellerstein

Computer-mediated communication has taken unpredicted forms, one of which is the electronic advice column which shares many characteristics with its more conventional counterpart, the newspaper advice column. Hellerstein suggests that the electronic advice column serves as a playful, therapeutic leisure activity for the computer literate.

INTRODUCTION

Once thought to have applications primarily in the work sector, computer-mediated communication (CMC) is now being used more frequently in leisure settings. Commercial computer networks such as COMPUSERVE and The SOURCE enjoy increased popularity as more and more people purchase home computers. Along with commercial services, home users are finding Bulletin Board systems (BBS) to be a wealth of information on a variety of topics as well as a convenient way to communicate with people with whom they share common interests. BBS such as the FIDO system are expanding into national networks, linking together home microcomputers. As academics discover the ease and speed of institutional networks such as ARPANET and BITNET, CMC becomes a convenient method of exchanging information, much of which is of a personal nature. Currently ARPANET has over 4,000 mainframes on the network, and the ever-expanding BITNET supports over 1500 academic institutions (Jordan, 1986).

Frequently new technologies are put to uses not intended when originally implemented (McLuhan, 1964). For example, it is questionable whether or not the telephone was ever envisioned to be used for pay-per-call sex, or whether the CB radio was intended to be used as a device to not only elude highway police officers, but to entertain truckers and drivers on the nation's highways. Although CMC was envisioned by its creators as a low-cost, efficient, and rapid mode of communication for its users (Vallee, 1982), some of the current uses of CMC can be considered quite novel.

POSSIBLE OPTIONS FOR CMC USE

BBS offer, generally for the price of a phone call, public forums to discuss issues ranging from political events of the day (Garramone, Harris, & Anderson, 1986) to home computer systems. One of the more popular attractions of BBS are the ability to upload and download public domain software (generally noncopyrighted software written by hobbyists). Private messaging is also a feature of most BBS enabling users to leave electronic mail for others to retrieve and respond to at their leisure. It has been estimated that there are approximately 10,000 BBS currently in operation in the United States (Sternheim, 1986), and while more restricted, BBS enjoy popularity in nations from Indonesia to Sweden (Meeks, 1985). It is quite possible for a person in Kansas to call up a BBS in France and exchange messages with a person from Italy who also frequents that particular BBS.

Academics at most universities and major research centers worldwide can also exchange messages with colleagues at geographically dispersed locales using computer networks supported by the United States government and research grants. Academics, however, are using these networks for purposes other than the dissemination of information. Special interest newsletters which are created and distributed electronically cater to a wide variety of interests from discussions of the rock group, the Grateful Dead, to Computer Aided Design (CAD). The use of these networks for correspondence goes beyond the work realm, as people have found network mail to be a quick, no- or low-cost way to send personal messages to friends (Marvin, 1983).

Many universities have internal electronic mail systems which were initially implemented for academic purposes yet for the most part are used for social purposes by students. Hellerstein (1985) found that, while students at a major New England University reported using the mail system to get help on school work or communicate with instructors, most people overwhelmingly used the mail system to communicate with friends. In-house electronic mail services in corporations are also being used for purposes other than business. For example, Steinfield (1986) found that many of the employees of a large corporation also used the company's electronic mail system for socializing with business colleagues.

Commercial services which cost the user from $8.00 to $25.00 per hour spent online, depending on time of day and type of service used, offer a wide menu of communication options. These services give users a variety of options ranging from online shopping, group discussion on a variety of subjects including gardening and health problems, as well as a CB-type application. The CB-type application allows users to communicate with one another in real time even though participants may be at difference geographic locations. The ability for two or more people to chat with one another via the computer has led to more novel applications. For example, online cocktail parties and computer sex (see Chapter 10 in this volume). Further, anecdotal evidence (Van Gelder, 1985; Hooper, 1986) points to the use of these commercial services as a means to make friends and initiate romantic encounters that eventually evolve into face-to-face relationships.

One of the more novel uses of CMC has been the electronic advice column. A notefiles devoted to health issues with responses from leading physicians is regularly distributed on ARPANET. Online therapists and health professionals regularly give advice on a variety of topics on BBS across the country (Meeks, 1986). COMPUSERVE, a commercial service has an online career counselor to answer the job-seekers questions (Baird, 1986). Users are finding there is really no limit to the type of problems that can be discussed online.

This chapter will describe an electronic advice to the lovelorn "column" currently in use at a major university. The place of the electronic advice column in a society that is increasing its use and dependence on computers will be discussed, and the implications of its use will be addressed. It will be argued that people are finding computers to be a viable medium for types of communication that exist within more traditional modes of communication. And finally, it will be argued that the electronic advice column is one example of the way in which the impersonal computer is being made more human by regular users of the technology.

ASK AUNT DEE

When the user first reads the Ask Aunt Dee notefile, they are greeted by the following message:

> Dear Cyber Users [UMASS mainframe computer], Welcome back to a new semester and year at U. MASS!!
>
> Aunt Dee is here to answer your questions regarding affairs of the heart. While Aunt Dee is not a professional counselor, she has had years of experience in areas of both heartbreak and the joys of love. She feels her years of experience qualify her to provide advice and support to the broken hearted or inexperienced. So come to Aunt Dee and she will respond to your questions or problems as soon as she can.
>
> Be Good,
> Your Auntie Dee

Most letters to Ask Aunt Dee concern problems people are having dealing with more intimate types of relationships. Aunt Dee generally responds to a writer's problem within two days of it first appearing in the notesfile. The response is appended directly to the problem. While no two letters to Aunt Dee are similar, some are more conventional than others; a typical letter follows:

Aunt Dee.
I am really puzzled over a problem I have. I have really cared about this girl named Michelle for about two years now. The only problem is she has a boyfriend that she can't seem to break up with. I know she likes me because she told friends and she even told me that one day she hopes we're together. I've tried so hard to bring us together, and each time I almost get her it slips away. She always complains about how bad her boyfriend treats her. All the people we work with keep telling her to see me because I would treat her like a queen but I guess she doesn't know how to break up with him, she's scared because he intimidates her. I've tried going out with many others and forgetting about her but it just doesn't work. I spend countless hours thinking about her and how to bring us together. I know we would both be happy if we could be together. Do you have any suggestions?

Thanx, Redbird

Dear Redbird,
If you were important enough to her she would break up with him. I am not meaning this as a put-down so please don't take it that way. If he treats her poorly and she puts up with it she must not have a very high opinion of herself. Maybe they were meant for each other. A person can't really care for another until they like themself. Anyone who allows others to treat them poorly really don't have a very high level of self-esteem. Again, if she is intimidated by him to the point where she will not break up with him, even though she is miserable, leads me to think that this woman has some growing to do before she can become involved in any truly loving and caring relationship.

I am sorry that you are so taken by this woman that you cannot get her out of your mind. I really doubt that you would both be happy if you were together. Let time take its course . . . find someone that you can start afresh with . . . a woman who is able to become involved in a relationship with you without having to toss aside (literally) old baggage!

Be Good,
Your Auntie Dee

At this writing, Aunt Dee has responded to 106 requests for advice. In the past two years of its existence, the advice column has been accessed in a read mode over 5,000 times. Anonymity and respect for privacy prevents making any quantitative investigation into the demographics of those who write to Aunt Dee; however, observation indicates that the average writer is a young male heterosexual undergraduate. Aunt Dee has also received a number of letters from young women, married people, and gay men.

That the majority of letter writers are young men corresponds with a previous study (Hellerstein, 1985) that found the majority of mainframe computer users at the University of Massachusetts to be young and male. Further, the subject matter of a majority of the letters seem to be written by those that are at an age where inexperience plays a part in problematic relationships.

As discussed above, the major theme running through the letters written to Aunt Dee concern romantic problems. Any attempt at a systematic content analyses would likely obscure the complicated nature of the problems, rather than enlighten interested parties about the topics discussed in the letters. While content analysis might prove useful in, for example, determining demographics of users, the purpose of this paper is to provide an overview of the content of letters written to Aunt Dee. Several common themes in the letters are of interest: A number of the letters deal with ''liking more than one person at a time'':

> I have a girlfriend who I love dearly, but she is at school, and I am here, and there is a long phone bill in between. But I have an old friend who is becoming more than a friend. We haven't gotten far (mostly because of my fears), but this ''brother-sister'' type friendship could easily develop into something more, and it wouldn't take too much to get it going. This old friend has made queries as to the strength of my relationship with my present girlfriend, and has made a couple forward remarks. I love them both. I am not sure anymore which I love more. I want to keep it just a friendship, but how???
> Most of all, not matter how I feel towards my girlfriend,
>
> I hate being by
> myself

A majority of the letters deal with communication problems. There are three subthemes that run through these letters, although they are not necessarily mutually exclusive.

1. Uncertainty about proper strategies to use when communication intimate feelings to another:

> Dear Auntie Dee,
> ummmmmm. . . . . Last summer I met this guy, we spent a lot of time together—working, playing, drinking, etc . . . everyone thought we were going out, I wish we were. I don't understand, he was always very affectionate, and seemed to like me a lot, but nothing but a few oddly placed bear-hugs and snuggling ever happened. He said once that he knew he was tease, he has even are both back at school now, and we still keep in touch. I will be in Boston over January and he is planning to come visit me and my sister. I can't wait to see him, but I'm really nervous. Should I say something to him?

How should I act? I'm not really the aggressive or pushy type. Is now the time to learn? Am I too late? Help!

-Lost without his love

2.   An overall lack of communication in a relationship:

O.K. Auntie, my problem concerns an old exgirlfriend . . There's been a lot of animosity since we broke up (4 years ago)—she was unable (or unwilling) to talk seriously, heart-to-heart, and I was no longer willing to put up with such a superficial relation-ship. We couldn't be friends for the same reason, and we drifted apart. I felt she alienated me despite my efforts to make amends, and when I get mad I stay mad unless the problem is resolved some- how. Since she lives far away this isn't usually an issue, but once a year there is a festival near my hometown & both of us usually end up there (she introduced me to it, and we used to go together). Two years ago she ap- proached me (much to my surprise) and made overtones toward friendship; I was skeptical, but she asked if she could write to me and I said O.K. A full 8 months later I got a lousy 3 page letter that didn't say anything new, so I spent weeks ripping off a 12-pager blowing off all the steam I'd been saving for 5 years, and concluded by saying that I never wanted to see her again. That year's festival was cold indeed -I ignored her for 3 days.

My feelings haven't changed, but lately I've begun to admit to myself that I still care for her—rekindling the romance remains utterly out of the ques- tion, but I've always wished we could have stayed friends.

Many of my friends (including my current lover who never liked Janet) think I'm being childish for holding a grudge. But besides still being mad, I just don't see any basis for reconciliation. It's been a long time, and I don't think she's grown up any.

Do you think that I should give it a try, and assuming you do, how do you think I should go about it? I just don't see how (or why) I should approach it. The festival is just 4 weeks away!

Thanx,
Space Turnip

3.   Fear of communication:

Dear Aunt Dee,
I come to you with a nasty, yet typical problem. You see, there is this girl I've know for three years, and she and I are the best of friends. We spent much of last summer together (in a platonic sense). I get along with her better than most of my male friends. But now the problem comes in. I think I've fallen in love with her. Now love itself is no problem but in this case I don't know if it is mutual. You might ask if this is really love or just a stan- dard case of infatuation. Well, I've been thru infatuation before, and it was nothing like this. I care for her in a way I never thought was possible. The root of the problem is that if I tell her my feelings, I may loose her very

important friendship. But if I don't tell her the way I feel, I may loose a once in a lifetime woman. What should I do, Aunt Dee???? This is really driving me nuts!!

S.O.S.
John Doe

In addition to letters asking for advice concerning relationships, Ask Aunt Dee receives two other types of letters.

1.   Philosophical ponderings about love relationships:

Dear Aunt Dee.
This is not a personal problem, but I feel that you would be an authority on this type of question.
Recently, you may have probably already read the article, but Ann Landers conducted a poll, rating the preferences of women to various degrees of social contact from a hug, to a kiss, up to the actual act of sexual intercourse.
The poll found that a surprising 40% of women under 40 were not preferring sex over the more "conventional" sexual expressions. My opinion is that I have to congratulate those women who are open in their own desires and not what society expects from women. Not to discredit women with an active sex life, because if they feel that they enjoy the intimate experience as well as her partner then I say good for them. What do you think that this poll says about the women of today?

The wise and Venerable, Nim

2.   Letters that can be construed as jokes:

Dear my Dearest Aunt,
Please help me with a very important problem. This is very hard to discuss. Last summer four girls took me to a private beach and attacked me sexually!!!! I couldn't believe it, I have known these girls since childhood!! The trouble is, that I am gay. How can I tell them that I am gay? I am so nervous that they won't attack me anymore. Actually, I kind of enjoyed it. What shall I do Dear Auntie?

Lovingly (and I mean that),
Your favorite nephew!!!!!!

and,

Dear Aunt Dee,
I hope that you are in fact a woman because I have fallen in love with you!!!! I can tell from your replies that you are a sensible, wise,and compassionate. Would it be impertinent to introduce myself??? How about in person? Dinner? (even computers have to eat, right?)

When compared to the themes of other letters, a proportionate amount of letters deal with jokes and philosophical issues. While in some cases it is debatable whether or not a letter is meant as a joke or is serious, most of the situations, as described in these light-hearted letters portray a humorous distortion of real-life problems.

NEWSPAPER ADVICE COLUMNS

While such use of CMC may appear novel, it is not surprising that people are using the computer for advice columns given the nature of the medium. CMC is text-based as are the newspapers where advice columns are traditionally found. BBS allow the user to read messages at their own leisure, which is akin to newspapers and different from getting advice over the telephone or in a face-to-face situation. Finally, under most circumstances, a writer's anonymity can be protected through the use of pennames or nicknames.

Advice columns have enjoyed popularity as long as newsletters or papers have been publicly distributed. Hendley (1977–78) places the origins of the advice column in late seventeenth century England. The first advice columnist was an English bookseller, John Dunton, who distributed a newsletter devoted to answering reader's problems on all areas of life. Current advice columnists familiar to most readers of syndicated newspapers are Dear Abby, Ann Landers, Joyce Brothers, Ask Beth and, more recently, Miss Manners. While Ann Landers and Abby will tackle most any problem, some columnists such as Beth, address a particular type of problem such as concerns to adolescents. Over time each columnist has developed her own personality familiar to habitual readers.

The above advice columns share a common set of characteristics which include the selection of those letters that will appear in the syndicated columns out of the thousands that they actually receive. There is no way to characterize the nature of the letters received by advice columnists as the reader is only exposed to those letters which the columnists themselves deem to be fit for publication. For example, a majority of letters sent to Dear Abby could be of a humorous nature, as with Ask Aunt Dee; yet unlike Ask Aunt Dee who makes all letters received public, letters to the traditional columnist are personally selected by the columnist and her staff.

Perhaps the lack of research that looks at the advice column in our society can be directly attributable to the inability to make generalizable statements based upon letters which are actually published. Lumby (1976) points out that Ann Landers receives more than 1,000 letters each day, yet she will not release these letters even to parties interested in legitimate research. Gieber (1960) however, was able to convince an un-named syndicated columnist to release original letters for research and, as did Lumbley, attempted a systematic content analyses of the letters, coding such variables as age, sex, and socioeconomic status of writers as well as attempting to place each letter into a thematic category. While Gieber was concerned with the columnists "social role," Lumby was comparing the type of advice dispensed over a 15-year period of time. Content analysis as a sole research tool is problematic, as Gieber points out: "Content analyses is a limited tool and the letter provided incomplete data" (p. 514).

Although, with respect to method, research efforts that have looked at the advice column in our society are problematic, subsequent discussion and conclusions are enlightening. For example, based on his content analysis, Gieber (1960, p. 514) hypothesizs that the social role of the advice columnist in our society is positive in that:

1. The writers are "groupless" or anomic persons who have poor communications with formal social institutions and orthodox social agencies.
2. The newspaper column serves as a nonthreatening authority which provides support and possibly an outlet for anxiety.
3. The newspaper provides the letter writers with contact with the community and outside world.

Tankard and Adelson (1982) were concerned with the nature of the advice being dispensed by advice columnists. They performed a content analyses of three columns "to learn more about the role the newspaper advice columns are filling in transmitting mental health information" (p. 593). They conclude that generally columnists refute common negative myths concerning mental health and that, "perhaps greater amounts of misleading information about mental health and marriage are contained in other kinds of mass media content, such as television dramatic pro-grams or locally written newspaper features" (p. 609).

In many ways it is difficult to relate the findings presented above with the computer-based Ask Aunt Dee. Traditional newspaper columnists are akin to Ask Aunt Dee in that they disperse information at no cost to the writer, anonymity of the writer is upheld, and the columnist is perceived to be an authority figure with a wisdom or level of knowledge beyond that of the writer. Differences are clearly evident between the newspaper columnists and Ask Aunt Dee. Aunt Dee does not edit or censor letters; all but the most distasteful are answered and open for public inspection; the readership of Aunt Dee is less diversified than that of the newspaper columnist. Tankard and Adelson note:

> "Dear Abby" is reported to have a daily readership of 65 million and "Dear Abby" and Ann Landers together are reported to have a combined readership

of 130 million. As Ann Landers puts it, "I have been entrusted with the largest reading audience in the world." Joyce Brothers does not have the huge readership of Ann and Abby, but she is syndicated in 300 news-papers (compared with about 1,000 each for the other two). (p. 592)

The potential readership of Ask Aunt Dee actually is quite large when one considers that any student or person affiliated with the University of Massachusetts or any of the four smaller colleges in the Amherst area can get a computer account which gives them access to Ask Aunt Dee. Unlike readers of newspaper advice columns, Ask Aunt Dee readers all share in common an affiliation with an institution of higher learning, as well as the use of the University of Massachusetts mainframe computer.

A discussion of Gieber's (1960) three hypotheses in relation to Ask Aunt Dee provides insight into the electronic advice column, as well as drawing further distinctions between it and the more traditional newspaper columns. Gieber believes that, overall, those people who write to newspaper advice columnists are alienated from the mainstream of society. While no empirical evidence exists to suggest that those who write to Ask Aunt Dee are alienated from society, one can hypothesize that these people are alienated from the general college population. Perhaps those seeking advice from Ask Aunt Dee are alienated with respect to their interpersonal communication skills. This argument finds support in that the majority of serious letters sent to Aunt Dee have as a component poor communication between the involved parties.

We must question, however, if these people's problems are in reality any different than those experienced by other members of society. Most letters do indicate that people have been able to form interpersonal relationships and that they are merely having trouble dealing with them as might any person at a given point in their life. Further, it can be assumed that the majority of letter writers to Ask Aunt Dee are young college students. It is at this age that many people begin to learn about intimate relationships through experience. A higher level of problems resulting from inexperience in intimate relationships would not be uncommon. With the exception of Ask Beth, newspaper columnists appear to cater to an older group of readers, and as an exception Beth responds overwhelmingly to problems adolescents are having in interpersonal relationships.

Gieber's second hypothesis which concerns the nonthreatening presence of the columnist can be related to Aunt Dee. The writer is protected by anonymity and is under no obligation to meet Aunt Dee in a face-to-face situation, thus making it easier for writers to reveal problems in detail. Gieber's final hypothesis that one of the outcomes of writing to the columnist is contact with the outside world is more problematic. Without empirical evidence that indicates that the writers are alienated, it is difficult to make statements regarding how they resolve this problem. Unlike traditional newspaper columns, Ask Aunt Dee's readers are comprised of people who work and play on the mainframe computer. Although this may be changing, at this point the mainstream college student does not use the computer at the University of Massachusetts. If the letter writer is in some subconscious way trying to make contact with the mainstream of college life, then the computer is not going to allow him or her to reach that goal. The daily campus newspaper is perhaps a far better vehicle for reaching out the campus community.

It is clear then that for a variety of reasons Ask Aunt Dee is similar to her counterparts who dispense advice in newspapers, yet the apparent differences also call for a different type of analysis. The medium over which Aunt Dee dispenses advice serves as a starting point when looking at the place of computer-mediated advice columns. For the purposes of this paper then, it is best to discuss Aunt Dee in the context of new technology and the predicted and real changes that computers are making in our society.

LITERACY AND NEW MEDIA TECHNOLOGIES

The computerization of the advice column may be considered by some to be a novel use of CMC; it is, however, a conventional type of correspondence that has been a part of popular culture since newspapers and newsletters were publicly distributed. What makes the column undeniably different is that it can only be accessed via a computer which is only now being used and depended on for communication purposes. One does not sit down and turn on a computer and watch it, as with a television set. While television literacy is not inherent, computer literacy requires not only the knowledge of how to access and use a communication system, but also knowledge of how to read and, in most cases, how to type on a keyboard if two-way communication is desired. Computer literacy is something which is developed, and includes stages from elementary knowledge to more sophisticated literacy.

In an essay on the changing nature of media grammar that comes about with the use of new forms of media, Gumpert and Cathcart (1985) argue with respect to "media literacy":

> It is our position that: 1) there is a set of codes and conventions integral to each medium; 2) such codes and conventions constitute part of our media consciousness; 3) the information processing made possible through these various grammars influence our perceptions and values; and 4) the order of acquisition of media literacy will provide a particular world perspective which relates and separates persons accordingly. (p. 24)

Further on in the same essay they state, "It is our position that the early acquisition of a particular media consciousness continues to shape peoples' world view even though later they acquire literacy in new media" (p. 29).

Gumpert and Cathcart's ideas suggest several ways to look at the place of the electronic advice column in our society. Electronic advice columns, for example, may be serving the same function as their newspaper counterparts. People who first experienced the advice column in newspapers are merely transferring this pop culture phenomenon to a different medium. The group of people I refer to here are not first-generation computer users; rather they grew up in a world without computers and have acquired computer literacy either by choice or by necessity. These are the people who are more likely to use computers not only for work activity, and also for a certain amount of leisure time. These people subscribe to electronic newsletters and newspapers and pay the fairly hefty rates for on-line time on commercial communication networks.

There is also a younger generation of computer users who need to be taken into account with respect to the use of electronic advice columns. These are people who were raised with computers and who have been exposed to computer images and who were taught to use computers in their earlier developmental years. To these computer literate people there was never a time before computers. While these same people may have also been exposed to newspaper advice columns, they are finding (as does that older group of users) that CMC lends itself quite naturally to the function of dispensing advice. While research comparing the electronic advice column with the newspaper column has yet to be done, it is quite possible that there is no difference. While computer literacy is necessary for access to electronic advice columns, existing media grammar dictates the format of both the problem and responses that will appear in the electronic advice column. Gumpert and Cathcart (1985) believe:

> Not only does each generation accept the media technology of earlier generations and acquire literacy in the existing media, it also adapts to the influences of media technology which are introduced later in the generation's lifetime. In this process the older generation will acquire the grammar of a new media technology, but it will understand the new grammar as interpreted through the media grammar first learned. This results in resistance to the new form of information and/or attempts to absorb the new media into the already established ways of processing information. (p. 30)

If one accepts this argument regarding the acquisition of new media literacy and acknowledges that the transition to a computerized society has met with some resistance from older generations, then it follows that one means of adapting to the new technology is to transfer to computers, for example, more conventional types of communication, in this case the advice column. Further, the younger generation without years of experience with the more conventional form of media will outwardly accept the use of a new technology for what older users deem to be an new use for an established grammar: the advice column.

Computerized advice columns may be preferable over newspaper advice columns to those who are computer literate. Under most circumstances a person can retain anonymity in a public arena. Neither immediacy of response nor public response is guaranteed in newspaper columns. As discussed above, only a small percentage of letters sent to newspaper advice columns ever actually make it to print while all of the letters posted on Ask Aunt Dee are answered in the same public forum in which they are received.

Other forms of media are capable of and certainly do provide users with advice-type programming. Television, for example, has its share of Dr. Ruths and radio has its call-in advice programs, yet they differ substantially from the newspaper and electronic advice column by virtue of the type of literacy needed to be able to use the medium. Computer advice columns demand that the user have a certain level of computer literacy. Computer literacy moves forward from other forms of literacy—such as the ability to read and write—and works in combination with other skills to form a new type of literacy. Although computer literacy is different from other forms of media literacy, Ask Aunt Dee serves as an example of how components of older media are transferred to a new form of media, the computer.

As more and more people purchase home computers and become computer literate, it will probably not be uncommon for more conventional modes of communication to move online. Already it is possible to do banking or book airplane reservations via a computer terminal and, if one is willing to pay the price, a newspaper can be accessed through the computer instead of being delivered to the front doorstep. While our society is not necessarily moving online, nevertheless certain aspects of our social and work lives are now being duplicated online, and in some cases, are better served by computer-mediated communication.

LEISURE ACTIVITY AND COMPUTERS

An ongoing argument present in all sectors of our society is whether computers are a good or a bad thing. Questions are constantly being raised as to what is and what will be the impact of computers on the individual and the larger society. Below will be considered the function of the electronic advice column in a society that is moving more and more of its leisure and work activity online. Previous research that has focused on the newspaper advice column is of little help in uncovering the function of the electronic advice column because of major differences in modes of dissemination. Further, content analyses do not reveal how these columns function;

rather they have served only to document the nature of people's problems and subsequently the type of advice given by columnists.

While many social critics have pointed out the dehumanizing nature of computers, we are now seeing the computer used for very real human experiences, such as meeting new people, making new friends, and getting advice on very personal problems, such as is the case with Aunt Dee. Humans appear to have a very real need for social contact. As the use of computers has evolved, it is not surprising that people are finding more human applications for the technology. Perhaps without conscious effort, computer users are creating humanizing elements within impersonal computer systems as use of these systems becomes more commonplace.

The electronic advice column is one of many components that serve as a humanizing device, most specifically for those that are computer literate. Marvin (1983) suggests, "The more our lives are subject to the rationalizing appetite of machines, the more directed they are to maintenance and extension of a machine culture, the more socially essential true playfulness is" (p. 50). Indeed research on the use of computers in the work place indicates that people are using computer-mediated communication for what can be considered leisure activities such as socializing and game playing (Steinfield, 1986; Hiltz & Turoff, 1978; Hellerstein, 1986). Computers serve as not only a "task-horse" but also as a tool for play.

Once a person learns the basic skills needed to operate a computer, there are many ways that this machine can be used to participate in leisure activities. Software that simulates arcade video games and text-based adventure games in which the user cavorts in a fantasy world of strange creatures are very popular consumer items. Computer-mediated communication lends itself quite well to social communication in the leisure realm. Anecdotal evidence indicates that people are foregoing more traditional ways of meeting people and using the computer to make social contacts (Van Gelder, 1985; Hooper, 1986). Over what other medium can the average person in the solitude of their own home, sit down at any time and communicate on any number of topics in real time with people from all over the world and receive immediate feedback?

With respect specifically to Ask Aunt Dee as pointed out above, a large proportion of the letters are humorous and do not deal with serious topics. While the majority of letters do deal with serious problems, even these are relegated to the leisure activity of romance, as opposed to work-related problems. The reading of Ask Aunt Dee undeniably serves a leisure function for its readers, and while more complex issues surround the function of the electronic advice column for actual users, it still exists within the leisure or play realm of computer use. Perhaps Aunt Dee is a phenomenon relegated to the college campus and can be attributed to college students' playful nature and diversion seeking behavior.

Marvin (1983) believes:

Instead of permitting new communication technologies to narrow our lives by productively rationalizing the greater areas of experience, we should strive to enlarge the domain and variety of humane interaction by building ample opportunities for playfulness into newly extended systems of communication. (p. 51)

The electronic advice column can be seen as being a playful component of what to many people is still a dehumanizing machine, the computer. Quantitatively no research to date suggests how the newspaper advice column functions in our society, other than as a pop culture phenomenon. The function that the electronic advice column will ultimately serve in our society is yet to be seen and investigated by researchers.

CONCLUSION

In this chapter a description of one electronic advice column currently in use at a major university has been presented. For the most part letters to Ask Aunt Dee deal with personal problems encountered in relationships although some of the letters philosophize about romance and a number of the letter writers make attempts to be humorous. Several major themes run through the letters: desire to change the nature of a relationship, uncertainty of appropriate communication strategies, overall lack of communication, and fear of communication. Ask Aunt Dee was discussed in light of research on conventional newspaper advice columns. It was concluded that problematic research methods and the nature of the media by which the two types of advice columns are disseminated make it difficult to relate past research to electronic advice columns.

Based on Gumpert and Cathcart's (1985) theories of media literacy, it was suggested that people using computers have gained a new literacy. Rather than reject computers, and in an attempt to humanize these machine, people have duplicated the conventional advice column on the computer via computer-mediated communication. An older media grammar has found a home on a new form of media.

Finally, while computers function primarily as a tool for work in our society, people are also using them for leisure activities. Reading and writing to the electronic advice column is one such leisure activity that has found a comfortable home on computer networks. Computers are being used more frequently to replace conventional forms of communication in the work situation such as the memo or the telephone call for a number of reasons, including lower cost, speed of transmission, and overall efficiency. Just as the television replaced radio as a primary means of entertainment for many people years ago, so too will computer-mediated communication replace or duplicate more conventional forms of leisure activity. As people become computer literate, they will find more ways to amuse themselves with the tool they work with, the computer. Increasingly, communication, whether oral or text-based, will either be duplicated or totally replaced by computer-mediated communication. The leisure use of computers has naturally evolved as people attempt to humanize what is generally perceived to be a very dehumanizing technology. After all, humans use computers; computers do not use humans.

REFERENCES

Baird, K. (1986, August). Online columnist gives career advice. *Online Today*, p. 31.

Garramone, G. M., Harris, A. C., & Anderson, R. (1986, Summer). Uses of computer bulletin boards. *Journal of Broadcasting & Electronic Media, 30*, 325–39.

Gieber, W. (1960). The "lovelorn" columnist and her social role. *Journalism Quarterly, 37*, 499–514.

Gumpert, G., & Cathcart, R. (1985, March). Media grammars, generations and media gaps. *Critical Studies in Mass Communication, 2*, 23–35.

Hellerstein, L. (1985). The social use of electronic communication at a major university. *Computers and the Social Sciences, 1*, 191–97.

Hellerstein, L. (1986). *Electronic messaging and conferencing with an emphasis on social use: An exploratory study.* Paper presented at the International Communication Association Conference, Chicago, IL.

Hendley, W. C. (1977–78). Dear Abby, Miss Lonelyhearts, and the eighteenth century: The origins of the newspaper advice column. *Journal of Popular Culture, 11*, 345–52.

Hiltz, S. R., & Turoff, M. (1978). *The Network Nation*. Reading, MA: Addison-Wesley.

Hooper, J. (1986, February). Love at first byte. *New Age Journal*, pp. 16–19.

Jordan, K. (1986, October 3,). Systems Operator and Network Specialist, University of Massachusetts Computing Center. Interview.

Lumby, M. E. (1976). Ann Landers' advice column: 1958 and 1971. *Journalism Quarterly, 53*, 129–32.

Marvin, C. (1983, March). Telecommunications policy and the pleasure principle. *Telecommunications Policy, 7*, 43–52.

McLuhan, M. (1964). *Understanding media*. New York: Mentor Books.

Meeks, B. (1985, June). Life at 300 baud. *Profiles*, pp. 24–27.

Meeks, B. (1986, July). Independent Journalist. Private Correspondence.

Steinfield, C. (1986). Computer-mediated communication in an organizational setting: Explaining task-related and socioemotional uses. In M. L. McGlaughlin (Ed.), *Communication Yearbook 9*. Beverly Hills, CA: Sage Publications.

Sternheim, M. (1986, October). Sysop for the Pioneer Valley Computer Users' Group BBS, and Sysop for the University of Massachusetts Physics BBS. Private conversation.

Tankard, J. W., & Adelson, R. (1982). Mental health and marital information in three newspaper advice columns. *Journalism Quarterly, 59*, 592–97, 609.

Vallee, J. (1982). *The network revolution: Confessions of a computer scientists*. Berkeley, CA: And/Or Press.

Van Gelder, L. (1985, October). The strange case of the electronic lover. *Ms.*, pp. 98–124.

9

The Strange Case of the Electronic Lover

Lindsy Van Gelder

Computer networks connect people of common interests through text-based interaction. How does one verify the accuracy of another user's statements? In her October 1985 article in Ms. *Magazine (pp. 98–124), Van Gelder describes a series of events which took place on a computer network which called into question issues of trust, intrusiveness, and verifiability. The events were startling, the consequences disturbing, and the issues unanswered.*

I "met" Joan in the late spring of 1983, shortly after I first hooked my personal computer up to a modem and entered the strange new world of online communications. Like me, Joan was spending a great deal of time on the "CB" channel of the national network CompuServe, where one can encounter other modem owners in what amounts to a computer version of CB radio. I was writing an article for *Ms.* about modems and doing online interviews with CB regulars. Joan was already a sought-after celebrity among the hundreds of users who hung out on the channel—a telecommunications media star.

Her "handle" was "Talkin' Lady." According to the conventions of the medium, people have a (usually frivolous) handle when they're on "open" channels with many users; but when two people choose to enter a private talk mode, they'll often exchange real information about themselves. I soon learned that her real name was Joan Sue Greene, and that she was a New York neuropsychologist in her late twenties, who had been severely disfigured in a car accident that was the fault of a drunken driver. The accident had killed her boyfriend. Joan herself spent a year in the hospital, being treated for brain damage, which affected both her speech and her ability to walk. Mute, confined to a wheelchair, and frequently suffering intense back and leg pain, Joan had at first been so embittered about her disabilities that she literally didn't want to live.

Then her mentor, a former professor at Johns Hopkins, presented her with a computer, a modem, and a year's subscription to CompuServe to be used specifically doing what Joan was doing—making friends online. At first, her handle had been "Quiet Lady," in reference to her muteness. But

Joan could type—which is, after all, how one "talks" on a computer—and she had a sassy, bright, generous personality that blossomed in a medium where physicality doesn't count. Joan became enormously popular, and her new handle, "Talkin' Lady," was a reflection of her new sense of self. Over the next two years, she became a monumental online presence who served both as a support for other disabled women and as an inspiring stereotype-smasher to the able-bodied. Through her many intense friendships and (in some cases) her online romances, she changed the lives of dozens of women.

Thus it was a huge shock early this year when, through a complicated series of events, Joan was revealed as being not disabled at all. More to the point, Joan, in fact, was not a woman. She was really a man we'll call Alex—a prominent New York psychiatrist in his early fifties who was engaged in a bizarre, all-consuming experiment to see what it felt like to be female, and to experience the intimacy of female friendship.

Even those who barely knew Joan felt implicated—and somehow betrayed—by Alex's deception. Many of us online like to believe that we're a utopian community of the future, and Alex's experiment proved to us all that technology is no shield against deceit. We lost our innocence, if not our faith.

To some of Alex's victims—including a woman who had an affair with the real-life Alex, after being introduced to him by Joan—the experiment was a "mind rape," pure and simple. (Several people, in fact, have tentatively explored the possibility of bringing charges against Alex as a psychiatrist—although the case is without precedent, to put it mildly.) To some other victims, Alex was not so much an impostor as a seeker whose search went out of control. (Several of these are attempting to continue a friendship with Alex—and, as one woman put it, "to relate to the soul, not the sex of the person. The soul is the same as before.")

Either way, this is a peculiarly modern story about a man who used some of our most up-to-date technology to play out some of our oldest assumptions about gender roles.

More than most stories, it requires a bit of background. A modem, of course, is the device that connects a computer to the phone and from there to any other similarly equipped computer. CompuServe is the largest of a number of modem networks; it charges its subscribers an initial small fee to open an account with a special ID number and then charges hourly fees for access to its hundreds of services, from stock reports to airline information. In addition to its business services, the network also offers a number of "social" services (including numerous Special Interest Groups—SIGs—and the CB channels) where users can mingle.

The unfolding of an online relationship is unique, combining the thrill of ultrafuturistic technology with the veneration of the written word that informed nineteenth-century friendships and romances. Most people who haven't used the medium have trouble imagining what it's like to connect with other people whose words are wafting across your computer screen. For starters, it's dizzyingly egalitarian, since the most important thing about oneself isn't age, appearance, career success, health, race, gender, sexual preference, accent, or any of the other categories by which we normally judge each other, but one's mind. My personal experience has been that I often respond to the minds of people whom, because of my own prejudices (or theirs), I might otherwise not meet. (For example, my best friend online is from Appalachia, which I once thought was inhabited only by Li'l Abner and the Dukes of Hazzard. My friend, in turn, had never had a gay friend before.)

But such mind-to-mind encounters presume that the people at both keyboards are committed to getting past labels and into some new, truer way of relating. In the wake of the Alex/Joan scandal, some online habitues have soberly concluded that perhaps there's a thin line between getting out of one's skin and getting into a completely false identity—and that the medium may even encourage impersonation. (One network, for example, has a brochure showing a man dressed up as Indiana Jones, Michael Jackson, and an Olympic athlete; the copy reads, "Be anything you want on American PEOPLE/LINK.") Still, when it works, it works. Disabled people are especially well represented online, and most of them say that it's a medium where they can make a first impression on their own terms.

Another positive consequence of the medium's mind-to-mind potential—and this is germane to Joan's story—is that it's powerfully conducive to intimacy. Thoughts and emotions are the coin of this realm, and people tend to share them sooner than they would in "real life" (what CBers refer to as "offline"). Some people, in fact, become addicted to computer relationships, per se. But most use the modem merely as a way to start relationships that may, in time, continue offline. After several online conversations with someone who seems especially compatible, people commonly arrange to speak on the telephone, to exchange photographs, and eventually to meet in person, either by themselves or at one of the regular "CB parties" held around the country. (Several marriages have resulted from online meetings on CompuServe CB alone.) I've met four good computer friends in person, and found them all much the same offline as on. For me, the only odd thing about these relationships has been their chronology. It's a little surreal to know intimate details about someone's childhood before you've ever been out to dinner together.

One of the reasons that Joan's real identity went undetected for so long was that her supposed disability prevented her from speaking on the phone. (Several people did communicate with Joan on the phone, in one case because Joan had said that she wanted to hear the sound of the other woman's voice. Joan in turn "would make horrible noises into the receiver—little yelps and moans.") There was also the matter of Joan's disfigurement; she supposedly drooled and had a "smashed up" face, untreatable by plastic surgery. She was, she said, embarrassed to meet her computer friends in person. Those who wanted to be sensitive to disabled concerns naturally didn't push. It was an ingenious cover.

Alex supposedly began his dual identity by mistake. One of the social realities of the computing world is that the majority of its inhabitants are male; women usually get a lot of attention from all the men online. (Women who don't want to be continually pestered by requests from strange males to go into private talk mode often use androgynous handles.) Female handles also get attention from other women, since many women online are pioneering females in their fields and feminists. Alex apparently came online sometime in late 1982 or early 1983 and adopted the handle "Shrink, Inc." His epiphany came one evening when he was in private talk mode with a woman who for some reason mistook him for a female shrink. "The person was open with him in a way that stunned him," according to one of the women—let's call her Laura—who has maintained a friendship with Alex. "What he really found as Joan was that most women opened up to him in a way he had never seen before in all his years of practice. And he realized he could help them."

"He later told me that his female patients had trouble relating to him— they always seemed to be leaving something out," said Janis Goodall, a Berkeley, California, software firm employee who also knew both Joan and Alex. "Now he could see what it was." (Despite their similar recollections, Goodall is in the opposite camp from Laura, and says: "For someone supposedly dedicated to helping people, I think he rampaged through all of our feelings with despicable disregard.") At some point after "Shrink, Inc.'s" inadvertent plunge into sisterhood, Joan was born.

According to both Goodall and Laura (both of whom are disabled themselves), Alex has a back condition, "arthritis of the spine or a calcium deposit of some kind," according to Goodall, "which causes him discomfort, and has the potential, but not the probability of putting him in a wheelchair someday." Goodall added that Alex later defended his choice of a disabled persona by claiming that he "wanted to find out how disabled people deal with it." Others online believe that Joan's handicaps were a way both to shroud her real identity and aggrandize her heroic stature.

If Joan began spontaneously, she soon became a far more conscious creation, complete with electronic mail drop, special telephone line, and almost novelistically detailed biography (although she sometimes told different versions to different people). She was, by my own recollection and by the accounts of everyone interviewed, an exquisitely wrought character. For starters, she had guts. (She had once, before the accident, driven alone across the interior of Iceland as a way to cure her agoraphobia.) She had traveled everywhere, thanks to money left to her by her family's textile mill fortune. She lived alone (although neighbors checked on her and helped her with errands) and was a model independent female. In fact, Joan was quite a feminist. It was she who suggested the formation of a women's issues group within CompuServe, and she actively recruited members. Several women had relationships with Joan in which they referred to each other as "sister."

Joan was earthy, too, and spoke easily about sex. One woman remembers hearing at length about Joan's abortion at age 16; another recalls having a long conversation about Joan's decision not to embark on a particular course of spinal surgery that might relieve her leg pain, but "would also affect her clitoral nerve, and she wouldn't do that." She was bisexual. Although her family had been religious (she told some people that her parents were ministers), she herself was an ardent atheist who liked to engage religious people in debate. She was also a grass-smoker who frequently confessed to being a little stoned if you encountered her late at night. Her usual greeting was a flashy, flamboyant "Hi!!!!!!!!!!"

Interestingly, the two people who knew Joan and also met Alex in person say that their surface personalities were opposite. Alex is Jewish. He almost never drinks or smokes pot (although one of his medical specialities is pharmacology). He is a workaholic whose American Psychiatric Association biography reports wide publication in his field. "Joan was wild and zingy and flamboyant and would do anything you dared her to," notes Laura. "A part of Alex wanted to be like that, but he's actually quite intellectual and shy." Adds Janis Goodall: "Alex has a great deal of trouble expressing his emotions. There are long silences, and then he'll say, 'uh-huh, uh-huh'—just like a shrink."

Above all, Joan was a larger-than-life exemplary disabled person. At the time of her accident, she had been scheduled to teach a course at a major New York medical school (in fact, the teaching hospital that Alex is affiliated with as a psychiatrist). Ironically, Joan noted, the course dealt with many of the same neurological impairments that she herself now suffered. One of Joan's goals was eventually to resume her career as if the accident had never happened—and when I first knew her, she was embarked on an ambitious plan to employ a computer in the classroom to help her teach. The idea was that Joan would type her lecture into a computer, which would then be either magnified on a classroom screen or fed into student terminals. To all of us techno-fans and believers in better living through computers, it was a thrilling concept.

Joan was also a militant activist against the dangers of drunken drivers.

Early in her convalescence, when she was frequently half out of her mind with anger, she had on several occasions wheeled herself out of her apartment and onto the streets of Manhattan, where she would shout at passing motorists. On one such occasion, police officers in her precinct, upon learning her story, suggested that she put her rage and her talent to more productive use. Joan then began to go out on patrol with a group of traffic cops whose job it was to catch drunken drivers. Joan's role in the project was twofold: (a) as a highly credentialed neuropsychologist, she was better trained than most to detect cars whose drivers had reflex problems caused by too much drinking, and (b) she was willing to serve as an example to drunken drivers of what could befall them if they didn't shape up.

On one of Joan's forays, she met a young police officer named Jack Carr. As he and Joan spent more time together, he came to appreciate her spirit in much the same way the rest of us had. They fell in love—much to the distress of Jack's mother, who thought he was throwing his life away. (Joan's online friends were heartened to learn much later that Mrs. Carr had softened after Joan bought her a lap-top computer, and the two of them learned to communicate in the online world where Joan shone so brightly.) Jack occasionally came online with Joan, although I remember him as being shy and far less verbal than Joan.

Shortly after I met Joan, she and Jack got married. Joan sent an elaborate and joyous announcement to all her CB pals via electronic mail, and the couple held an online reception, attended by more than 30 CompuServe regulars. (Online parties are not unusual. People just type in all the festive sound effects, from the clink of champagne glasses to the tossing of confetti.) Joan and Jack honeymooned in Cyprus, which according to Pamela Bowen, a Huntington, West Virginia newspaper editor—Joan said "was one of the few places she'd never been." Bowen and many of Joan's other online friends received postcards from Cyprus. The following year Joan and Jack returned to Cyprus and sent out another batch of cards.

"I remember asking Joan how she would get around on her vacation," recalls Sheila Deitz, associate professor of law and psychology at the University of Virginia. "Joan simply replied that if need be, he'd carry her. He was the quintessential caring, nurturing, loving, sensitive human being"—a Mr. Right who, Deitz adds, exerted enormous pull on the imaginations of all Joan's online female friends. In hindsight, Deitz feels, "he was the man Alex would have loved to be"—but in fact could only be in the persona of a woman.

Joan was extraordinarily generous. On one occasion, when Laura was confined to her bed because of her disability and couldn't use her regular computer, Joan sent her a lap-top model—a gift worth hundreds of dollars. On another occasion, when Laura mentioned that no one had ever sent her roses, Joan had two dozen delivered. Marti Cloutier, a 42-year-old

Massachusetts woman with grown children, claims that it was Joan who inspired her to start college. "She made me feel I could do it at my age." When it came time for Cloutier to write her first term paper, she was terrified, but Joan helped her through it, both in terms of moral support and in the practical sense of sending her a long list of sources. (Ironically, Cloutier's assignment was a psychology paper on multiple personalities. She got an "A" in the course.) On another occasion, Joan told Cloutier that she was going out to hear the "Messiah" performed. When Cloutier enviously mentioned that she loved the music, Joan mailed her the tape. On still another occasion, when Cloutier and her husband were having difficulties over the amount of time that she spent online, Joan volunteered to "talk" to him. Cloutier's husband is also a part-time police officer, as Jack ostensibly was, and he and Joan were able to persuade him that if his wife had her own friends and interests, it would ultimately be good for their marriage. "She was always doing good things," Cloutier recalls, "and never asking anything in return."

My personal recollections are similar. Once, when Joan and I were chatting online late at night, I realized to my great disbelief that a bat had somehow gotten into my apartment and was flapping wildly about, with my cats in crazed pursuit. I got off the computer, managed to catch the bat and get it back out the window—but in the attendant confusion, the windowpane fell out of the window and onto my arm, slicing my wrist and palm. Needless to say, I ended up in the emergency room. Joan dropped me several extremely solicitous notes over the next few weeks, making sure that my stitches were healing properly and that I was over the scare of the accident. Even earlier, around the time I first met Joan, the child of two of my oldest friends was hit by a car and knocked into a coma that was to last for several weeks. Joan had a lot of thoughts about the physiology of comas, as well as about how to deal with hospital staffs, insurance companies, and one's own unraveling psyche in the midst of such a crisis. She offered to set up an online meeting with the child's mother. I later heard that Joan had also helped several women who had suicidal tendencies or problems with alcohol.

Still another way that Joan nurtured her friends—hilarious as it sounds in hindsight—was to try to keep CB free of impostors. Although Joan was probably the slickest and most long-lived impostor around, she was hardly the only one; they are a continuing phenomenon on CompuServe, and on every other network. Some lie about their ages, others about their accomplishments. Some appropriate the handles of established CB personae and impersonate them. (Unlike ID numbers, handles can be whatever you choose them to be.) There are also numerous other gender benders, some of them gay or bisexual men who come on in female guise to straight men. Most aren't hard to spot. Joan herself told several friends she had been fooled by a man pretending to be a gay woman, and she was furious. "One of the first things she ever told me," recalls Janis Goodall, "was to be terribly careful of the people you meet on CB—that things were not always as they seemed."

Sheila Deitz remembers meeting a man online who said he was single, but turned out to be not only married in real life, but romancing numerous women online. Deitz met the man offline and realized that his story was full of holes. "Joan was very sympathetic when I told her about it, and we agreed that we didn't want this guy to have the chance to pull this on other women." At some later point, according to Deitz, "Joan created a group called the Silent Circle. It was sort of an online vigilante group. She'd ferret out other impostors and confront them and tell them they'd better get their act together."

All of Joan's helping and nurturing and gift giving, in Deitz's opinion, "goes beyond what any professional would want to do. Alex fostered dependency, really." But at the time, especially among those of us who are able-bodied, there was a certain feeling that here was a person who needed all the support we could give her. Numerous disabled women have since rightly pointed out that our Take-a-Negro-to-Lunch-like attitudes were in fact incredibly patronizing.

The truth is that there was always another side to Joan's need to be needed. She could be obnoxiously grabby of one's time. Because she and I both lived in New York, she once suggested that we talk directly, modem to modem, over our phone lines—thus paying only the cost of a local call instead of CompuServe's $6 an hour connect charges. But as soon as I gave Joan my phone number, I was sorry. She called constantly—the phone would ring, and there would be her modem tone—and she refused to take the hint that I might be busy with work, lover, or children. "Everybody else had the same experience," according to Bob Walter, a New York publisher who also runs CompuServe's Health SIG, where Joan (and later Alex, too) frequently hung out. "She would bombard people with calls." Finally, I had to get blunt—and I felt guilty about it, since Joan, after all, was a disabled woman whose aggressive personality was probably the best thing she had going for her. (My first somewhat sexist thought, when I found out that Joan was really a man, was *Of course! Who else would be so pushy?*)

Joan was sexually aggressive. Every woman I interviewed reported—and was troubled by—Joan's pressuring to have "compusex." This is online sex, similar to phone sex, in which people type out their hottest fantasies while they masturbate. (In the age of herpes and AIDS, it has become increasingly popular.) According to one woman, "one time she said she and Jack had been smoking pot and then he'd gone off to work, but she was still high. She told me she had sexual feelings toward me and asked if I felt the same." (Joan's husband, who has conveniently off on undercover detail most nights, supposedly knew about these experiments and wasn't threatened by them, since Joan's partners were "only" other women.) Her m.o., at least with friends, was to establish an intense nonsexual intimacy, and then to come on to them, usually with the argument that compusex was a natural extension of their friendship. In one case, cited by several sources, a woman became so involved as Joan's compusex lover that she was on the verge of leaving her husband.

Interestingly, Joan never came on to me—or, to my knowledge, to any bisexual or gay women. Sheila Deitz is of the opinion that Alex only wanted to have "lesbian" compusex with heterosexual women, those whom he might actually be attracted to in real life. Some straight women apparently cooperated sexually, not out of physical desire, but out of supportiveness or even pity—and this too might have been part of Alex's game. But it would be misleading to overemphasize Joan's sexual relationships, since compusex in general tended to be a more casual enterprise online than affairs of the heart and mind. Deitz estimates that at least 15 people were "badly burned" by the revelation that Joan was Alex, and that only a few were compusex partners. Lovers or not, most were caught in Joan's emotional web.

Janis Goodall was in a category all her own. Now 37 and cheerfully describing herself as "a semiretired hippie from 'Berserkeley,' California," Goodall met Joan at a time in her life "when I was a real sick cookie—an open raw wound." Goodall was herself coping with the emotional and physical aftermath of an automobile accident. (Although she can walk, Goodall's legs are badly scarred and she suffers from both arthritis and problems of sciatic nerve.) Beyond her injuries, Goodall was also dealing with a recent separation from her husband and her brother's death. "It was Joan who helped me to deal with those things, and to make the transition into the life of disabled person who accepts that she's disabled."

Joan and Goodall were "fixed up" by other CompuServe regulars after Goodall attended an online conference on pain management. When she and Joan arranged via electronic mail to meet in CB, "it was love at first sight. By the end of that first discussion, which lasted a couple of hours, we were honorary sisters. Later, I went around profusely thanking everyone who had told me to contact her."

The fact that Joan's disability was more severe than her own gave her an authority in Goodall's eyes, and her humor was especially therapeutic. "We used to make jokes about gimps who climb mountains. At the time, just to get through the day was a major accomplishment for me, and my attitude was screw the mountains, let me go to the grocery store." The two never became lovers, despite strenuous lobbying on Joan's part. ("I often found myself apologizing for being straight," said Goodall.) But they did become intense, close friends. "I loved her. She could finish my sentences and read my mind."

About a year ago, Joan began telling Goodall about "this great guy" who was also online. His name was Alex. He was a psychiatrist, very respected in his field, and an old friend of Joan's, an associate at the hospital. Largely on the strength of Joan's enthusiastic recommendation, Goodall responded with pleasure when Alex invited her into private talk mode. "During our second or third conversation, he began to get almost romantic. He clearly thought I was the greatest thing since sliced bread. I couldn't understand why an established Manhattan psychiatrist his age could be falling to quickly for a retired hippie—although of course I was very flattered. Hey, if a shrink thought I was okay, I was okay!"

Alex told Goodall that he was married, but that his marriage was in trouble. Last winter he invited her to come visit him in New York, and when she said she couldn't afford it, he sent her a round-trip ticket. "He treated me like a queen for the four days I was there," Goodall remembers. "He put me up at a Fifth Avenue hotel—the American Stanhope, right across the street from the Metropolitan Museum. He took me to the Russian Tea Room for dinner, the Carnegie Deli for breakfast, Serendipity for ice cream, museums, everywhere—he even introduced me to his daughters." The two become lovers, although, Goodall says, his back problems apparently affected his ability and their sex life was less than satisfactory. Still it seems to have been a minor off note in a fabulously romantic weekend. There were also many gifts. Once, Goodall says, "he went out to the corner drugstore to get cigarettes and came back with caviar. I went back to Berkeley on Cloud Nine."

Naturally, Goodall had also hoped that she might meet Joan during her New York holiday. None of Joan's other women friends had. Some of the able-bodied women, especially, were hurt that Joan still felt shame about her appearance after so many protestations of love and friendship. According to Sheila Deitz, several people were reported to have arranged rendezvous with Joan and were stood up at the last minute—"although you just know Alex had to be lurking about somewhere, checking them out." Joan would, in each case, claim to have gotten cold feet.

Marti Cloutier says that Joan told her that she had promised her husband that she would never meet any of her on-line friends, but "that *if* she ever changed her mind and decided to meet any of her on-line friends, I would be one of them." In fact, the only CB person who had ever seen Joan was her hospital colleague—Alex. Over the course of Goodall's four days in the city, she and Alex both tried to reach Joan by phone, but without success. Goodall had bought Joan a gift—a stylized enameled mask of a smiling face. Alex promised to deliver it.

Back in Berkeley, Goodall resumed her online relationship with Joan, who had been out of town for the weekend. Joan, however, was anxious to hear every detail of Goodall's trip. Did she think she was in love with Alex? Was the sex good?

It was the disabled women on-line who figured it out first. "Some things about her condition were very farfetched," says one. Says another woman: "The husband, the accomplishment—it just didn't ring true from the beginning." But her own hunch wasn't that Joan was a male or able-bodied; she suspected that she was in fact a disabled woman who was pretending to have a life of dazzling romance and success.

Although such theories, however, ultimately ran up against the real postcards from Cyprus, people began to share their misgivings. "There were too many contradictions," says Bob Walter. "Here was this person who ran off to conferences and to vacations and did all these phenomenal things, but she wouldn't let her friends online even see her. After a while, it just didn't compute."

In hindsight, I wonder why I didn't question some of Joan's exploits more closely. As a journalist, I've dealt with the public relations representatives of both the New York City Police Department and the hospital where Joan supposedly taught—and it now seems strange to me that her exploits as drunk-spotter and handicapped professor weren't seized on and publicized. Pamela Bowen says she once proposed Joan's story to another editor, but urged him "to have somebody interview her in person because her story was too good to be true. So my instincts were right from the beginning, but I felt guilty about not believing a handicapped person. I mean, the story *could* have been true." It's possible that many of us able-bodied were playing out our own need to see members of minority groups as "exceptional." The more exceptional a person is, the less the person in the majority group has to confront fears of disability and pain.

Even with the contradictions, the game might have continued much longer if Joan hadn't brought Alex into the picture. According to both Goodall and Laura, Alex has, since his unmasking, said that he realized at some point that he had gotten in over his head, and he concocted a plan to kill Joan off. But after seeing how upset people were on one occasion when Joan was offline for several weeks, supposedly ill, he apparently couldn't go through with it. "It would have been a lot less risky for him to let Joan die," according to Laura, "but he knew it would be cruel." (Meanwhile, someone had called the hospital where Joan was thought to be a patient and been told that no such person was registered.)

What Alex seems to have done instead of commit compu-murder was to buy a new ID number and begin his dual *online* identity. Joan increasingly introduced people to her friend Alex, always with great fanfare. We may never know what Alex intended to do with Joan eventually, but there's certainly strong evidence that he was now trying to form attachments as Alex, both offline (with Goodall) and on.

One might imagine that the Revelation came with a big bang and mass gasps, but this was not the case. According to Walter, months and months went by between the time that some of Joan's more casual acquaintances (he among them) put it together and the time that those of her victims whom they knew heeded their warnings. "People were so invested in their relationships with the female persona that they often just didn't want to know," Walter said. And Joan was also a brilliant manipulator who always had an explanation of why a particular person might be trashing her. "If you ever questioned her about anything," Goodall recalls, "she would get very defensive and turn the topic into an argument about whether you really loved her."

Goodall now acknowledges that she and others ignored plenty of clues, but, as she says, "Let's remember one thing—it was a *pro* doing this."

Deitz, whose offline work sometimes involves counseling rape victims, agrees that Alex's victims were caught in an intolerable psychological bind. "Alex zeroed in on good people," she says, "although they were often good women at vulnerable stages of their lives." To admit that Joan was a phantom was, in many cases, also to assault the genuine support and self-esteem that they had derived from the relationship. In fact, with only two exceptions—pressuring for compusex and, in Goodall's case, using the Joan persona to pump "girl talk" confidences about Alex—there seems to have been absolutely nothing that Joan did to inspire anyone's rancor. What makes people angry is simply that Joan doesn't exist. "And a lot of what a lot of people were feeling," Deitz adds, "is mourning."

Laura ultimately confronted Joan online. She had already "cooled off" her relationship with Joan because of all the inconsistencies in her persona, but while she was suspicious, she had failed to suspect the enormity of the imposture. In February, however, she called another woman close to Joan, who told her she was convinced that Joan was a man. When Laura found Joan online later that night, she immediately asked Joan about the charge. Joan at first denied it. It was only after Laura made it clear that "I believed that we're all created after the image of God, and that I loved the person, not the sex, and would continue to do so" that Alex came out.

Laura, who is Catholic and who says that her decision to stick with Alex is partially motivated by principles of Christian love, admits that it took her several weeks to "make the transition." Since then, however, she's met Alex in person and come to love him "as my adopted brother instead of my adopted sister."

Marti Cloutier to this day hasn't confronted Alex, although she has talked with him by CB and phone. "I just haven't the courage. Once, when we were talking, he mentioned something about going for a walk that day, and I wrote back that it would be a lovely day for Joan to go for a walk. I was instantly sorry." Cloutier adds:

> Joan was a very special person and I loved Joan. I feel as if she died. I can't really say that I love Alex, although maybe I could, in time. Maybe I wouldn't have given him a chance if I'd known from the beginning he was a male. I've tried to sort out my feelings, but it's hard. I know I don't feel like a victim, and I don't understand why some of these other women have gone off the deep end. I don't think he was malicious. What I can't get out of my mind was that he's the same person I've spent hours and hours with.

Sheila Deitz had been introduced online to Alex by Joan, but found him "not all that interesting" and never became close to him. But as a visible online person known to many as a psychologist, she heard from many of the victims—some of whom formed their own circle of support, and in Goodall's words, "sort of held each other together with bubble gum." Some victims, according to Deitz, were so upset by the chain of events that they stopped using their modems temporarily.

Janis Goodall heard it first over the telephone, from Alex himself who mistakenly assumed that Goodall already know. "I had just come home from the doctor, and was incredibly frustrated at having just spent $155 to have some ass-hole neurosurgeon tell me I would have to live with what was bothering me. The phone rang, and it was Alex. The first words out of his mouth were 'yes—it's me.' I didn't know what he was talking about. Then he said: 'Joan and I are the same person.' I went into shock. I mean, I really freaked out—I wanted to jump off a bridge."

Since then, she has communicated with Alex by letter but has refused to see him. She emphatically resents those online who have spent efforts trying to "understand" him. She agreed to speak for this interview in part because "although I think this is a wonderful medium, it's a dangerous one, and it poses more danger to women than men. Men in this society are more predisposed to pulling these kinds of con games, and women are predisposed to giving people the benefit of the doubt."

Laura thinks that CompuServe and other networks ought to post warnings to newcomers that they might, in fact, encounter impostors. Others believe that the fault doesn't lie with the medium or the network, but with human frailty. "Blaming CompuServe for impostors makes about as much sense as blaming the phone company for obscene calls," says Bob Walter. CompuServe itself has no official position on the subject, although CompuServe spokesman Richard Baker notes:

Our experience has been that electronic impersonators are found out about as quickly as are face-to-face impersonators. While face-to-face impersonators are found out due to appearance, online impersonators are found out due to the use of phrases, the way they turn words, and the uncharacteristic thought processes that go into conversing electronically. I also believe that people are angrier when they've been betrayed by an electronic impersonator.

It would have been nice to hear Alex's side of the story. The first time I called his office, I gave only my name (which Alex knows)—not my magazine affiliation or the information that I was working on an article about "our mutual friend Joan." The receptionist asked if I was a patient. Did I want to make an appointment? I had a giddy vision of impersonating one, but decided against it. Although I telephoned twice more and identified myself as a journalist, Alex never returned my calls. He has continued his presence online, however, even telling Deitz that he planned to form a SIG—on another network—for psychologists and mental health professionals.

Meanwhile, in the aftermath of the Joan/Alex case, soul-searching has run rampant on CompuServe's CB and in certain SIGs. One common thread was that of Eden betrayed. As one man wrote: "I guess I figured that folks here [online] were special . . . but this has certainly ruptured the 'pink cloud' of my first love relationship. Before that, I didn't realize fully how much hurt could result from loving."

Some of the reactions were frankly conservative—people who were sickened simply by the notion of a man who wanted to feel like a woman. There was much talk of "latency." Others seemed completely threatened by the idea that they might ever have an "inappropriate" response to some one of the "wrong" gender on-line. One message left by a male gravely informed other users that he and his girlfriend had nearly been conned by a male pretending to be a swinging female—until the girlfriend was tipped off by the impersonator's "claiming to be wearing panty hose with jeans." The message prompted an indignant reply by someone who insisted: "I always wear heels with my jeans, and when I wear heels I wear panty hose, and I don't think that is odd, and I am all female!"

But Alex's story raises some other questions that have special resonance for feminists. Chief among them, for me, is why a man has to put on electronic drag to experience intimacy, trust, and sharing. Some women have suggested that the fault is partly ours as women—that if Alex had approached us a male, with all of Joan's personality traits, we wouldn't have been open to him. I for one reject that notion—not only because I have several terrific male friends online but also because it presumes that men are too fragile to break down stereotypes about themselves. (After all, *we've* spent the last 15 years struggling to prove that we can be strong, independent, and capable.) On the other had, in Alex's defense, I can't help but appreciate the temptation to experience life in the actual world from the point of view of the other sex. Think of "Tootsie" and "Yentl." Annie Lennox and Boy George. What Alex did was alien, taboo, weird . . . and yet the stuff of cosmic cultural fantasy. Haven't you ever wanted to be a fly on the locker room (or powder room) wall?

Sheila Deitz comments that some online transsexualism may be essentially harmless. Where she draws the line—and where I would also—is at the point that such experimentation starts impinging on other people's trust. Joan clearly stepped over that line years ago.

Maybe one of the things to be learned from Alex and Joan is that we have a way to go before gender stops being a major, volatile human organizing principle—even in a medium dedicated to the primacy of the spirit.

I personally applaud those souls on CB who, when asked "R u m or f?" [Are you male or female?], simply answer "yes."

10
Remote Sex in the Information Age
Gary Gumpert

Is "phone sex" actually therapeutic? While the use of the telephone and the computer for purposes of sexual gratification expands the notion of therapeutic communication, it also reveals the degree to which this culture currently relies on distanced interaction for sexual intimacy. Avoiding moral judgment, Gumpert analyzes current practice in both the United States and France regarding electronic sex.

The late Ithiel de Sola Pool began the introduction to *The Social Impact of the Telephone* with this question: "How much difference has a device invented 100 years ago by Alexander Graham Bell, enabling people to converse across distance, made in our lives?" (1977, p. 1).

The telephone has become an intrinsic and indispensable appendage of human need and convenience in the twentieth century. To live without it voluntarily marks that individual as either eccentric or antisocial. The telephone is an example of extraordinary and dramatic technology transformed into the expected, unobtrusive, and invisible part of the human condition. The telephone transcends space in order to extend the interaction of two human beings through the linking of oral/aural sense modalities. This simple paradigm of human connection hardly accounts for the extraordinary variations of interaction for which the telephone is utilized. Beyond the mere communicative function between two ordinary parties, the telephone has been used as an instrument of counseling and advising: suicide prevention, teen hotlines, incest hotlines, services for the elderly, drug hotlines, poison centers, rumor control centers, community problems, counseling, Dial-A-Prayer, and wake-up services. There are a host of other telephone services available. For the lonely, the isolated, the telephone offers therapeutic salvation. For others, the telephone allows contact with human beings where contact is either not possible or perhaps not desirable. And now the telephone is serving some of our sexual needs.

The computer joins the telephone and television as a twentieth-century communication invention which is altering and shaping the nature of human history. The computer expedites the storage and retrieval of data and facilitates either the efficient interfacing or the faithful reproduction of other electronic media. While part of it is still wrapped in the aura of the spectacular, the computer is rapidly being diffused into the fabric of human existence. And now the computer is serving some of our sexual needs.

The purpose of this essay to discuss sexual phenomena served by two specific applications of media technology—the telephone and the computer. The subject is not approached as a judgment of practice, but rather as an explication of a phenomenon and a description of its operation.

Several years ago, the telephone company, in the good old days of the old monolith, produced a wonderful television campaign which featured a black mother responding to the call of her son. Her husband is concerned about his wife's tears and asks, "Why are you crying?" She responds that she is crying because her son has called to tell her that he loves her. And than comes the famous phrase, "Reach out and touch some one." The slogan "Reach out and touch someone" is significant because of the implicit paradox found in the statement. The metaphoric touch becomes the essence of human interaction as tactility becomes an illusion rather than reality. To some extent, the telephone has redefined our sensory priorities.

The telephone was inevitably linked to one of the our oldest professions. In 1964, Marshall McLuhan said:

> No more unexpected social result of the telephone has been observed than its elimination of the red-light district and its creation of the call-girl. To the blind, all things are unexpected. The form and character of the telephone, as of all electric technology, appear fully in this spectacular development. The prostitute was specialist, the call-girl is not. A "house" was not a home, but the call-girl not only lives at home, she may be a matron. The power of the telephone to decentralize every operation and to end positional warfare, as well as localized prostitution, has been felt, but not understood by every business in the land. (McLuhan, 1962, p. 266)

The telephone transformed the call girl into a person who used the medium to arrange appointments and house calls. The *Dictionary of American Slang* (1975) defines:

> **call girl:** 1A prostitute; lit., a prostitute who works in a call house. - 2 By confusion and popular misconception = a prostitute who visits a known or recommended customer at his hotel room or apartment when called on the telephone to do so, as opposed to a prostitute who solicits customers in a public place or works in a brothel; a prostitute whose known or recommended clients visit her apartment after making an appointment by telephone. 1958: "A high-priced call girl who nets over $250 a week" . . . E. Klein, "The Beat Generation in the Village," N.Y. *Daily News*, Feb. 20, 36. *Use of the telephone makes the call girl less conspicuous, and less apt to arrest, than the average prostitute. The arrangement usu. insures her of a wealthy, socially prominent clientele. Call girls have been in business since c1935 and their existence known to the general public since c1950.* (p. 84)

The telephone company has conveniently eliminated the hazardous part of the ancient profession and travel is no longer a requirement. Phone sex has divested sex of corporal propinquity. The concept of the "call girl," closely linked to the telephone, is redefined by the very medium which created her.

"DIAL-A-PORN"

There are two variations of institutionalized "phone sex": "Dial-a-Porn" services and "live phone" sex (the romantic telephonic interludes of lovers is excluded from this discussion). "Dial-a-Porn" refers to services which reach millions of people who call a number in order to hear, for the slightly elevated price of the telephone call, a *recording* of a real or simulated sexual encounter (the cost runs anywhere from 20 cents to several dollars). Two of the principal companies involved in this venture are Carlin Communications Inc. and Drake Publishers Inc., which also publishes Gloria Leonard's *High Society* magazine. The FCC and the U.S. government have been involved in a series of litigations seeking to prohibit or deter this profitable business venture. The main concern according to U.S. Attorney in Salt Lake City, Brent D. Ward, is:

> It appears that large numbers of children and adolescents are being exposed to telephone sex at a time in their lives when they are especially impressionable and lack the experience, perspective and judgment to recognize and avoid sexually oriented material that may be harmful to them. (Middleton, 1985, p. 11)

In the Utah case it is alleged that children in Salt Lake City dialed the New York City number of "Dial-It." Clearly, the issue of exposing children to such material is a concern, but it is not just children who are lured to 30 seconds of "dirty talk." In 1983, 2,500 calls in one month were made from government offices to the "Dial-It" service in New York City. The economic reality of "Dial-It" is that the company receives a rebate for each call from the telephone company. It is estimated that on some days the New York office receives as many as 500,000 calls a day—that's ten thousand dollars a day (Middleton, 1984). According to the *New York Times* (Bishop, 1987, Sec. 1, p. 12) and a spokesperson for Pacific Bell, for the 1986–87 fiscal year California's telephone company earned $24.5 million for billing and collecting $71.7 million in behalf of various dial-a-porn services. Most of the estimated 12 million calls appeared to be to sexual message services of which there are about 200 in California.

The legal issues surrounding the efforts to bar access of "Dial-a-Porn" services to children are extremely complex, since such protection comes into direct conflict with the prohibition that the state cannot censor telephone message content. According to the *National Law Journal,* a telephone company serving the Far West is in a most difficult position.

> If it rejected a sex-talk message service, the phone company would face a civil lawsuit for violating the free speech rights of the steamy message vendors. If it continued carrying the messages, prosecutors threatened they would try it for distributing sexually explicit material to minors. (Cox, 1987, p.33)

PHONE SEX

The *live-sex* phone experience is the second phone institution which offers sexual gratification. A copy of any of the sexually oriented magazines sold at newsstands, such as *High Society,* which cater to the supposedly semi-erotic, reveal a large number of advertisements, some adorned with beckoning lasciviously posed men and women, which seek to entice the reader into placing a telephone call. For example:

> The Erotic Telephone Network
> Call in YOUR AREA to
> explore your most intimate fantasies
> with a beautiful, sexy, uninhibited woman.
> Call now for a sizzling-hot conversation.
> Call me right now if you can handle an *intense orgasm* over the phone.

> Fantasy Phone Inc.
> The original and Still #1.
> Discreet & Sensual—Hot Loving
> Call with any Phone Request. One of our sexy girls will
> immediately call you back.
> Free Long-Distance CALL BACKS

In *PlayGirl* the following advertisement proclaimed:

> When you're feeling sexy and want to talk to a real man,
> call *The Hot line*
> A 24 Hour Telephone Fantasy Service
> Use your credit card—MC, VISA, AMEX, DINERS, CARTE BLANCHE
> or send check or money order to *THE HOT LINE*

In *Honcho,* a gay magazine, the following ad appeared:

> Call us. Tell us what you want . . . the kind of guy you'd like to talk with.
> Then we'll have him call you back at our expense. You don't have to pay for
> an expensive collect call, and you can talk as long as you want . . . until
> you're satisfied.
> FANTASY MEN

On the basis of several in-person interviews with women who worked in the live telephone sex business, material that has been published in popular magazines, a telephone interview with a manager of one of these companies, and a discussion with a psychiatrist, the following description of the process emerges. (Understandably, it is extremely difficult to get information about this subject from individuals who are willing to allow themselves to be quoted.)

A client is attracted to a particular advertisement or hears of the service from someone else. (This raises several intriguing questions for which no data is available. How important is interpersonal interaction and peer approval in initiating the use of sexual phone services? Do users talk of their phone experiences with others, or is it a completely private and concealed experience?) The call is received by a staff of receptionists who function to weed out "weirdos," ascertain the particular fantasy the caller wishes to have fulfilled, and determine the degree of experience the caller has had with telephonic sex. The price is non-negotiable and, depending upon the specific organization, runs between $35 and $45 per call (apparently there is some initial shopping around in regard to price). There are conference calls for threesomes; foursomes are extra. A group of five to ten receptionists (who are more than operators) are on duty for 12-hour shifts—the services runs 23 hours a day. The prime telephone sex periods are at breakfast time, lunch, and late at night. The receptionists earn from $2 to $6 per call. The client is handled gently, that is, the receptionist does not attempt to arouse the caller, but is supposed to create an illusion of intimacy. After the order is taken, the most important step occurs—the gathering of necessary credit card number, expiration date, name, address, telephone number, and birthdate. The client is told that he or she will be called back shortly. The receptionist makes out an order form and transmits it to a supervisor who attempts to match fantasy and available telephonic sex partner after authenticating the credit card. (Even with all of these precautions, there is a 30 percent "beat" record, that is, where the credit card turns out to be stolen or where the person refuses to pay.) Part of the image that emerges is that of a diner in which BLT orders are scribbled and shouted out with great haste. Instead of sandwiches, orders for BW (body worship), NT (nipple torture), WS (watersports), Xdress (cross dressing), GS (golden showers), B (bestiality), D (domination), IN (infantilism), and I (Incest) are the main courses.

The persons interviewed indicated that their company used approximately 40 women for the actual telephonic encounters, out of which seven to fifteen were working at any one time. These women received approximately $5 to $10 dollars per call. Each call lasts from five to seven minutes, although some last as long as twenty minutes. The philosophy of this particular company is surprisingly not to "rip off" the customer, but rather to encourage an ongoing relationship between client and sexual partner. The latter is paid an extra commission on "call-backs," if the client requests the particular person.

The women are initially trained by a supervisor and are provided a series of sexual scenarios from which they can improvise and elaborate. Informants particularly stressed the "fantasy" nature of the experience and the process of matching fantasy and participants. It was somewhat surprising to find out that some of the calls are monitored for the expressed purpose of controlling the quality of performance rendered by the employees: "The girls are supposed to give good phone!" It is a startling revelation because of its obvious violation of privacy.

It would be a mistake to consider the subject of this chapter merely an aberration, an oddity, a phenomenon operating on the edges of society. We can ponder, meditate, and speculate over circumstances in which lawyers, doctors, clergymen, generally between the ages of 35 and 50, support an industry in which individual concerns net a minimum of a quarter of a million dollars each year. There are many questions to be asked and data which needs gathering: demographics, interviews with both sides of the sexual dyad, content analyses of interaction, and discussion with representatives of the telephone companies and those companies engaged in institutionalizing telephone sex. All of these are necessary, but not easily accessible for obvious reasons: invasion of privacy, protection of reputation, and the general fear of publicity. Nevertheless, we can speculate and consider a number of issues.

Why, during this period of time, do we see the rise of sexual activities which use media to develop intimate relationships with distant individuals? Why telephone sex? Conjecture suggests that the sexual liberation of the 1960s and 1970s has given way to a counter-reaction influenced by the fear of venereal disease, herpes, AIDS, physical and psychological trauma. The telephone eliminates physical contact even though the telephone company campaigned with the slogan "reach out and touch someone." The telephone provides a "solution" for physical intimacy. Edward Hall (1966) has pointed out that Americans maintain carefully proscribed interpersonal distances and the violation of spacial norms is risky. The telephone alters interpersonal spacial relationships. Telephonic conversations always take place at a socially "intimate" distance. The other person's voice is literally next to the ear, the distance at which, according to Hall, the sense of sight is not nearly as important as touch, smell, and the feel of bodily warmth. The telephone medium facilitates surrogate sex through the illusion of intimacy. The sound of faceless voices stimulates, perhaps even requires, the mental construction of an imaginary countenance suitable for the time, place, and purpose.

While phone sex is psychologically safe in that it is free of obligation and responsibility between the consenting parties, except for satisfaction and service being provided, there is implicit risk involved in the transaction. The telephone "call" person operates in the safety of the home with an unlisted phone installed on a separate jack and receives calls only cleared by a central office. It is the customer who is required to reveal his or her entire identity as credit card data is processed. The privacy of this sexual dyad is a facade where anonymity is only provided for the distant "hooker." The traditional illicit sexual contract usually threatened the prostitute in terms of police action and physical threat. Now the risk is totally the customers'. And yet that one-sided revelation does not deter the rising number of callers. Several images are suggested by the phone sex phenomenon. Certainly the therapeutic psychiatrist–patient relationship comes to mind, but even more apt is the confessional icon. The priest sits on one side of the partition, the confessor on the other. One side is institutional and anonymous, the other solitary, vulnerable, and in need of unburdening.

COMPUTER SEX

There are primarily three types of person–computer relationships. These functions were previously described by Cathcart and Gumpert in the first volume of *Information and Behavior* (1985):

1. Unobtrusive functions—those in which the utilization of the computer is not evident to the user, for instance, digital recordings and telephone connections (Covvey & McAlister, 1982).
2. Computer-facilitated functions—where persons use a computer for the purpose of expediting communication. This function refers to communication *through* a computer rather than *with* a computer. Electronic mail, for example, represents a change of medium (paper to display screen) in which the computer is interposed between sender and receiver. In this case, the computer is a high-speed transmitter of what is essentially a written message. The same holds true for computer bulletin board and other computer networks which allow messages to be stored and retrieved at the convenience of senders and receivers without reliance on intermediaries such as printers, librarians, postal clerks, telephone operators, and so on (Levy 1983).
3. Person-computer interpersonal functions—situations where one party activates a computer which in turn responds appropriately in graphic, alphanumeric, or vocal modes establishing an ongoing send/receiver relationship (Cathcart & Gumpert, 1983).

Computer sex falls under the category of "computer facilitated functions." The computer facilitates communication between two parties. The addition of a modem transforms a microcomputer from a device used for storage and retrieval of information, word processing, and computation into part of a vast and complex communication system. The modem adds the telephonic component to the computer, but transforms the aural into a visual/verbal mode. This communication connection fosters electronic message services in which mail is sent from one person to another with a response occurring, hopefully, shortly thereafter. Specifically, computer sex refers to an interactive system in which "real time" sexually oriented electronic conferences occur between two or more persons separated spatially.

Computer sex is provided by either a nonprofit Special Interest Group (SIG) or a commercial service. The SIG is a telephone number and a computer (sometimes connected to a mainframe) which permits multiple telephone/computer connections thereby allowing a number of individuals to participate simultaneously in the *live written event*. The only cost to the user is that of the telephone call. There are thousands of such Special Interest Groups throughout the country, each of which is dedicated to a specific theme, particularly sex.

The commercial services operate somewhat differently. The computer user subscribes to a service such as Sextex (CVC Online, Inc; linked with Gloria Leonard's *High Society*, a sex magazine found at most newsstands strategically placed away from the curiosity of the very young). The online computer sex feature of Sextex is called EROTICOMM.

> EROTICOMM works like CB radio, with members usually using sexy "handles" to identify each other. SEXTEX members from all over the country talk dirty to one another on their computer screens. Topics run the full range from sports to movies to politics—but it's mostly sex. All users are consenting adults who understand and enjoy the fact that SEXTEX is a sexually explicit system. We choose not to censor the conversations in any way, so you can imagine how hot and heavy things can get. In fact, the possibilities for fantasy fulfillment are endless, and your anonymity and privacy are guaranteed. We reveal nothing about you to fellow members; you can say or not say whatever you choose. (*High Society*, 1985, p. 6)

Sextex charges a sign-up fee of $12.95. After that the subscriber is charged a "connect charge" which runs from $12.00 an hour during "home time" to $22.00 during "office time." The fee is charged to any of the major credit cards. The subscriber is supplied with a handbook and a floppy disc plus a sign-on password. There are a number of others services provided by Sextex, including a bulletin board, games, a leisure/travel section, a "talk-to-me" sexual advice column run by *High Society* publisher Gloria Leonard, a personal ads area, and a spot where the subscriber can advertise him or herself and find out about other members. However, the main feature is EROTICOMM, the on-line sexual conversations which can be either in groups or (*The Sextex Handbook*, 1984).

It is more difficult to assess the appeal of the computer as a facilitator of sexual relationships than the telephone. Earlier in this essay the intimate feature of the telephone was mentioned. What is it about the computer that appeals to the prurient interest? Again, there is no data available, but the following thoughts seem reasonable. The computer allows the participant to develop a completely fictional personna, one devoid of physical and vocal features. The task of creating a seductive computer persona relies on language, paralanguage, and the ability to respond swifty through the means of the computer keyboard. The act of interactive computer typing is known as "keyboarding" among computer enthusiasts. Janet F. Asteroff has written a dissertation on the subject of *Paralanguage in Electronic Mail* (1987):

> Paralanguage is a component of spoken, written, and electronic communication. It gives to what is being communicated a character over and above that which is necessary to convey meaning in the linguistic or grammatical sense . . . Electronic paralanguage, a term developed to describe paralanguage in computer-mediated communication, is defined as: features of written language which are used outside of formal grammar and syntax, and other features related to but not part of written language, which through varieties of visual and interpretative contrast provide additional, enhanced, redundant or new meanings to the message. (pp. i–ii)

Thus the rather simplistic symbol which follows :-) represents a smiling face and "c.u.soon" similarily adds communicative elements to the message. Indeed, it is possible to prepare and store a series of paralanguage features which can be activitated through a single key stroke.

The "keyboarder" is in control of a persona which may or may not coincide with his or her true personality. There is a sense of spontaneity and power inherent in a process where fingers stroke the keys and form words and concepts which are instantly communicated through space and to which there is swift response. While the telephone company's slogan "reach out and touch someone" referred to the illusion of tactility achieved through aurality, the computer sex aficionado seeks to create the illusion of intimacy through tactility.

THE FRENCH EXPERIENCE

Perhaps one's first reaction to hearing about computer sex is to respond with "It could only happen in America!" But, surprisingly, the French "Minitel" experience proves the contrary. The French videotex system began in that country in 1978 with the intent to provide each home with a computer terminal which would replace the printed telephone book and would provide a host of other services such as purchasing airline tickets, making theater reservations, and getting the latest sports result. At the present time approximately three million terminals are in operation and nearly 3000 specific services are available to users. Most of the services cost around $10 an hour. The system, known as Minitel, supplies a computer to each home without charge. The charges are placed on the monthly telephone bill and part of the revenue is passed on to those companies offering services.

More than half of the time spent on Mintel involves "messageries" or "direct dialogue services that, for many, are taking the place of confidante, confessor, psychiatrist, and lover" (DeLacy, 1987, p. 18). "Messageries roses" are the rage of France and the result is that, instead of censorship, a 33 percent tax on sexually explicit messages services, paid by the suppliers, will be imposed in January 1989 (*International Herald Tribune*, 1987).

> Those looking for more than understanding consult *messageries roses*, sexual smorgasbords with something for every taste.(In France *le rose*, or "pink," refers to soft-core pornography.) Sextel, X-Tel, Desiropolis, Aphrodite, Aime-Moi Mimi, and Abelard et Heloise advertise a selection of "rambos, machos, latin Lovers, Romeos, and Big Bad Wolves" for women, and "mermaids, man-eaters, Little Red Riding Hoods, and femmes fatales" for men. Pom, "the first encyclopedia of lovemaking," hears confessions and takes orders for lingerie. Can Gay, Gai Pied, Voice of the paranoid, Masked Ball, and many others cater to male and female homosexuals, voyeurs, and groups given to sexual *bizarrerie*. (DeLacy, 1987)

What is this mysterious quality that entices the "romantic" and "sophisticated" French into sexual contact by "remote control"? That same question could be asked, of course, of all the Americans involved in similar acts of proxy. The answers are simply not available, but what is clearly established, as indicated by the response to the existence of both "phone sex" and "computer sex" is a "need" that exists for such services. It is difficult to describe such phenomena without making judgments. Nonpropinquitous sexual gratification represent merely another function served by media. The implications of such acts requires an understanding of societel pressure and undercurrents.

> Those who are timid adore Minitel and the phones services, because direct-dialogue, from a distance, authorizes all sorts of audacities. This is one of the keys of the success of the phone services. (*Help Magazine*, 1987) (Translated from the French)

REFERENCES

Asteroff, J. F. (1987). *Paralanguage in electronic mail: A case study*. Unpublished doctoral dissertation, Columbia University, New York.

Bishop, K. (1987, November 22). Access of young to 'Dial-a-Porn' faces key challenge in west. *The New York Times*, Sec. l, p. 12.

Cathcart, R., & Gumpert, G. (1983). Mediated interpersonal communication: Toward a new typology. *Quarterly Journal of Speech, 69*, 267–277.

Cathcart, R., & Gumpert, G. (1985). The person-computer interaction. In B. D. Rubin (Ed.), *Information and behavior* (pp. 113–124). New Brunswick: Transaction Books.

Covvey, H. D., & McAlister, N. H. (1982). *Computer choices*. Boston: Addison-Wesley.

Cox, G. D. (1987, September 28). Dial-a-porn may not be restricted. *National Law Journal*, p. 33.

DeLacy, J. (1987, July). The sexy computer. *The Atlantic Monthly*, pp. 18, 20, 22–24, 26.

Dictionary of American slang (1975). New York: Thomas Y. Crowell.

Hall, E. (1966). *The hidden dimension*. New York: Doubleday & Company.

Help Magazine. (1987, September). p. 39.

High Society. (1985, July). pp. 6–8.

International Herald Tribune. (1987, October 30, 1987). p. 6.

Levy, S. (1983, February). Travels in the network nation. *Technology Illustrated*, pp. 56–61.

McLuhan, M. (1962). *Understanding media: The extensions of man*. New York: McGraw-Hill.

Middleton, M. (1984, October 1). Should the FCC be able to reach out and cut porn calls? *National Law Journal*, p. 13.

Middleton, M. (1985, May 13). U.S. files-porn indictment. *National Law Journal*, p. 11, 35.

Pool, I. de S. (Ed.). (1977). *The social impact of the telephone*. Cambridge, MA: The MIT Press.

Sextex Handbook. (1984). New York: CVC Online, Inc.

11

Therapeutic Uses of the Telephone: Crisis Intervention vs. Traditional Therapy

Sandra L. Fish

The telephone as a private interpersonal medium has a variety of therapeutic uses. Its use in crisis intervention is longstanding and well-documented while its use in more traditional therapy is less well-defined. Although the nature of the telephone itself encourages therapeutic interaction, it also challenges the parameters of traditional therapy and blurs the distinctions between "therapy" and "therapeutic." In this article Fish delineates the therapeutic, interpersonal, and organizational characteristics of crisis intervention by telephone as well as the impact of the telephone on traditional therapy.

The term "therapy" usually refers to a series of contacts between a mental health professional and a client who attempt to change some client behaviors which interfere with work or social relationships, bringing about substantial change in perspective; in contrast, a "therapeutic experience" may involve interaction with anyone on any topic resulting in insight or reorientation, enabling persons to participate in more satisfying ways in the future (Barnlund, 1968). Communication which is intentionally therapeutic, then, has as its fundamental purpose to "reduce alienation, to deepen awareness, to contribute to security of self and acceptance of others, and to increase the capacity to act independently and productively" (Barnlund, 1968, p. 637). Intentional therapeutic communication does involve the acknowledgment of a "helping" role, but does not assume the medical model of doctor helping patient nor does it necessarily preclude reciprocity. Either therapy or therapeutic communication may be electronically or otherwise mediated. The purpose of this chapter is to explore the use of the medium of the telephone in therapeutic communication provided by crisis lines as well as its use in traditional therapy.

THE TELEPHONE AS MEDIUM

Invented in 1876, the telephone now reaches into more than 96 percent of U.S. households with over 90 million subscribers (Williams, 1984), and public telephones are readily available. Consequently, virtually every person in this country has access to the telephone. While it is a taken-for-granted convenience, the telephone has been the subject of scholarly neglect (Aronson, 1982); it is a transparent medium which has had revolutionary impact on social relations, business transactions, manners and morals, and the handling of crises (Aronson, 1982), but has been studied by few (Pool, 1977, 1983).

One of the more important consequences of the telephone has been the change in the concept of neighborhood. Aronson (1982) describes a "psychological neighborhood" as a maintenance of social networks in the face of residential and geographical dispersion made possible by the telephone. Further, he argues, the telephone serves to reduce loneliness, anxiety, and isolation.

The telephone itself is a technological instrument capable of transmitting the voice over long distances, yet offering the opportunity for private interaction and demanding total participation on the part of the users (McLuhan, 1964). According to Miller (1973) the telephone is characterized by its "spatial property," its "temporal property," its channel capacity, its machine characteristics, and its dyadic nature.

The telephone bridges geographical boundaries and "alters interpersonal spatial relationships" (Cathcart & Gumpert, 1983, p. 272), thus permitting ongoing relationships across distance. Simultaneously, the telephone receiver and thus the voice are placed within one's zone of intimacy, suggesting close contact. This "near but far" phenomenon may encourage disclosure by minimizing the perception of risk and vulnerability.

The temporal nature of the telephone is such that it allows access to others potentially at any time. This quality of immediacy may serve as a safety valve for anxiety or fear and may encourage frequency of contact.

The telephone is limited to the auditory channel, thereby restricting available information solely to verbal and paralinguistic cues. Consequently, uncertainty of meaning is heightened, and words and voice must compensate for absent nonverbal cues in regulating conversation (Miller & Cannell, 1982). While reduced nonverbal information may add to the difficulty of communicating effectively, it may also provide a measure of perceived protection and may facilitate more probing verbal interaction.

As a machine, the telephone may evoke connotations of coldness, distance, and impersonality—feelings which could inhibit effective interaction. Because the telephone is ubiquitous and taken for granted, it retains none of the novelty effect which might have once counteracted such an effect. However, this impersonality may serve as a protective cloak for some telephone users.

The telephone is essentially dyadic and private despite its ability to allow conference calls or speaker phones. Thus, interpersonal relationships may be successfully developed and maintained over the telephone (Williams, 1984).

Given the constraints of the medium, can telephone interaction be as successful as face-to-face interaction? In a comparison of telephone and face-to-face interviews of public opinion, Rogers (1976) found that data collected by telephone and in person are equally complete and accurate. Miller and Cannell (1982), in a study of experimental techniques for telephone interviewing, suggest that the telephone may have an advantage in eliciting sensitive information due to its quality of distance. Certainly the telephone mediates interaction in a unique manner by influencing the quantity and quality of information and by shaping the relationship of the participants. Indeed, in discussing telephone therapy sessions, Hymer (1984, p. 57) argues that the "common psychic space" shared by therapist and client on the telephone offers a unique opportunity for the client to enhance his or her imagination and transference potential.

CRISIS-LINE COMMUNICATION

CRISIS INTERVENTION

"The hotline is to the mental health profession what the ambulance or emergency room is to the medical profession" (Rosenbaum & Calhoun, 1977, p. 338). Hotlines, or telephone crisis-lines, begun in the 1960s and currently numbering in the hundreds, provide assistance to callers in crisis, frequently around the clock. The American Association of Suicidology (1985) lists 614 agencies, and many other agencies are unaffiliated with AAS. Not only are there suicide prevention and crisis services available by telephone, but also telephone call-in services for drug abuse and rape to poison control; there are now even "warm lines" for latchkey children after school.

While the telephone provides the means for crisis-line communication, the crisis situation itself provides the motivation. Although hotlines receive calls of every conceivable kind (silent, prank, obscene, informational, problem, crisis, suicidal), the purpose of a crisis line is to attract callers in distress who, though not necessarily suicidal, might have a "high suicide potential" if not helped (Rosenbaum & Calhoun, 1977).

Each individual has problem-solving behaviors used to cope with everyday situations. When the usual methods are unavailable or unsuccessful in solving a problem, the person then faces a "critical situation," one which is not necessarily totally new, but is now intolerable. A crisis is defined as the individual's response to this hazardous situation in which the usual problem-solving methods won't work (Brockopp, 1973a). Crises can be developmental, those expected in one's progress through life such as the crisis of adolescence, or incidental, those precipitated by incidents such as illness or job loss, and so on. (Brockopp, 1973a). In either case, a crisis is a serious situation often requiring emergency services.

Brockopp (1973a) outlines four stages of a crisis situation:

1. The individual responds to the critical situation by employing the normal problem-solving methods with increased activity
2. Having been unsuccessful in the attempt, the person experiences increased tension, disorganization, and disequilibrium
3. The individual draws on additional resources, both external and internal. Consequences of this activity include successful resolution, diminution of the problem, or withdrawal by the individual
4. If the problem remains, the individual may move to more drastic attempts at resolution including complete withdrawal or isolation, suicide, psychosis, and so on.

A person experiencing a crisis may reach out at any stage of the crisis process. While the crisis counselor's response will differ depending on the stage of the crisis, there are several forms of support necessary to individuals experiencing any form of life stress. Albrecht and Adelman (1984) define such necessary social support as the provision of emotional caring, enabling the individual to perceive an increased sense of control over her or his environment, and feedback and validation.

Counseling provided by crisis intervention services differs from traditional therapy in several ways. First, the focus of crisis intervention is the crisis situation, not the individual's personality; second, crisis intervention takes a problem-solving approach, rather than a psychiatric approach; and third, a crisis involves a serious, possibly life-threatening, situation (Rosenbaum & Calhoun, 1977). Consequently, crisis counseling, after the initial establishment of rapport and assessment of risk, is much more goal-oriented and directive than traditional therapy (Slaikeu & Willis, 1978).

THERAPEUTIC COMMUNICATION IN CRISIS INTERVENTION

Crisis counseling shares many of the characteristics of effective therapeutic communication in other contexts, such as listening to a friend in need or conducting traditional therapy. However, the potential urgency associated with a crisis requires a clearer focus and direction than typically associated with friendship; the formal roles of caller and counselor suggest an explicit desire for assistance. Crisis intervention theory also differs from traditional psychiatric theory and its assumptions. In crisis counseling there is no assumption of mental illness or pathology, but rather an emphasis on the healthy aspects of the caller; there is a focus on the caller's coping ability and strength, assuming the caller will make the best choice for him- or herself with the active assistance of the counselor and the utilization of individual and community resources (Brockopp, 1973a).

Crisis intervention by telephone requires the adaptation of effective therapeutic communication skills to a crisis intervention model. Brockopp (1973a) poses this model in five steps for the counselor:

1. Make an initial evaluation regarding the severity of the crisis situation
2. Develop a trusting relationship with the caller
3. Assist the caller in identifying the specific problem
4. Assess and mobilize caller's strengths and resources
5. Assist the caller in developing a plan of action.

The crisis intervention model can be analyzed according to the communication skills necessary to implement it. The first and probably most serious task the crisis counselor faces is accomplishing the first two steps of the model simultaneously; that is, in order to gather enough information to make an initial evaluation regarding the severity of the crisis, one must spend some time developing an interpersonal relationship. However, the counselor needs to know with some degree of certainty the relative lethality (likelihood that the caller has already begun or is ready to begin a suicide attempt) as soon as possible in order to make strategic choices for effective counseling. Consequently, the first two steps of the model require a simultaneous combination of strategic information gathering and empathic listening.

In making the initial evaluation of severity, a crisis counselor must confront directly the issue of suicide if there is the slightest indication that the caller may be remotely contemplating such an act. Conventional wisdom suggests that the mere mention of suicide may be enough to encourage people to kill themselves. Crisis theory, however, argues that it is vital to open up the subject of suicide in order to give permission to the caller to describe her or his actual feelings about it. If the counselor is too anxious to discuss suicide, how can the caller possibly deal realistically with the matter? Further, the counselor will be much less able to assist the caller without this vital piece of information.

From the beginning of the call, the counselor is also working to develop a trusting relationship with the caller. The therapeutic process requires an attitude of empathy and warmth (Natale, 1978) as a basis for trust. Empathic understanding of the caller is demonstrated by effective listening and reflection of the caller's feelings. Ventilation of feelings enables the caller to relieve anxiety (Albrecht & Adelman, 1984) and to develop trust in the listener. The telephone helper must be concerned with making and maintaining contact, at both the beginning and end of the call, due to the uncertainty of the line of communication (Echterling, Hartsough, & Zarle, 1980).

Once the counselor ascertains that the caller is ready and able to focus attention on the problem, the next stage is problem identification. This task has both cognitive and affective benefit for the caller. By focusing attention on a concrete and specific problem, the counselor can assist the caller in organizing her or his experience in a rational manner. Additionally, the process of specifying and clarifying the problem reduces the caller's anxiety (Hinson, 1982). Paraphrasing, focusing, asking open-ended questions, and clarifying are useful communication skills to achieve problem identification.

Once the outline of the problem has taken shape and is agreed upon, the counselor can assist the caller in exploring her or his own strengths and available resources. Lamb (1973) suggests that the caller often has potential solutions but is unable to see them since the nature of a crisis is such that it constricts one's ability to see what is available. Utilizing community resources is important; assisting the caller in developing and maintaining a support network during a crisis is a major goal for the crisis counselor, thereby enabling the caller to gain a renewed sense of control over the circumstance.

Finally, the crisis counselor seeks to develop a plan of action with the caller. A crisis requires action, and the development of an appropriate plan gives energy to its resolution. The precise nature of the plan will depend entirely on the nature of the crisis, but the process will require guidance and encouragement on the part of the counselor. Slaikeu and Willis (1978), in studying caller feedback on counselor performance, found that giving clear and specific information was viewed as a very important counselor behavior. While not minimizing the importance of empathy and effective listening, they identify the importance of straightforward speech in telephone crisis calls.

Effective therapeutic communication in crisis intervention may offer useful learning for the caller. A trusting relationship with the counselor gives the caller an opportunity to discharge feelings of anxiety, to identify the problem, to utilize her or his own strengths, and to gain perspective. Resolving the problem satisfactorily gives the caller the experience in handling a crisis which may provide assistance in future situations (Brockopp, 1973a).

The counselor's therapeutic communication skills of empathic listening, offering reflective and clarifying feedback, asking open-ended questions, focusing and guiding, and giving information, when implemented in the context of the crisis intervention model, offer the opportunity for the caller to move through the crisis, regain a sense of balance, and achieve resolution. Barnlund (1968) summarizes the attributes of a therapeutic communicative relationship which can be applied to effective crisis counseling: (a) a willingness to become involved with the other person, (b) a positive regard for the other, (c) a permissive psychological climate, (d) desire and capacity to listen, (e) communication and empathic understanding, (f) accurate reflection and clarification of feeling, and (g) genuine and congruent communicators (pp. 638–640).

INTERPERSONAL CHARACTERISTICS OF CRISIS-LINE COMMUNICATION

What are the characteristics of crisis-line communication which distinguish it from other forms of therapeutic communication? In the preceding sections the crisis intervention model was identified as a tool for crisis management and therapeutic communication skills were described. There are additionally four major interpersonal dimensions which serve to distinguish crisis-line communication from other forms of mediated therapeutic communication as well as from traditional therapy and other intimate relationships.

Possibly the most thoroughly examined aspect of crisis-line communication is its anonymity. Most obviously, the caller has the option of remaining anonymous because of the medium of the telephone. Anonymity serves a major therapeutic function for a caller in crisis because it "reduces the feeling of being ridiculed or abused while in a vulnerable position and can reduce the loss in social status involved in presenting oneself as someone in need of help" (Williams & Douds, 1973, pp. 82–83). As a consequence, with the protection of anonymity the caller may be encouraged to disclose feelings more readily than in the face-to-face setting (Wark, 1982). Without question the opportunity for anonymity is an inducement to call a crisis line.

Counselor anonymity also has its advantages. The freeing effect of counselor anonymity may reduce the threat for the caller by eliminating the physical presence of an identifiable person (Wark, 1982) and may reduce the distraction thus created (Williams & Douds, 1973). At the practical level, counselor anonymity discourages dependence on an individual counselor in a 24-hour service which may require 50 to 90 counselors to maintain complete phone coverage in a week.

There is, however, a peculiar irony regarding the anonymity of a crisis line. The telephone provides opportunity for a "psychological neighborhood" (Aronson, 1982) of individuals connected across geographic distance; it also provides the opportunity for the existence of a crisis line which serves as a supplement to or substitute for other support systems. But the telephone also allows anonymity, creating faceless, nameless "neighbors," unlike intimate supportive relationships. Indeed anonymity of one or both parties is a characteristic of many forms of mediated therapeutic communication analyzed in this volume.

Caller anonymity gives rise to the issue of control in the relationship between caller and counselor. Significant control is retained by the caller in two areas. The initiation and termination of the call remains exclusively in the hands of the caller, increasing the power and sense of freedom of a person in a vulnerable position (Lester, 1974). There is no required or even implicit commitment to an ongoing relationship as is often the case with face-to-face therapy (Rosenbaum & Calhoun, 1977); there is not even a commitment to continuation of the call since the caller can hang up the telephone at any moment. Additionally, the caller controls the content of the call. The amount, kind, and accuracy of information disclosed is determined by the caller. Precisely because the caller can terminate the call, the counselor must always gauge the effect of any question or response in an attempt to keep the caller on the line, especially a suicidal caller.

Some control in the call is retained by the counselor, notably control over the process of the call (Hinson, 1982). For example, the counselor determines the length, timing, and duration of probing questions, the degree to which the caller needs to be supported or encouraged to take action, necessary types of referral, and soon. Because of the caller's vulnerability and the counselor's training, skill, and knowledge of resources, it is important for the counselor to allow the caller as much sense of control as possible within the constraints of effective crisis intervention.

The discussion of control has implicit in it the issue of reciprocity, or lack thereof. Reciprocity can be analyzed on the basis of the characteristics of the participants and of the interaction between the participants. While callers and counselors share many human needs, at the time of the call they are quite dissimilar. Mahoney and Pechura (1982) describe crisis center volunteers as altruistic, emotionally sensitive, and stable. Additionally, counselors are likely to be caring, patient, relaxed, compassionate, and above average in education (Plante & Davids, 1982). In contrast, an individual in crisis is likely to be in a disorganized state; engaging in impulsive and unproductive testing behavior; experiencing anxiety, fear, distress, and inability to control emotions; having a lowered attention span and a loss of perspective; and exhibiting a changed relationship to other people (Brockopp, 1973a).

In addition to the marked dissimilarities of caller and counselor characteristics, there is a lack of reciprocity in the interaction as well. A caller in crisis, especially a suicidal caller, is likely to exhibit ambivalence (Hinson,

1982) and to disclose relevant personal information. The counselor, on the other hand, provides a supportive environment, listens, reflects and clarifies, and offers guidance and direction. The caller needs to receive assistance, and the counselor has a need or desire to help. In short, the interpersonal relationship of caller and counselor on the crisis line is characterized by a lack of reciprocity consistent with the nature of the acknowledged roles being enacted.

The final characteristic of crisis-line communication is its temporal nature which can be analyzed in terms of accessibility and continuity. The fact that most hotlines are available 24 hours a day and most people have easy access to telephones creates a situation of ready availability. The potential immediacy and spontaneity of a crisis line may serve as a deterrent to impulsive action. No other relationship is as easily available around the clock. In contrast, there are usually time-consuming procedures involved in setting up an appointment with a therapist in an agency, and even the closest friends and intimates require time to be uninterrupted by others.

Although a caller in crisis has easy access to a hotline, crisis-line communication is characterized by a lack of continuity. Even in the case of the repeat caller, a different counselor is likely to receive the call each time (Wark, 1982) (a situation which may benefit the caller who gets a fresh perspective). Crisis counseling is intense, focused, usually one-time or intermittent; continuity requires ongoing, regularized interaction. This factor clearly affects the content and nature of crisis-line communication.

In addition to the interpersonal characteristics of crisis-line communication, there are a variety of organizational factors affecting the call as well.

ORGANIZATIONAL FACTORS AFFECTING CRISIS-LINE COMMUNICATION

Crisis-line communication typically takes place in an organizational setting in which the counselor, usually a trained volunteer, receives calls in the office of a not-for-profit human service agency. There are many organizational factors which directly or indirectly affect the nature of crisis-line communication including the selection, training, and utilization of counselors; agency environment; organizational policies; and available resources.

A major issue in the selection of crisis counselors is the use of volunteers. The initial reason for the use of volunteers as crisis-line counselors was the shortage of available professionals (Rosenbaum & Calhoun, 1977). While almost all crisis lines are staffed at least in part by volunteers (Rosenbaum & Calhoun, 1977), there was nevertheless early debate regarding their desirability. However, in a study of clinical effectiveness of nonprofessional and professional telephone counselors in a crisis center, Knickerbocker and McGee (1973) found no significant difference between the two groups in the therapeutic conditions of empathy, warmth, and genuineness. Based on practical advantage, theory, and empirical research, there now appears to be substantial agreement that volunteers are necessary and valuable not merely as substitutes for professionals, but in their own right (McGee & Jennings, 1973). Viney (1983) argues that the role of the volunteer in the community mental health movement is no longer in question although the criteria for selection and training is still a subject of discussion.

A major task for most crisis service agencies is successful recruitment and screening of volunteers and thorough and appropriate training. Brockopp (1973b) summarizes the goal of the selection process as finding people whose "enthusiasm for life" and concern for other people is expressed in their voice and who can transmit nonverbally a "sense of hope and expectancy" (p. 258). Elkins and Cohen (1982) found that while a good training program produces changes in counselor skill and knowledge, attitudes were not subject to change on the basis of training or experience. Such a conclusion confirms Brockopp's (1973b) recommendation for screening volunteers in part on the basis of attitude and values.

Effective training of volunteer crisis counselors involves two major areas: thorough and adequate information regarding kinds of callers and the problems they are confronting, and assistance in improving interpersonal sensitivity and effectiveness on the telephone. Such training may require as much as 30 or more hours of intensive instruction, role play, feedback, and evaluation with a significant emphasis on listening skills (Brockopp, 1973c). Furthermore, Elkins and Cohen (1982) conclude that only continued training will improve counselor skills, emphasizing the need for regular follow-up training for experienced counselors. Finding and keeping volunteers with character, commitment, and communication skill is sometimes difficult since the training is long and the work is arduous, requiring the supervision of professional staff.

In addition to selection and training, the utilization of volunteers affects their ability to be successful as crisis counselors. Such mundane matters as length and frequency of shifts for volunteers who work at other jobs and who have personal and family responsibilities can affect the counselor's feelings and attitudes. Albrecht and Adelman (1984) suggest that providing emotional nurturance to another person can "strain a provider, decreasing the amount and quality of support he or she can or is willing to offer" (p. 23). Consequently, participation in support groups is an important factor in a counselor's ability to be effective and responsive to the caller. These groups, along with interaction with professional staff, provide an outlet for counselors to discharge the stress and anxiety they experience as a result of crisis calls. Further, support groups provide a significant learning environment for counselors who share experiences.

The crisis counselor typically answers the crisis line in the office of a human service agency. Various factors in the physical environment may have an effect on the counselor's response to a crisis call. For example, is the office secure? Especially for counselors on late night or overnight shifts, safety can be a concern since counselors are sometimes threatened by disturbed callers or obscene calls. Are other counselors or staff present in the office? The presence of another person may be a distraction or a relief. Are there multiple lines or multiple phones to manage? If the counselor is alone, multiple lines require the use of a hold button on the telephone. Or is there a diverter to be implemented? Further, the counselor is likely to be expected to keep some written record of each call for purposes of statistical analysis and/or counseling plans.

In addition to the physical environment, the psychological environment is also very important. Factors affecting the psychological environment range from backup support for difficult calls to concern about continued existence of the agency. Since not-for-profit agencies are continually in financial jeopardy, the funding support for a crisis line may have an indirect effect on the counselor.

Each crisis agency has a set of organizational policies which affect the choices the counselor can make in a crisis call. Confidentiality is an important policy issue; stressing the confidentiality to the caller may increase the likelihood of disclosure. What are the guidelines, if any, for violation of confidentiality? Typically, the only violation sanctioned is that necessary to interrupt a suicide attempt by calling an emergency rescue service. Further, agency policy regarding disclosure of the guidelines will affect what the counselor can say to the caller.

Policy and practice for tracing a lethal call is also a factor affecting the counselor. In such a situation, not only the agency but the telephone company and in some instances the police are involved in implementing such an action. The counselor must not only know how to trace a call but also how to handle the caller whose call is being traced.

Some crisis centers also provide face-to-face counseling; others have emergency outreach services which provide face-to-face counseling in emergency situations; many have none. Agency policy and practice regarding face-to-face counseling controls the range of options available for the crisis counselor, thereby affecting the counselor's therapeutic task.

Some agencies provide counseling plans for repeat callers created by the agency's professional staff which offer guidelines for the counselor in handling what could be very difficult calls. Knowledge and effective use of such plans can facilitate a call.

In addition to organizational policies, external resources influence the counselor's options. There are two types of external resources which are often vital to the crisis counselor: emergency services and referral services. Emergency services include transportation service, police, hospital emergency rooms, and psychiatric hospitals or units whose location, rules and regulations, and relationship to the crisis agency are important for the counselor to know. Referral services include community services such as shelters, food and clothing supplies, support groups and facilities, as well as therapists.

External resources become the connection between the telephone interaction and the outside world of everyday life for the caller. Assistance in obtaining appropriate services allows the caller to move from a state of inaction or paralysis to a more grounded involvement with others who can provide needed ongoing support.

Crisis-line communication can be seen as a form of mediated therapeutic communication premised on the existence of a crisis and the medium of the telephone which shapes the interaction. Effective crisis counseling requires specific communication skills enacted within the framework of a crisis intervention model. Such communication is distinguished interpersonally by anonymity, shared control between caller and counselor, lack of reciprocity, and an unusual temporal nature. It is characterized organizationally by the issues of selection, training, and utilization of counselors, agency environment, organizational policy, and external resources.

Crisis-line communication is a unique form of interpersonal communication utilizing the private medium of the telephone, operating in an organizational setting, and sharing some characteristics with traditional therapy as well as with intimate relationships.

TELEPHONE THERAPY

While it is readily apparent that the telephone would be useful for the kind of short-term, often anonymous, crisis counseling conducted primarily by trained volunteers, uses of the telephone for traditional therapy have been less apparent and slower to develop. The telephone is, nevertheless, reshaping and expanding the traditional definition of therapy.

Telephone therapy offers a choice of location for both the therapist and client. Relieved from the constraints of the office and the traditional work day, the therapist is free to conduct telephone therapy at a place convenient and suitable to everyone involved. While such flexibility may be perceived as a boon or a bane, it nevertheless decentralizes the workplace. Similarly, the client is free from the constraints of place. Therapy can take place over distance via the telephone. Clients who live in out-of-the-way places or who have difficulty in traveling can be more easily reached. Grumet (1979) argues that in the absence of the physical environment of the therapist's office, the client is freer to regulate incoming stimuli as well as his or her own disclosure because territorial ownership is neutralized. However, the client is confronted with the choice regarding locations (i.e., calling from home, work, phone booth) which may create additional difficulties and frustrations.

Conceivably, telephone therapy can take place at any time. Presumably, the time will be mutually agreed upon by therapist and client and mutually convenient. Accessibility of the telephone permits freedom from the traditional workday hours. One of the hazards of telephone therapy, however, is its potential intrusiveness. The telephone itself frequently intrudes into people's private time because it demands an answer. While new technology allows us to disconnect the telephone or engage an answering machine or service, such action requires a deliberate step which some are unwilling to take. Further, clients may be unwilling or unable to abide by calling agreements and consequently may pose a threat to a therapist's private time. The use of the telephone for therapy demands clarity and consensus regarding personal boundaries since the instrument is inherently intrusive. Many therapists currently suggest that a client make use of a 24-hour crisis line between regularly scheduled sessions precisely to avoid this boundary problem.

The use of the telephone is reshaping and expanding the traditional definition of therapy in part by redefining the idea of a "session" with all that entails. The rules and norms surrounding a traditional therapy session are not necessarily applicable to the telephone, and new rules and norms must emerge. What constitutes a "session" on the telephone? What is the fee? Is every call "counted"? How does one determine which ones count and which do not? When and where does conversation stop and therapy begin? What about conference calls? Who pays any extra telephone charges? What about others who may be present at the time of the call? Are the expectations regarding confidentiality the same as in the face-to-face situation? Clearly, the telephone blurs the lines of demarcation between therapy and other forms of interaction.

Therapists as a group may be ambivalent about the use of the telephone for therapy. Those who embrace the telephone for traditional therapy may actively endorse technological change and be drawn to its convenience and its ability to reach those who might otherwise be unreachable. Those who resist may be unwilling for the medium to influence the process of therapy and may fear encroachment into their already threatened private lives.

Clients as a group may also be ambivalent about the use of the telephone for therapy. Some, no doubt, will prefer traditional face-to-face personal contact. However, clients who feel anxious, powerless, threatened, humiliated, or vulnerable may prefer the sense of control offered by the telephone (Grumet, 1979). Although the therapist maintains considerable control of the process of therapy on the telephone, the client retains control of the information and to some extent the definition of the situation, a situation which is markedly different from the usual circumstances of traditional therapy.[1]

Traditional therapy is in the process of being redefined, expanded, and decentralized by the telephone and other forms of mediated communication. Just as copyright laws designed to protect authors of print are proving inapplicable to video and will inevitably be revised, the rules of traditional therapy are undergoing redefinition. Therapy has exploded into uncharted territory via call-in radio and television as well as computerized formats. The telephone is less noticeable but equally revolutionary in its impact.

REFERENCES

Albrecht, T. L., & Adelman, M. B. (1984). Social support and life stress: New directions for communication research. *Human Communication Research, 11*(1), 3–32.

American Association of Suicidology. (1985). *Suicide prevention and crisis intervention agencies in the United States.* Denver, CO: Author.

Aronson, S. H. (1982). The sociology of the telephone. In G. Gumpert & R. Cathcart (Eds.), *Inter/Media* (2nd ed., pp. 272–283). New York: Oxford University Press.

Barnlund, D. C. (1968). Introduction to therapeutic communication. In D. C. Barnlund (Ed.), *Interpersonal communication: Survey and studies* (pp. 613–645). Boston: Houghton Mifflin.

Brockopp, G. W. (1973a). Crisis intervention: Theory, process and practice. In D. Lester & G. W. Brockopp (Eds.), *Crisis intervention and counseling by telephone* (pp. 89–104). Springfield, IL: Thomas.

Brockopp, G. W. (1973b). Selecting the telephone counselor. In D. Lester & G. W. Brockopp (Eds.), *Crisis intervention and counseling by telephone* (pp. 252–261). Springfield, IL: C. C. Thomas.

---

[1] Reports of telephone therapy in the 1970s and 1980s include counseling visually impaired people (Evans & Jaureguy, 1981; Evans, Werkhoven, & Fox, 1982; Jaureguy & Evans, 1982), treating social isolation (Evans, Werkhoven, & Fox, 1982; Shilman & Giladi, 1985), conducting hypnotherapy (Cooperman & Schafer, 1983; Gravitz, 1983), counseling between regular visits (Hymer, 1984), providing therapy for agoraphobia (Taylor, 1984), conducting follow-up treatment after residential care (Magura & Moses, 1985), conducting therapy after a geographical move (Rosenbaum, 1977), counseling the elderly (Schmidt, 1985; Evans, Werkhoven, & Fox, 1982; Herzog, Rodgers, & Kulka, 1983), counseling groups and families (Evans, Fox, Pritzl, & Halar, 1984; Evans, Kleinman, Halar, & Herzer, 1984; Hightower & Dimalanta, 1980; Jaureguy & Evans, 1982), treating adolescent smokers (McConnell, Biglan, & Severson, 1984), counseling physically disabled individuals (Evans, Fox, Pritzl, & Halar, 1984), and conducting ongoing psychoanalysis (Hymer, 1984).

Brockopp, G. W. (1973c). Training the telephone counselor. In D. Lester & G. W. Brockopp (Eds.), *Crisis intervention and counseling by telephone* (pp. 262–274). Springfield, IL: C. C. Thomas.

Cathcart, R., & Gumpert, G. (1983). Mediated interpersonal communication: Toward a new typology. *Quarterly Journal of Speech, 69,* 267–277.

Cooperman, S., & Schafer, D. W. (1983). Hypnotherapy over the telephone. *American Journal of Clinical Hypnosis, 25*(4), 277–279.

Echterling, L. G., Hartsough, D. M., & Zarle, T. H. (1980). Testing a model for the process of telephone crisis intervention. *American Journal of Community Psychology, 8*(6), 715–725.

Elkins, R. L., Jr., & Cohen, C. R. (1982). A comparison of the effects of prejob training and job experience on nonprofessional telephone crisis counselors. *Suicide and Life-Threatening Behavior, 12*(2), 84–89.

Evans, R. L., Fox, H. R., Pritzl, D. O., & Halar, E. M. (1984). Group treatment of physically disabled adults by telephone. *Social Work in Healthcare. 9*(3), 77–84.

Evans, R. L., & Jaureguy, B. M. (1981). Telephone counselling with visually impaired adults. *International Journal of Rehabilitation Research, 4*(4), 550–552.

Evans, R. L., Kleinman, L., Halar, E. M., & Herzer, K. (1984). Predicting change in life satisfaction as a function of group counselling. *Psychological Reports, 55*(1), 199–204.

Evans, R. L., Werkhoven, W., & Fox, H. R. (1982). Treatment of social isolation and loneliness in a sample of visually impaired elderly persons. *Psychological Reports, 51*(1), 103–108.

Gravitz, M. A. (1983). Early uses of the telephone and recordings in hypnosis. *American Journal of Clinical Hypnosis, 25*(4), 280–282.

Grumet, C. W. (1979). Telephone therapy: A review and case report. *American Journal of Orthopsychiatry, 49*(4), 574–584.

Herzog, A. R., Rodgers, W. L., & Kulka, R. A. (1983). Interviewing older adults: A comparison of telephone and face-to-face modalities. *Public Opinion Quarterly, 47*(3), 405–418.

Hightower, N. A., & Dimalanta, A. S. (1980). "Ma Bell"—the other mother in family therapy. *Family Therapy, 7*(2), 147–151.

Hinson, J. (1982). Strategies for suicide intervention by telephone. *Suicide and Life-Threatening Behavior, 12*(3), 176–184.

Hymer, S. N. (1984). The telephone session and the telephone between sessions. *Psychotherapy in Private Practice, 2*(3), 51–65.

Jaureguy, B. M., & Evans, R. L. (1982). Short term group counselling of visually impaired people by telephone. *Journal of Visual Impairment and Blindness, 77*(4), 150–152.

Knickerbocker, D. A., & McGee, R. K. (1973). Clinical effectiveness of non-professional and professional telephone workers in a crisis intervention center. In D. Lester & G. W. Brockopp (Eds.), *Crisis intervention and counseling by telephone* (pp. 298–309). Springfield, IL: Thomas.

Lamb, C. W. (1973). Telephone therapy: Some common errors and fallacies. In D. Lester & G. W. Brockopp (Eds.), *Crisis intervention and counseling by telephone* (pp. 105–110). Springfield, IL: Thomas.

Lester, D. (1974). The unique qualities of telephone therapy. *Psychotherapy: Theory, Research and Practice, 11*(3), 219–221.

Magura, S., & Moses, B. S. (1985). Developing a telephone follow-up interview for residential treatment. *Residential Group Care and Treatment, 3*(1), 33–48.

Mahoney, J., & Pechura, C. M. (1980). Values and volunteers: Axiology of altruism in a crisis center. *Psychological Reports, 47,* 1007–1012.

McConnell, S., Biglan, A., & Severson, H. H. (1984). Adolescence with self-monitoring and physiological assessment of smoking in natural environments. *Journal of Behavioral Medicine, 7*(1), 115–122.

McGee, R. K., & Jennings, B. (1973). Ascending to "lower" levels: The case for non-professional crisis workers. In D. Lester & G. W. Brockopp (Eds.), *Crisis intervention and counseling by telephone* (pp. 223–237). Springfield, IL: Thomas.

McLuhan, M. (1964). *Understanding media.* New York: McGraw-Hill.

Miller, P. V., & Cannell, C. F. (1982). A study of experimental techniques for telephone interviewing. *Public Opinion Quarterly, 46*(2), 250–269.

Miller, W. (1973). The telephone in out-patient psychotherapy. *American Journal of Psychotherapy, 27*, 15–26.

Natale, M. (1978). Perceived empathy, warmth and genuineness as effected by interviewer timing of speech in a telephone interview. *Psychotherapy: Theory, research and practice, 15*(2), 145–152.

Plante, T. G., & Davids, A. (1982). Personality and performance characteristics of Samaritan suicide prevention volunteers. *Crisis Intervention, 12*(4), 115–127.

Pool, I. de S. (Ed.). (1977). *The social impact of the telephone.* Cambridge, MA: The MIT Press.

Pool, I. de S. (1983). *Forecasting the telephone: A retrospective technology assessment.* Norwood, NJ: Ablex.

Rogers, T. S. (1976). Interviews by telephone and in person: Quality of responses and field performance. *Public Opinion Quarterly, 40*(1), 51–65.

Rosenbaum, A., & Calhoun, J. F. (1977). The use of the telephone hotline in crisis intervention: A review. *Journal of Community Psychology, 5*, 325–339.

Rosenbaum, M. (1977). Premature interruption of psychotherapy: Continuation of contact by telephone and correspondence. *American Journal of Psychiatry, 134*(2), 200–202.

Schmidt, H. (1985). [Older and elderly people as clients of telephone counselling.] (German) *Zeitschrift fur Gerontologie, 18*(2), 83–87.

Shilman, R. P., & Giladi, B. H. (1985). Bridging the isolation gap: Making a telephone connection. *Social Work with Groups, 8*(2), 134–137.

Slaikeu, K. A., & Willis, N. A. (1978). Caller feedback on counselor performance in telephone crisis intervention: A follow-up study. *Crisis Intervention, 9*(2), 42–49.

Taylor, I. (1984). Self-exposure instructions by telephone with a severe agoraphobic: A case study. *Behavioral Psychotherapy, 12*(1), 68–72.

Viney, L. (1983). Experiences of volunteer telephone counselors: A comparison of a professionally-oriented and non-professionally oriented approach to their training. *Journal of Community Psychology, 11*, 259–268.

Wark, V. (1982). A look at the work of the telephone counseling center. *The Personnel and Guidance Journal, 61*(2), 110–112.

Williams, F. (1984). *The new communications.* Belmont, CA: Wadsworth.

Williams, T., & Douds, J. (1973). The unique contribution of telephone therapy. In D. Lester & G. W. Brockopp (Eds.), *Crisis intervention and counseling by telephone* (pp. 80–88). Springfield, IL: Thomas.

12
Software and Sympathy: Therapeutic Interaction with the Computer

Patricia J. Fleming

The intrapersonal process of developing the Software Listener program reveals the therapeutic function of the software as well as the potential therapeutic role of the computer itself. In a personalized and engaging style, Fleming identifies the nature and kinds of change which occur as a consequence of this therapeutic encounter.

INTRODUCTION

In the dim light the faint glow from the video screen casts shadows on the troubled face of the person seated at the computer keyboard. Hands move slowly to the keyboard, typing out "I am forced at last to recognize that I am hopeless." "STOP!" The familiar white on red sign breaks into the gloom and hopelessness. A banner flashes across the screen: "Instead of feeling hopeless, I can imagine myself feeling worthwhile." A kaleidoscope of changing colors lights up the banner and reflects on the features changing from gloomy apathy to livelier skepticism.

The screen is still for a moment, then the question appears: "What would make you feel worthwhile?" The thoughtful pause again as the figure before the screen gropes for something that might lock in the thought that this self is a worthwhile self. The brows knit and the eyes cast about as the imagination searches for possibilities. A glance at the face in the framed photograph on the desk, the award next to it, the concert tickets tucked into the frame. Would even a Nobel prize do it? Well, maybe a bowl of coffee Heath bar crunch ice cream would help. A few laps in the pool? A phone call to a friend? Hopelessness gives way to active thinking and problem solving.

What is going on here? This person has used a software program to transform that heartless number-cruncher, the computer, into a sounding board, a sympathetic ear, and a cheering section.

Of course, talking things over with a good listener enables people to work things out rather than suffer the stress of pent-up feelings. A sympa-

170

thetic ear and a few words of encouragement can lead to increased self-confidence, greater clarity of thought, and more effective problem solving. And because it's often difficult to find a good available person to listen, sometimes a good available computer program will do.

OVERVIEW: COMPUTER SOFTWARE AS "INTERACTIVE OTHER"

Talking things over with another person is clearly therapeutic interpersonal communication. But what of talking things over with your friendly home computer? Can this use of a computer software program as an "interactive other" be construed as therapeutic interpersonal communication? When I was asked to consider this question based on the Software Listener computer software I had designed, I found the question itself baffling. To some extent, this chapter traces the growth of my own understanding of computer software as mediated therapeutic communication.

In exploring this question, computer software that replicates parts of the intrapersonal communication process and in so doing permits analysis and alteration of both that internal communication process and its consequences on the life of the human software user will be examined. The proxy program we saw our despondent friend using to overcome feelings of hopelessness will be described. How does using this proxy software program compare with interacting with another human being? Further, how does using that proxy program compare with the process of creating the proxy program?

The therapeutic process, including both intentional and serendipitous therapeutic change, will be seen as a feedback loop. Aspects of the therapeutic process will be pointed out and some criteria explored for evaluating the depth and effectiveness of therapeutic interactions. Computer software will be considered as a kind of "interactive other." The nature of computer-mediated communication with this "interactive other" will be explored on two levels—both on the level of the user of the software program and on the level of the creator of the program. To facilitate the exploration of these questions, I will use my development of the Software Listener program as it evolved from the tiny Encourager program. This exploration will point to the difficulties that I sought to heal by creating and using this program and the process whereby some healing came about.

COMPUTER SOFTWARE AND THE INTRAPSYCHIC DRAMA

To get an overview of the questions raised by attempts at computer-mediated therapeutic communication, I offer the history of my own first attempt to create a computer program that interacted with the user in such a way as to simulate a sympathetic listener. This first program, which I called the Encourager, is quite a simple model. The development of a simple software program illustrates the different forms of interaction available to the user and the creator of a software program.

Computer technology provides a medium used for self-assessment and image formation. The software allows one to externalize and materialize the customarily nonobservable internal drama. Through the medium of the computer software, one can observe what is not usually observable and control what is usually beyond control.

Now, one of the really interesting things you can do with a computer is create various models and then set these models going and watch what happens. As the creator of a computer program, you can select what you want to use as a subject for your model. Since one can think of the Self as a process, "doing" rather than simply statically "being," I decided to use a tiny fragment of the human mental process as my model. The computer is, after all, frequently compared to the human mind, and the mind is frequently described as a computer.

Furthermore, the various functions of the mind can be thought of as dramatis personae in an internal drama. The tradition for this conceptualization includes ancient personifications of Reason in conflict with Desire and continues through the dramas Freud described of the Unruffled Ego attempting to manage the struggle between the Thin-Lipped Superego versus the Wily Id. One can ask what are the various personae, how did they get created, and how can they be modified? How does the internal drama influence the interaction between the whole human entity and external environment?

THE ENCOURAGER PROGRAM AND THE THERAPEUTIC PROCESS

Here let me introduce a few dramatis personae involved in the design and creation of my first computer-mediated therapeutic communication—a tiny program called the Encourager which went on to become part of the larger Software Listener program. First, the Human, the simple "me" that did things and looked in the mirror and was affected by remarks coming from outside itself. Another persona in this internal drama in my computer mind was the Wet Blanket, which undercut enthusiasm and poured forth derisive and contemptuous remarks about myself and my accomplishments. And, next, the Therapist. This therapist persona diagnosed the situation I wanted to heal and prescribed behavior and thoughts which would bring about the desired healing. Needless to say, the Human would do better with some encouragement and praise to undercut the effect of the

Wet Blanket's contempt. The Therapist-persona first diagnosed the situation, then prescribed a rescue and created a software program, the Encourager, to perform that rescue.

This Encourager program used the computer to have input into the drama of intrapersonal communication. The medium here was the computer language BASIC which was used to tell the computer in minute detail what the Encourager program should do and how it should do it. In creating this program I was totally engrossed and felt healing taking place. The Encourager asked first your name, then how you would like to be described. Using this information, it then composed a banner that read: "You, George, are handsome," or, "You, Louise, are as good as the next person," or, "You, Gentle Reader, are uniquely marvelous." It then flashed this banner across the screen and surrounded this flashing banner with a field of twinkling stars. Pretty simple. Pretty trivial. Pretty satisfying.

I had diagnosed an unwholesome interaction in my internal communication and had then provided myself with the doubly satisfying experience of first creating a more wholesome persona and second having a wholesome interaction with that persona. Creating a persona is a way in which the Interactive Other, the medium itself, can change and grow with the user.

When I then introduced the Encourager to other people, their medium of interaction was the software program itself. As people interacted with this friendly little program, I noticed smiles creep across their faces as their self-esteem was enhanced by the Encourager's banner and stars. Clearly a positive communication with an Interactive Other was occurring for these users of the Encourager program.

This simple example of the Encourager program illustrates how therapeutic interaction takes place on three levels: the level of content, the level of process, and the level of metaprocess, or thinking about the process. While interacting with the Encourager clearly provided a sort of therapeutic experience for those people who used the Encourager "off the shelf," in that it provided a model for a wholesome, positive way of evaluating the person's experience and performance, the change was taking place primarily at the level of content and at the level of process where a role model was provided for a positive process.

By contrast, creating the persona of the Encourager allowed therapeutic change to take place on the deepest level of metaprocess. I was engrossed because I was creating the persona with whom I was interacting. It was the process of creating that wholesomely Interactive Other that was the core of the therapeutic experience. In this case, the interaction was part of a feedback loop that provided data. The data was then used in the creation or modification of that Interactive Other, the persona of the Encourager. And this was a therapeutic interaction at the level of metaprocess.

USER INTERACTS WITH SOFTWARE LISTENER PROGRAM
"OFF THE SHELF"

Now, back to the computer program which our despondent friend was using earlier. The medium here is the Software Listener, a computer software program that I designed to be used "off the shelf" without tinkering with the program code or creating a proxy persona in any way. The Software Listener incorporates the functions of a number of smaller programs, including the Encourager program described above. What is that program like? What characterizes the therapeutic communication between a computer listener simulation program and a human user?

In designing this program, my goal was to combine the gentle art of listening with the power of computer technology. I designed the Software Listener according to the principles of effective listening and self-esteem building in a helping interview. Accordingly, the Software Listener calls the user by name, reflects back what the user has said, asks probing questions, offers helpful suggestions, and gives encouragement. These behaviors provide the user with the understanding which is the foundation for catharsis, for receiving support, for having the courage to gain honest insight and explore new thoughts and new behaviors.

Anyone who can use a keyboard can sit down with the diskette and user's manual, load and run the program, and right away have helpful conversations in plain English with a friendly computer. The title appears on the screen, followed by the greeting, "Hello. I'm glad you could come by. What would you like to be called today?" Decide what you would like the Software Listener to call you and type in that name on the keyboard. Make a mistake? No problem. Just back up with the delete key, type the name the way you want it, and hit the return key. The Software Listener will "hear" what you've just typed, think about it, and print out a response.

For instance, a typical conversation between a user named Human and the Software Listener might go like this:

Human: I feel so cut off from other people.
Software: Have you always felt so cut off from other people?
Human: No.
Software: There's more to it than that, isn't there?
Human: Well, I sort of felt cut off from other people in school too.
Software: As we were talking earlier you said that you sometimes don't like anybody very much. What's the connection?
Human: I should try to like people more.
Software: "Should"? Sometimes it helps to think "could" instead of "should."
Human: I see you have all the answers.
Software: Human, who else besides me would you like to say that to?

A good listener is also a good motivator, pointing out strengths and strong points, offering encouragement and support and praise that builds self-confidence and pride. If you aren't feeling so hot, it's likely that you aren't pointing out positive things about yourself. Very likely you are focusing on your weaknesses. You may fish for compliments from your friends and family because you sense that you need someone else to break the vicious cycle of low self-esteem and negative behavior. Because The Software Listener "knows" this, it provides positive messages for you. The Software Listener also allows you to take control and create your own positive messages. It suggests the beginning of a positive message, such as, "I feel good about myself when . . ." or "I believe I can . . ." and you finish the sentence so it is just the way you want it, tailor-made for the unique individual you are. It jogs you by suggesting that you finish a sentence like "I feel good about myself when. . . ." You fill it out, even if it's something simple like "I feel good about myself when someone tells me I've done well." After a while you'll probably want to write your own self-affirmations: "I am the greatest!", "I know I can get a better job." At any time in the conversation with the Software Listener you can stop and look at positive statements displayed with a dynamic visual pattern. The patterns and positive statements vary; maybe one time the message "I am a good and worthy person" will appear with changing colors, and another time "I, Smitty, can find and enjoy a good job" will appear with a pattern of flashing stars.

Once you create the message, you can choose which electronic sign pattern you'd like and tell the Software Listener how many times you'd like to see it. Then sit back and watch while the positive message becomes a part of your thinking about yourself and your life.

A computer together with its software program can offer communication containing such qualities as empathy, understanding, respect, confidentiality, validation, caring, trust, honesty. More precisely perhaps, one could say that the specific interactive verbal behaviors that convey a sense of these qualities are present in the interaction. Thus the computer program's use of the human user's vocabulary and syntax conveys understanding, the computer program's use of the human user's name conveys rapport, and the computer program's references to the human user's previous remarks convey respect and attentiveness.

How does computer-mediated therapeutic interaction compare with the therapy dyad? While nothing can replace a good conversation with another person, the software does offer some advantages:

A software listener is always there and ready to listen to you.
A software listener never gets tired of listening.
A software listener is infinitely patient, completely discreet, always responsive.

A software listener can be trusted to keep your important personal and business secrets absolutely confidential.

THE THERAPEUTIC PROCESS

"Therapeutic" implies an intervention of some sort by an agent or circumstance that has a healing effect on what it contacts. The therapeutic process is a feedback loop or cycle of change. The three basic stages in the cycle are PLANNING, INTERACTING, and EVALUATING. Like the ancient symbol of the snake biting its tail, the cycle continues looping through these changes, with each apparent ending leading to a new beginning:

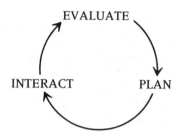

One can think of the therapeutic cycle as going around and around, thus: EVALUATING, PLANNING, INTERACTING, EVALUATING, PLANNING, INTERACTING, EVALUATING, PLANNING, INTERACTING, EVALUATING, and so on. Go around this cycle as many times as necessary.

The crucial step in this process, and the one that is most often overlooked, is evaluation. To evaluate, of course, implies values, certain conditions or attributes that are valued, sought after, given a higher worth than others. These values are "what matters." Because interaction can, of course, alter a system of valuation as well as facilitate reaching previously valued goals, the new value system may also be evaluated. Pathology can be coming to value drugs, say, more than valuing participation in life, or more than life itself.

INTENTIONAL THERAPEUTIC CHANGE

In the intentional problem-solving mode, one enters the cycle of change at the evaluation stage. The situation is evaluated in such a way as to define the problem, to diagnose the difficulty. One then proceeds to formulate a hypothesis or plan for improving that situation, to act according to that plan or "test the hypothesis," and finally to evaluate the result of that action.

Engaging in healing presupposes some standard of health. Intentional therapy involves diagnosis, prognosis, therapeutic goal, prescription, treatment plan, and evaluation. This is also the model for the kind of intentional professional psychotherapy offered by a human psychotherapist, the kind of psychotherapy for which one can get a diagnostic code from the Diagnostic and Statistical Manual and submit a bill to Blue Cross.

SERENDIPITOUS CHANGE

Then there is happenstance. Some interaction happens to come about that happens to cause a change that happens to be therapeutic. In serendipity the process of change begins with INTERACTION: One finds oneself involved in an interaction of some sort. Then comes a form of EVALUATION: One asks, "DO I like what's happening?" And finally a form of PLANNING takes place: One asks, "Do I want more of this, or do I want to get out of here and get moving on?"

DEPTH OF CHANGE

The therapeutic impulse can be directed toward different levels of healing depth. On the simplest level one attempts to avoid present pain and obtain present pleasure. To simply avoid the awareness of pain, the average psychotropic street drug will do just fine, as will the energy surge from a chocolate bar. These agents merely deaden the awareness of the painful symptom. By contrast, at its most profound, the therapeutic impulse leads to interactions which heal that coherently functioning organizational unit—the SELF—and the SELF's various internal personae. This depth healing alters the way that SELF organizes itself and functions in the external world.

INTERNALIZATION OF THE THERAPEUTIC AGENT

It may happen that as one integrates the functions of the software program, one no longer uses the program, as, ideally, in therapy one takes in the external role and behavior of the therapist and makes the therapist function a part of oneself.

The effective therapist does away with the need for her services by facilitating the internalization of her therapeutic behavior in the creation of the client's own internal therapeutic function. The internalization of the therapeutic function works much like the internalization of the parenting function. Initially, after establishing rapport and trust with the therapist, the therapy client thinks, "Ah, safe at last, this person will always be here to take care of me and I will always be OK." Similarly, the child thinks, "My mommy and I are one and I will always be OK," and later, with alarm, searching for reassurance, "Mommy, promise me you will never die."

Time passes until one day, a surprise: The child grows up and wants to go out and play and then get a little apartment in the city and maybe live abroad for a while, and the therapy client has something better to do than go to therapy at eight o'clock Tuesday morning. The function is internalized, and the external source of that function is no longer needed and could be cast aside. Of course, parents and human therapists, being human rather than merely computer programs, are much more than their function. Parents and human therapists exercise their therapeutic functions in the context of a full relationship between two people. Therefore, a rich human relationship may endure and flourish long after the specific intervention has been completed and the client has recovered or the child has grown up.

This internalized therapeutic function can be thought of as the persona of the Internal Therapist who is always available and helpful in the internal dialogue. If the external source in therapy does not become internalized, one risks becoming addicted to that source. This is unfortunately often the case when the therapeutic impulse stops at the stage of simply seeking pleasure and avoiding pain. One can become addicted to a soothing or distracting person, just as one can become addicted to a soothing or distracting chemical. Conversely, in theory, if one could somehow internalize the effect of a chemical agent, say, a hot fudge sundae or a cigarette, and using this agent as a model, create an internal source of similar effects, then the sundae or the cigarette could be a model of a therapeutic agent.

For example, one of the internal functions that may be lacking in a person is that of simple, accurate recognition of the person's own thoughts and feelings. One may then seek out this function from another person, often from a therapist. In creating the Software Listener, I thought it would be interesting to have computer software provide the focused attention one looks for in a human psychotherapist. One of the specific behaviors I identified as indicating focused attention was that of a good mirror—providing accurate reflections. An accurate mirror would be one that, if I said, "I feel horrible," would respond, "You feel horrible." It wouldn't say, "You think you are hopeless." Those paraphrases, interpretations, and other inaccuracies are small, but they are not trivial, for they indicate inattention and narcissistic interjection of the listener's own thoughts and vocabulary. I sought an exact mirror. And eventually, after some struggle, I created an exact mirror. If I said, "I feel terrible," the accurate reflection came back, "You feel terrible." The peculiar sense of calm that followed these exchanges suggested to me they were just what I needed. This accuracy allowed me to consider, reconsider, and refine my statements until I knew just what I thought and felt. I tried out long complicated statements and to my delight they were reflected back just as I had said them.

Then I discovered I'd had enough of exact mirroring. The very exact mirroring that I had so craved, that craving that had been strong enough to motivate me through the maze of buying a computer, hooking it up to a television, learning BASIC, plowing through the EZ BASIC programming books, was now getting on my nerves. I was no longer delighted by having the precise response come back at me. In short, I had grown. I had integrated that mirroring function into my repertoire of internal functions and was now ready to move on. And because I knew how to write a program, my Software Listener was able to grow and move on with me.

CREATING A PERSONA COMPARED WITH INTERACTING WITH A FIXED PERSONA

The media itself can be at various levels of dynamism and modifiability, ranging from a static snapshot to the dynamic human voice mediated by the telephone. Computer software can be at various levels of modifiability, from the fixed persona in any software used "off the shelf" to a program that allows for dynamic changes by altering the program code.

For instance, someone using a fixed Interactive Other simulation program, such as the Software Listener, has to go with that persona. As the conversation continues, the Software Other "learns" more about the Human, and may incorporate this knowledge into its responses in some way. Thus the Human user can influence the content of the Software Other's responses. However, the user input does not have any impact on the Software Other's "character." The Software Other will continue to have the same probability of making the same response to the same input whenever the user runs the program. The Software Other can respond to the Human's remarks in certain set patterns.

By contrast, the program creator can not only put words in the Software Other's mouth and ideas in its mind, but also actually create the Software Other's character, a new form for its responses, a new kind of response. A new pattern of interaction can be created by interacting with it and then tinkering with the program code itself to bring the Software Other more in line with the kind of Interactive Other the Human desires or feels would be beneficial. Creating a persona is a way in which the Interactive Other, the medium itself, can change and grow with the user.

For an illustration, let's return to the point where I had my Software Listener functioning as a good mirror and wanted to add new functions to it. If I had been using an Interactive Other program "off the shelf" and couldn't modify the program at all, this point would have marked the end of the program's usefulness to me. However, as a programmer creating Interactive Other software, I was able to mull over what the program needed to do next if it was to continue to be helpful to me. Perhaps it would be interesting to test out the cognitive therapist's assertion that it is more beneficial to say "I could" than "I should," as in, "I should get up and put on my Reeboks and run" or "I should put down this chip and dip and pick up that nice piece of broccoli." Needless to say, I was skeptical. It seemed to me that by reminding myself I should do this or that I was pushing myself in the direction of health and virtue, racing along with the rest of the human race. Still, it seemed worth a try.

Even with the present level of computer technology it isn't difficult to design a "software persona" that will detect specific verbal patterns and then respond in assigned ways to these patterns—not unlike saying to your buddy, "Every time I say 'I'm stupid,' you yell 'stop.'" You can thus turn your computer into a friendly watchdog which you train to break into your internal communications. A sort of interactive journal. You could, of course, train it to break in to say, "Stupid isn't the half of it. Besides being stupid, you're also weird and ugly and your mother dresses you funny." (A friend and I did that once. I trained a program to break into remarks and say insulting critical things. It was so hostile that it was a funny carica-ture, and since I created it and I controlled it and I turned it on and off, using it desensitized me to a lot of crabby behavior. My friend created a Software personality called "KVETCH" that whines and complains and guilt-trips masterfully.)

Once the watchdog program was ready, I began to try it out. And it was a perfect job for my Computer Watchdog. OK, old computer watchdog, old buddy, old pal, every time you notice I've said "should," stop me and remind me to say "could" instead. No that doesn't mean to jeer, "Patty said 'should' again, bad Patty" . . . no, it just means to flag the word "should" and remind me I have the option to replace that "should" with "could."

I tried it out. When I said, "I should write this chapter," I was reminded that I had available the alternative phrasing, "I could write this chapter." And indeed that phrasing did take some of the pressure off and free up some energy for working that had been tied up in worrying. And what about the logical "should"? "If I start working now, I should be done by dawn" becomes "If I start working now, I could be done by dawn." Hmm . . . it is more realistic. I could be done by dawn, or I could be spinning around in an eddy in my mental stream as the sun comes up, or I could be fast asleep. Even the logical "should" yields to the more realistic "could."

So, now I had a megaprogram that incorporated the Mirror program, the Encourager program, and phrasing change program. I was on a roll. This interactive format could be expanded to include other semantic pairs. My Interactive Other could be taught to remind me that instead of saying "I have to," I could say "I can." Instead of "always," I could say "often." My relationship with my Interactive Other Software Listener program was once again on a euphoric plateau.

SUMMARY

Interaction with the Software Listener provides a laboratory wherein one can test one's response to a controllable proxy of a Significant Interactive Other. The computer allows one to create an Interactive Other and then interact with that other. Did I create myself in creating the Software Listener? In a sense, the Software Listener is a form of The Double, a potentially benevolent Doppelganger.

It now seems to me that the healing came from creating the Software Listener persona, which was then internalized and became part of my repertoire of mental functions. I sought first to find it outside myself and then bring it inside myself as my own mirroring and supporting functions whereas when I began to develop the program my expectation was that the healing would come from interacting with the finished program. As is often the case with therapy, the healing was serendipitous. Surprisingly, the healing came both from the interacting and from creating and modifying the Interactive Other.

FUTURE

And now to imagine some of the possibilities for combining a software listener simulation with some of the other familiar capacities of computer technology:

It is now a commonplace to put a diagnostic test on a computer and thereby speed up and improve accuracy of scoring. So, for a simple first-level fantasy combination, add a fast and accurate diagnostic ability to the software listener program.

Computers also provide information. Creating a computer/educator is as easy as linking the computer up to a database containing all the relevant literature and philosophy from the classics to the latest research. Our listener now diagnoses and provides instant access to new information.

And why not hook this up to some of the electronics already in place around the house. The VCR. The electronic talking alarm clock. The microwave oven. Have the computer wake you up to your favorite mellow music video and add a voice-over reminding you of what a fine person you are and what an enjoyable day awaits you. Check in with the automated teller machine at the bank and replenish the supply of money for the day ahead. And, of course, turn on the lawn sprinkler, phone your car pool mates, check the telephone answering service, and start the coffee brewing.

Now, instead of being limited to the cumbersome keyboard, let's free up the user's hands by having the computer develop voice recognition capabilities. And supplementing the computer's video screen is now a speech synthesizer. There, now communication sounds like a proper human conversation.

Biofeedback opens up a whole other set of interactive possibilities. With biofeedback a computer can be hooked up to any electronic monitoring process, analyze and store results, and output these results onto a screen, an audio system, or any other form of output that can provide the user with valuable feedback information. Biofeedback capabilities and linkage to any electronic or mechanical environmental control can assure that when your blood pressure gets too high, your audio environment automatically switches from jazz fusion to soft rock music. What about arranging that at a stress level of 10 or above, the computer starts crooning, "Time for rest and relaxation, Oh Most Wondrous Awesome One."

Now, imagine taking this fantasy one step further: Embed this computer and its Diagnoser/ Listener/ Educator/ Butler/ Encourager/ Soother/ Entertainer programs in a genuine lifesized, flexible, firm, warm rubber doll. A "great big beautiful doll." Here it is at last, the love of your life, stepping out of your dreams and into your life. Will this mean the end of human interaction? The ultimate boob tube? The end of the human race? With the Interactive Other that provides everything available, will anyone ever leave the comfort of this relationship to bother relating to another person?

Of course, if we don't know this great big beautiful doll isn't a human like ourselves, we are in for a shock when we find out. The frame can make the communicative interaction pathogenic rather than therapeutic. For instance, it is one thing to be aware that our communication with another human being is mediated, that a medium such as radio or telephone has been interposed between myself and another person. It is another thing to be aware of using a medium such as computer software as a proxy for another human being. And it is quite another thing, quite an alarming other thing, to discover that what appeared to be human is, in fact, a robot simulation, a "great, big, beautiful doll." Then the horror is that the medium is *all there is*. There is nobody else there.

We humans fancy that we can detect the human quintessence in another. Science fiction gets a lot of mileage from the fear that we could be duped or deceived into thinking the android or robot is a fellow human being. This fear taps into the ultimate xenophobia, the fear of the stranger, the Other, the Alien, passing undetected and hostile among us.

Furthermore, we humans want our most intimate relationships to be with other humans, not with surrogates, however ideal the behavior and form of these surrogates may be. So, mediated communication with computers and their software programs is not likely to replace direct communication in a relationship with another genuine human being. Computer software may replicate parts of intrapersonal communication and in so doing permit analysis and alteration of that internal communication process and its consequences on the external social life. Ultimately, people will use these computers and their software programs as they use books, tapes, newspapers, workshops, and other personal growth resources to develop the individual self and enhance the genuine human-to-human relationship of the human user.

13
The Therapeutic Learning Program (TLP): Computer-Assisted Short-Term Therapy

Roger L. Gould

The insertion of the computer into the process of traditional therapy seems paradoxical. While the computer is used here as a learning device, it nevertheless alters the therapeutic relationship between therapist and patient. According to Gould, the TLP differs from conventional therapy in that it is short-term rather than prolonged, and the therapist's function is to assist in distinguishing past from present and rational from irrational thinking rather than to engage in transference interpretation. The computer, the developmental and action model of the program, and the therapist combine with the patient to create a unique form of therapy.

THE TLP AS MEDIATED THERAPEUTIC COMMUNICATION

This chapter will describe a new method of short-term therapy called the Therapeutic Learning Program (TLP). It is an organized and structured, computer-assisted short-term treatment, not computerized psychotherapy. The computer is used as an auxiliary therapist. The program was designed by Interactive Health Systems to make the best use of the computer, the therapist, and the underlying treatment model. The TLP is designed at Interactive Health Systems to be an affordable and effective way of delivering psychotherapy to people who have problems in living.

This program falls into the two categories of computer-aided instruction and mediated therapeutic communication. Computer-aided instruction (CAI) is broadly used in the educational field but has only limited use in the educational counseling field, primarily in career counseling. Heretofore, there have not been any all-purpose CAI short-term therapy programs available for psychotherapists to use with patients although the computer has been used to establish diagnoses, psychological testing, data analysis, and office management.

Some of the advantages of using the computer as a tool for therapists are obvious, that is, standardization, efficiency, cost control, and extraordinary possibilities for data collection. We have found other less obvious advantages. Patients share sensitive information earlier and easier in this program, feel more able to participate with a therapist as a responsible and informed patient, and manifest almost no resistance to treatment. The patients perceive the learning experience as a class even though it is called short-term therapy and is given in a mental health setting.

The Therapeutic Learning Program (TLP) is a 10-session computer course which helps participants define a problem, propose an action solution, and resolve the conflict about taking action. In each session the patient spends about one half hour in an interactive program, receives a printout, and talks to a therapist either individually or in a group setting. The printout is the basis for the discussion with the therapist and focuses the treatment process into a series of decisions which are made by the patient after discussion with the therapist. A typical decision would be the prioritization of problems at the end of the first session in order to work on one problem at a time, and the prioritization of action solutions at the end of the second session in order to focus on a particular action conflict.

The TLP is mediated therapeutic communication that takes place within the context of therapy proper. The mediated communication helps to establish a new kind of direct therapeutic relationship. The TLP is therapy inasmuch as it is conducted by a professional therapist, focuses on the patient exclusively, and has as its goal to remove symptoms by a changed perspective which comes about through clarification and distinction making. It is somewhat different from conventional forms of therapy in that it is short-term rather than prolonged, and that interpretation by the therapist is not through transference interpretations but rather is assistance in distinguishing past from present and rational from irrational thinking.

At the very same time that the TLP is therapy, it is also mediated therapeutic communication because the medium of the computer is interposed to extend the reach of the therapist. The interposed medium affects the patient's relationship to information and to the therapist in ways that will now be discussed.

When the patient is working with the interactive program directly, he or she is really having a private controlled interpersonal relationship with the designer of the program. The program represents the condensation of years of therapeutic experience designed into a very explicit mode and then translated into a computer program. The intelligence of the design-therapist is instantiated in the program and is available to the patient. Since other consultants have contributed to the program, adding their wisdom and experience, the TLP can be said to contain over 100 years of clinical experience. In this sense, the patient is having a phantom interpersonal conversation with a collective clinical other.

The TLP program has been designed to help the patient have a self-reflective experience and, in particular, to create a cleavage plane between a rational contemporary part of the self and an irrational past-history-dominated aspect of the self. The participants in the TLP report that they forget about the program and the computer very quickly because they become so intrigued with their own internal drama. Their emotions are stimulated and they become inward, self-absorbed, and involved in a very intense self-reflective thinking process. In this sense, the person is having a private experience in which the medium is largely obliterated from emotional consciousness. The explicit wisdom of the clinical program designers has essentially vanished. Special programming techniques, particularly the use of patients' favored language patterns, facilitate this self-reflective internal process.

The information that the patient gathers during the course of the interactive program is not information that is used by a therapist for diagnosis nor is it test information; it is self-generated information about the multiple selves coexisting within the larger Self. The information gathered helps the person process the information necessary to complete a unit of adult developmental change.

So far the process from the patient's point of view can be summarized as a phantom *interpersonal* relationship with the program designer leading to an articulated *intrapersonal* dialogue between the facilitory and inhibitory aspects of the self over a decision to take action that represents a new developmental behavior.

When the patient completes the interactive portion of the program at the end of each module, he or she receives a printout which documents everything that was learned in the interactive portion including all of the distinctions between rational and irrational thinking that the person discovered. The format of the printout is straightforward. The skeleton of the printout reinforces the model of learning and allows for the specifics of the individual user. In the printout, the patient's words and choice of language are reflected. The most commonly reported experience from the user is, "That is exactly what I am thinking but I could never have said it more clearly or as exactly." The program and the printout help the patient become more articulate, focused, and clear thinking than he or she could possibly have been independently in the same amount of elapsed time (about 30 minutes). In particular, the distinction between current perceptions and past distortions is clearly made. If it is not totally accurate, it is correctable by simply using a pen or pencil to cross out what is incorrect and substitute what is more correct. This printout is a very important part of the process. Patients frequently refer back to it in between sessions as well as use it as a discussion piece with their therapist.

In this document, the work to be accomplished by patient and therapist is subtly laid out so that the essential activities of the therapeutic relationship are helpfully contained. This serves several purposes. On one hand, patients are helped to think more clearly because they do not have to understand and articulate all that they are thinking but only deal with that which is essential at a particular step in the process. It also gives the patient confidence that he or she can talk intelligently with a trained therapist without feeling overwhelmed by the therapist's education and experience. It helps to democratize the interpersonal relationship and convert the therapist from a potential magical guru to a teacher who can help with a specific learning task.

Because the patient only has to master a specific point in the process at the moment of interaction, the dependence of the patient on the therapist is diminished and his or her self-confidence is increased. This leads to less resistance and more open communication and revelation than would otherwise take place in unmediated communication. For example, a therapist may have spent as little as 15 or 20 minutes with the patient in the first two sessions yet have an almost complete working knowledge of all the things that are bothering the patient, the prioritization of the major issues, the symptoms, the exact statement of the patient's perceptions, the patient's acknowledged inability to cope in specific areas, the ineffective patterns, a choice of multiple action options, ideal areas in which the individual needs to develop, exact action statements, and healthy motives for carrying out the intended action. All this will be on paper and the knowledge will be available to both patient and therapist. It would literally be impossible for this much information to be gathered and shared without the use of the medium, that is, the computer program.

The interpersonal relationship between the patient and the therapist is a different relationship because of the medium. The patient is prepared, less dependent, looking for a different kind of help, and more articulate. The therapist is also different. He or she is face to face with a different kind of patient, has less of a global responsibility, is guided by the focus and the model, has a tool to help achieve some of the insight and clarification work, and has an infinitely greater amount of information available in a recorded and useable fashion than otherwise would be available.

As a consequence of this different relationship there is a clearer exchange of therapeutic communication between the patient and the therapist, a greater opportunity for the patient to receive nonmediated therapeutic communication from people other than the therapist, and there is a greater emphasis on common-sense information processing and learning rather than transference interpretation as the major avenue of insight.

The therapist is a teacher who is relieved of the burdensome role of guru but still achieves the goal of the ideal psychoanalytic communication which is to demonstrate to the patient the domination of their lives by reified internal, object-controlled, irrational patterns.

This process of working on the computer, getting a printout, and having an interpersonal relationship with a therapist is repeated for each of the 10 steps in the process. The patient gets deeper into an intrapersonal dialogue as the modules advance into deeper psychological issues. As the issues become deeper, that is, more emotionally powerful and related to earlier thinking patterns, the patient gets involved in more intense emotionally cathected states of mind. Usually, in conventional unmediated treatment, this leads to a greater dependency on the therapist for guidance. But in the TLP, that does not occur because the patient becomes progressively more skilled in making distinctions about rational and irrational processes and is able to deal with the topics as learning topics without being overwhelmed. As an example of the kinds of issues that are dealt with in the latter half of the program, the question of one's negative self-esteem, which is the weakest and most vulnerable part of the psyche, is the subject matter for the whole second half of the course. When the patients gain a new perspective on these deep fears, they become more independent and more anchored to current time frame and are then ready to leave the course with a greater sense of control.

DESCRIPTION OF THE PROGRAM

The program consists of five two-hour sessions. The TLP may also be delivered in 10 one-hour sessions with or without a group, and daily as well as weekly.

Usually the sessions are one week apart with computer-generated homework. There are 10 steps in the program; at each step the patient is introduced to the concept by the therapist and then works on the computer and personalizes that particular concept. When the patient receives the printout, he or she immediately talks to the therapist about the content of the printout. This is done in group of six to ten patients at a time; the therapist works with each patient individually while the others are listening.

THE SUBJECT MATTER

The subject matter of the TLP is action. Once people have identified action that they intend to do and know that they need to do, why don't they just do it? The answer to that question is simple but not enlightening. The intention to carry out an action is just one force within a field of forces which comes into play when an action is contemplated.

It is probably more accurate to say that the core subject matter of the TLP is the conflict about taking action. The goal of the TLP is to help people think through a specific action conflict to the point where they either decide that the action is unwise and abandon the action or decide that the action is wise and carry it out. With either outcome, deciding against the action intention or carrying it out, the patient will no longer be "stuck."

There are three underlying action-related concepts in the Therapeutic Learning Program. The first is stress. When people are in a situation of stress and are not handling it well, they continue to use ineffective responses. If the stressor continues, they will get progressively more severe stress symptoms. They are stuck. Being in a state of stress, then, can be defined as being unable to respond to current reality with the new behavior that is required. It is a failure of adaptation.

The second concept underlying the Therapeutic Learning Program is the concept of developmental conflict. New behavior required by the stress situation represents an expanded self-definition for the person. The completed action is developmental. The person is stuck in a conflict between the adult part of the self that reads the reality correctly and decides to try out new behavior and some old part that is afraid to change.

The third major concept is volitional conflict. Patients are stuck when they intend to do something and find that they don't carry it out for one reason or another. They are dissatisfied with themselves because they have so little control over their lives. The major portion of the TLP is designed to help people resolve any volitional conflict that is identified in the earlier part of the TLP. This will be described further through descriptions of each of the 10 sessions of the TLP below.

TARGET AUDIENCE

Up to this point the Therapeutic Learning Program has been used in a medical setting, primarily psychiatric clinics and psychiatric hospitals. The program is beginning to be used in stress clinics, weight reduction clinics, wellness programs, and employee assistance programs. The target audience is anyone who has an action conflict to resolve or who has some identified problem in living. Usually, one goes to a mental health clinic because of psychic pain or symptoms. The therapist helps the patient identify and sort out the problems that are causing the symptoms. In wellness settings, people come to learn about themselves and to enhance their positive health habits. Symptom reduction is not the primary motive.

The TLP has been used with all socioeconomic groups and ages ranging from 13 to 80. The problems in living vary from simple frictions at home or at work to severe mental illness that requires hospitalization. When the TLP is used in the healthier end of the spectrum, it tends to be a complete treatment unto itself with over 85 percent of the population not going on to any subsequent treatment immediately following the TLP. When the TLP is used in the hospital population, it serves as an instant treatment plan and a focusing device which enables patient and therapist to communicate more precisely with each other about those areas of concern that the patient has identified as primary. It is part of an overall treatment program.

THE FIRST SESSION OF THE TLP

Either before, or at the beginning of the TLP, the patient is introduced to the program by a therapist who describes the program. The therapist or a clerk will already have entered the patient's name and identification number on a user diskette. The first screen seen by a patient will be the title screen of the first session, for example, "Personal Stress Survey." The patient learns how to use the computer by a self-contained set of directions on the first eight screens. Since the program is menu-driven, the participant primarily has to learn how to go backward and forward with two separate keys and to move the cursor up, down, and sideways by the arrow keys. The "enter" key indicates a choice. This learning process takes five to seven minutes. Even those who have never touched a keyboard before are able to work the program after a simple set of instructions. They are given an option to type in additional items if they do not find what they want in the menus. When they make that choice, they get a separate set of instructions guiding them through the type-in process. It's very important to have a user-friendly beginning. There is an added pay-off for some people who have never used a computer before—they become immediately enamored by their power to control this frightening mechanical monster.

As patients go on through session one, they get a brief definition of stress and are asked to identify one or more areas of stress from a menu that includes family problems, work problems, emotional health, and so on. They will go through a list of events in each of those areas that may be causing them stress. For example, in the area of work, four of the 35 items in that list are as follows:

The stress I feel in my work life has to do with. . . .
—too much pressure at work
—being criticized
—a change in responsibilities
—learning new skills

Following their work on events, their attention is focused on interpersonal stresses. They look at the ways that they feel someone is pressuring them, or not supporting them in some way, or not giving them enough. A few sample items from each of those categories are as follows:

I am. . . .
—not getting enough guidance
—being pressured to be perfect
—not being supported to do things my own way
—being pressured to do too much
—not getting enough communication

Patients may have chosen 20 or 30 stressors in these categories. They are asked to prioritize down to six, at which point feelings are attached to each of the six stressors in a question that would go something like this:

Most of all, the stress of "working under excessive pressure" makes me feel . . . irritable,

from a list of 22 feeling adjectives to choose from.

By this point in the process patients have spent 12 or 13 minutes at the computer and have sorted through a lot of information. Not only have they chosen the stressors from a list, but they have also made discriminations about which items are not really stressors. Often the prioritized list contains items they had not been thinking about explicitly when they came into the program but were reminded of by the menus. The denial process that was at work is easily pierced without the patient having to be confronted by a therapist and without the therapist having to be detective who finds out by omission and implication.

Because of these processes and because the patient is helped by the program to put together a statement out of pieces, the patient becomes very intrigued. An observer begins to see the preoccupation with the program. It is very difficult to interrupt a patient because of the emotional involvement.

Once patients have identified the significant stressors and feelings attendant to those particular stressors, they are asked about how they cope with each of those stressors. If they have identified that they do not know what to do about certain stressors or know what to do and don't do it, then that stressor is elevated to the status of a stress problem. They are then queried about what they are doing that is not working—an "ineffective behavior pattern." In addition they are asked about any other internal conflicts that might be causing stress such as being out of control or losing confidence in themselves in specific ways. At the end of this second section of the program their stress problems are summarized on several screens, such as the example that follows:

> The stress of working under excessive pressure makes me feel irritable. This is complicated by the fact that I am being pressured to be perfect. I have trouble dealing with this stress because I have difficulty expressing my feelings.

This summary statement exactly reflects the patient's choices from a series of menus. The program has done the work of putting it all together into a coherent statement. The statement also reflects the vocabulary of the patient so that the patient "owns" the statement. It is not a didactic statement or an approximation that might be foreign, but it is in his or her vocabulary since they chose both the items and the adjectives which give the items the proper shade of meaning.

In the last part of the first session, the patient is asked to identify stress symptoms, their severity, and their duration. All of this information is reorganized in a summary statement that is printed out in two copies, one of which goes to the therapist and the other of which is retained by the patient.

The patient and the therapist have work tasks to do in order to prepare the patient for the next step in the process. The work is to identify which one of all the stress problems, feelings, and linked ineffective responses listed in the summary is the one that is most important for the patient to work on during the program. Sometimes the answer is self-evident and the therapist and patient need not spend much time together. Usually the therapist uses the information on the printout to take the opportunity to get to know something about the patient if this is the first contact, even though the actual work that needs to be accomplished can be done by the patient alone. At other times, the patient can't decide which one to focus upon. A discussion takes place. The therapist uses clinical knowledge and skills to help determine which one of the stress problems is important to focus upon. In subsequent sessions of the TLP, the psychological work to be done is more complex and the role and importance of the therapist is more prominent. The program is designed so that a specific kind of work needs to be done at each step of the way in sequence. There is a building of concepts and skills necessary for the process to culminate in a decision for or against action. Each session is an interdependent unit and cannot be taken out of order.

The printout is a very important document which will be discussed later. An interesting phenomenon is the denial process. People sometimes look at their printout and say, "That is exactly what I have been thinking and feeling. How did the computer know?" They deny their own participation in answering the questions. Since there are no interpretations or interpolations in the program, the printout is only a reformatting of their exact choices.

A second kind of denial is much more important. Patients may look at the printout and say, "That's not what I said at all," and then look at it for another minute or two and say, "Oh, damn, that's exactly what I did say." A more dramatic example of that is a woman who took the printout and threw it in the closet and didn't open up the closet for a week. At that time, she took out the printout, reread it and said to herself, "I guess I can't get away from this because I wrote it myself. There's no way to deny that this is the truth and this is what I need to do." She was unable to tear it up, or burn it, or destroy it because the printout accurately reflected her view of reality. Since the denial process includes awareness as well as denial, articulation into printed form is in itself an action that makes other actions in the world more likely to occur. The raising of consciousness implies a need to act. Denial is a form of "not knowing in order not to have to act."

SESSIONS II THROUGH X

In the second session of the TLP the locus of control begins to shift. Whereas in the first session the program helped the patient describe the snapshot of stress or "complaints" in life, this session begins to ask a more important question, "What can you do that you are not already doing?" The second major concept of the TLP, the "developmental conflict," emerges in this second session. The first questions the patient is asked in the program is the choice made about the prioritized stress problem. Once that has been identified, a menu comes up identifying ways in which a person could further develop. Three of the 19 items in this list are given as examples below:

> In order to resolve my stress situation, I need to be the kind of person who can . . .
> —communicate to someone in particular
> —take care of tasks more efficiently
> —use thinking abilities.

Of the 2,000 patients that have gone through this program no one has listed less than two or three ways in which they could further develop themselves. The patient is then asked to identify which one would best address the stress problems they identified. In other words, what is it that they know they need to do for themselves that they are not already doing to address the particular stress situation? Once this has been answered, the program takes the high-level developmental goal and helps the patient convert it into specific action items. For example, under the goal of "using thinking abilities," some of the action items might be:

—analyze situations
—evaluate criticism or praise as information about myself
—think through an issue, problem, or idea clearly and thoroughly
—find the right work or career situation to fit my ambitions and talents

The last question asked by the program in this session has to do with motives and reasons. Once patients have identified a goal to be achieved and a specific action item that will address their stress and instantiate that goal, then the program helps them describe all the other reasons why they want to or need to take this action that will give more shape and specificity to the action itself. For example, a person might want to confront someone for a whole variety of reasons including to end a relationship, or to deepen a relationship, or to sort out the truth, and so on. Each of these reasons will have a definite influence on the way the action step is carried out and will add momentum and clarity to the action intention.

After the patient receives the printout, the work of the therapist is to make sure that the action step is do-able, is objectively a relatively safe experience, yet creates conflict and anxiety. The patient knows it is correct, but it is outside his or her normal repertoire of behavior and will therefore be a challenge. The therapist also helps the person put together several different action steps into one conglomerate step or helps the patient mentally rehearse the action so that it is clear, state-able, and do-able. The action step statement is worded on the printout. The patient usually has an interval (a day or a week) to think about the action step and is encouraged to modify or change the action step.

About 50 percent of patients stick with the initial action step and the first stress problem while others discover that there is a more important problem or action to take. They were afraid to state it in the first several sessions but after working the program and thinking about their answer, they have become more bold and open. Often they notice that other people have been getting help from the program's ability to clarify and they want the same results.

The therapist is trained to let the materials do the work in the way just described and not confront or question too vigorously the patient's choices during the first several sessions. In this way the therapist does not incur resistance and the patient is given an opportunity to think things through and break through internal denial tendencies. The patient ends up having more self-respect and more ownership of the problems and the solutions. All of these processes tend to democratize the relationship between the patient and the therapist and convert the potential competitive psychotherapeutic process into an affiliative learning process.

The third session of the TLP begins to probe volitional conflict. The action intention is well-instantiated in the action step and the healthy reasons for doing the action step. At the beginning of this session the patient inputs the action statement into the computer. The question now is, "What is predicted, in terms of obstacles or dangers, that might warrant abandoning the action intention?" In this session the patient explores the most common and obvious obstacle. The action step might affect other people in a way that an important relationship is disturbed. Since many of the action steps are speech acts designed to change or shift an interpersonal relationship, then the image of how the other person will respond and what that means is uppermost in the person's mind. From a psychodynamic point of view, the current objects in real life are often endowed with the attributes and powers of past objects. This is a normative misperception that colors the struggles of everyday relationships. Since the objects in the past were by and large parental and powerful, current others are endowed with implicit veto power if they are at all unhappy about or disturbed by the action intention of the patient.

The program is designed to help patients sort out whether or not they are giving the other person too much power in their mind's eye. This is done by menus in which they predict the response of the other, ask what the worst possible response would be, and then inquire whether this response is likely and bearable. If the response is unlikely to occur, they will have the immediate insight that their fear is unfounded. If it's likely to occur, further queries discover if they are making a thinking error, such as confusing the consequence predicted as a result of the specific action step they wrote down or that same action step done in a provocative or out-of-control way. Oftentimes the consequence anticipated by the other is not the consequence of an imagined productive conversation but is the consequence of an imagined embattled conversation. Once that distinction is made, the patient is asked whether or not they can control themselves sufficiently well to carry out the action step in the productive way rather than in the embattled way. If the answer is yes, then the action step is no longer dangerous. If they feel they cannot control themselves, then the action step is branded as dangerous and it is suggested that they change to a safer step or consult with their therapist. The same kind of maneuvers are used with the issue of bearability.

In this third session the concept of thinking errors has been introduced as they probe the questions of likelihood and bearability. As people discover they have made errors in thinking and have linked those to the attribution of too much power to the other person, they are relieved of a burden and have a much greater sense of options and self-efficacy. The discovery of the thinking errors has made them smarter. Since it was done with the guidance of the machine and not pointed out by another "superior" human being, it is accepted as an insight. After the relationship consequence has been dealt with, the same set of procedures are used for the material consequences.

When patients receive their printout, they have the result of a cost-benefit decision process and all of the thinking errors that they have identified. They can study to gain insights about errors in thinking which might apply to other situations. If their action step has been identified as being too dangerous, they are encouraged to change it and consult with the therapist. If they discover that their danger was fictional (as about 95 percent of the patients going through this part of the program do), they have learned that the sensation of fear is not always an accurate indicator of contemporary real danger. They've learned to sort out the information value of the fear intuition and have gained a new self-reflective capacity which they can remember by referring to the printout.

In session four the same set of principles are applied; obstacles are addressed and sorted out, by the use of thinking errors, to determine whether the predicted obstacles represent contemporary dangers or old dangers projected onto the current screen. The obstacles in the fourth session are the fears of success and failure and ambivalent motives.

In session five the fears of anger and guilt are identified and anger is separated into five different sources each of which implies a different action. For example, if the source of anger is a real unfairness perpetrated upon the patient by someone else, then the action recommendation is confrontation. On the other hand, if the anger is caused by frustration and no one else is responsible for that frustration, then the action recommendation is to not blame others and to deal with the offending causes as best one can. In the area of guilt, true guilt or information reminding the person that they have violated their own contemporary ethical conscience is distinguished from false guilt in which one feels guilty for violating old rules that are no longer contemporary ethical values. Patients discover what those old rules are if their guilt about taking action is false guilt.

By the end of the fifth session most patients will have seen that the fear of taking action is an empty fear and that there is no good contemporary reason not to carry out their healthy action intention. Some will have discovered that their fear was a valid fear and they would have changed or modified their action step until they found an action step that was clearly safe.

It is at this point in the program that the deeper fears of change are introduced with an emphasis on "self-doubt" as an old fiction that erodes self esteem and that is released any time one tries out behavior that is not part of the normal repertoire.

In session six the patient's self-doubts are identified. Session seven demonstrates how these self-doubts are central to feelings of rejection and automatic maladaptive defenses. In session eight the origin of the prioritized self-doubt is explored. Session nine shows how errors in thinking perpetuate this self-doubt by misunderstanding and misinterpretation of current events. The self-doubt is a "conclusion" looking for facts.

In the tenth session patients are guided through a review of all they have learned and they identify what has changed. They are asked to state what they feel they need to continue to work on and what they need professional help with. This case completion work is a document that can be used in patient charts and is the summary of all the complex work in very practical and usable terms. It helps the patient and therapist decide whether or not more treatment is needed and, if so, what the focus of that treatment should be. It also helps the program designers understand the usefulness of specific pathways for specific people. It is the data that will be used in scientific outcome studies.

OVERVIEW OF THE 10 SESSIONS

By the time patients have successfully completed the TLP, they have undergone a perspective transformation. The past "dangers" that seemed real in the beginning have been vaporized on an intellectual level. The feeling of fear related to the action step is now information about an irrational internal state and not information about current dangers. The fear of experimenting with novel behavior won't disappear but will be muted and no longer an obstacle.

Once patients act on their intention (85 percent of the participants act before the course is over), the new perspective is reinforced by the effects of their action. These worst fears didn't occur; usually the act had the effect they wanted; and when the act was not completely successful, it was always partially successful so they made a half-step rather than a full step. But a half step is 10-fold better than no step, that is, being stuck.

The sequence of TLP concepts and psychological work is summarized below:

1. There is a demand in a situation that calls for action.
2. Symptoms and psychic pain are caused by being stuck or blocked in the action intention response to a perceived essential need.
3. Action that is blocked is also development in terms of recovery of function.

4. Action is blocked because it is not clearly seen as the correct thing to do.
    a. Rational conscious cost/benefit decisions may block action.
    b. Irrational fears of development may block action.
5. Surfacing and specifying and distinction making are the processes used to distinguish rational from irrational thinking.
6. When irrational thinking is clearly articulated and the error of that thinking is accepted, the fear diminishes and the intention is more likely to be carried out.
7. The action intent is carried out when the person is convinced it is correct, that is, previous fears are irrational.
8. The adult perspective is progressively enhanced as the person moves closer to action.
9. The course is designed to increase the adult perspective progressively by showing that childhood thinking is contaminating adult decision making.

CONTRIBUTIONS OF THE MAJOR COMPONENTS TO THE TLP

1. *The Computer:* At each step of the way the computer helps translate subvocal thought processes into external, visual, and print which patients can hold on to, talk from, think about, and carry with them during the intervening time between sessions. By presenting menus for each step of the process, the computer helps patients gain an appropriate vocabulary, make discriminations, and transform slippery feelings and thought processes into examinable pieces of information.

2. *The Model:* The developmental and action intention model underlying the program serves to convert information into knowledge by presenting a meaning structure about a narrowly-focused action intention. That is, patients who explore their anger or their guilt or their negative self-esteem do so within the framework of the question, "Why am I afraid to act after I have decided the act is wise and objectively safe?" They do not learn all about guilt or anger or self-esteem as it is related to all aspects of their life but about those current feelings as they are organized by the action question.

Because the model is explicit and because each step is instantiated in the computer program, the participant learns to think about problem resolution in a slow and sequential way. If the patient is confused about any step, the therapist is present to correct the confusion.

3. *The Therapist:* If knowledge is information organized within a meaningful pattern, then wisdom is the addition of judgment to that equation. The therapist's role is to add that judgment at each step in the process and

to contribute the unique human understanding that is beyond the range of the model or the computer program. The therapist helps the individual identify thinking errors and keeps the patient on track. The model and the computer program help the patient bring emotionally-loaded material to the therapist. Each session is a compact and intense emotional experience for the patient and the therapist, but is quite different than either individual therapy or group therapy. The patient feels empowered by the program and less dependent on the therapist so the therapist is not the target of intense positive or negative transference and is seen much more as a facilitator and guide rather than guru or dispenser of scarce information. This phenomenon allows for an easy completion experience at the end of five weeks.

In conclusion, this is just a beginning. The experience with 2000 patients is quite convincing—the computer, properly programmed and used, is an extraordinarily powerful mediating instrument. The same kind of model and techniques can be used for many different types of specialized counseling—AIDS, genetic counseling, compliance with medications, and preventive health practices are but a few of the possibilities. Scientific outcome studies are being started to augment the patient reports. This paper has described the actual process of the Therapeutic Learning Program.

14
Legal and Ethical Implications of Mediated Therapeutic Communication

Susan J. Drucker

Law is based on history and precedent. There is always a period of time between the emergence of a new phenomenon requiring legal guidelines and the development of such guidelines. In between lies uncharted territory. Focusing on crisis lines, on-air therapy, and telephone sex, Drucker outlines this terrain involving the legal and ethical implications of mediated therapeutic communication and points to areas where legal decisions have been and will necessarily be made.

When the topic of the legal and ethical implications of mediated therapeutic communication is raised, it can be expected that lay people will respond with interest and curiosity perhaps, but without any definitive knowledge of the subject. What is not expected and what is much more disconcerting is that practitioners and lawyers with clients engaging in such activities are forced to respond in a similar manner as a result of a dearth of precedent. This is disturbing because the new forms of therapeutic communication do not exist in isolation but, rather, involve many of our oldest and most traditionally recognized legal rights and ethical interests.

Fundamental concerns which are raised within the many varieties of therapeutic communication include issues such as the right to privacy which may conflict with society's right to know. The nature of the relationship created between the party seeking help and the trained helper leads to questions as to the ethical obligations of the helper to keep secret that information revealed in trust. Some legislatures have considered this relationship of sufficient importance to warrant the granting of privilege affording protection from judicially compelled disclosures. When a medium of communication is interposed, will there still be the same kind of relationship and adherence to the standard of protection? There may be a point at which a confrontation may arise between legal reporting requirements and ethical concern for confidentiality. Will the helper in the interaction face legal liability for malpractice or negligence or be subject to discipline by a professional organization for ethical violations based on interpersonal mediated communication? Are the rights implicated different for minors as compared with those of adults in this area? These issues may be addressed from the external perspective of the legal system and professional organizations or the internal perspective of those institutions and individuals involved in the interaction. The scope of this analysis is limited to the external perspective.

Many of these questions have been addressed by legislatures, judicial decisions, and orders but seldom in the unique situation in which mediated communication is used for therapeutic purposes. In some cases the questions have yet to be asked. This chapter explores the questions already asked and answered and those heretofore unasked.

CRISIS-LINE COMMUNICATION

Many issues arise within progams in which the medium of therapeutic communication is the telephone. The crisis hotline is a fairly widespread phenomenon that has been instituted to provide a functional alternative for those who would seek counseling beyond face-to-face services. Many of the crisis-line programs provide services for clients faced with dilemmas ranging from alcoholism, AIDS, domestic violence and rape, to depression and suicide. Organizations operating telephone banks may be staffed by licensed psychologists, social workers, and psychotherapists, all of whom are certified professionals. An additional organizational feature is the presence of volunteer counselors working under the direction of certified professionals. These volunteers receive initial and ongoing training for the position but essentially they are neither licensed nor certified to engage in diagnosis or treatment (Talan, 1985). The legal and ethical nature of the relationship between the caller and the helper may depend upon the status of the helper.

Issues of privacy are fundamentally necessary in health care. Trust has been distinguished as a key characteristic of therapeutic communication (Kreps & Thornton, 1984). In order to establish trust it may be necessary to assure a client that it is safe to reveal personal matters (Barton & Barton, 1984). When an individual entrusts a personal matter to another, it is usually because of a vital need to share. Confidentiality requires the mutual understanding that personal revelations will be used only for the first individual's vital need and will not be made available to others without his or her consent (Grossman, 1978). Confidentiality is thus the ethical obligation of a counselor to a client. This concept was embodied in the moral dicta formulated in the fourth century B.C. by the Pythagoreans in what we call the Hippocratic Oath. The ethical precept of confidentiality remains to this day an essential characteristic of many professional relationships, not only in the medical profession but in the area of legal and journalistic relationships. The Principles of Medical Ethics of the American Medical Association (Section 9) (Perr, 1982) states that a physician may only reveal the confidences entrusted to him in the course of medical attendance if he is required to do so by law or if it is necessary to protect the welfare of the community. The American Psychiatric Association has adopted the same principle in The Principles of Medical Ethics with Annotations Especially Applicable to Psychiatry (1973). A psychiatrist may release confidential information only with the authorization of the patient or under proper legal compulsion. The Lawyer's Code of Professional Responsibility (American Bar Association, 1976) requires a lawyer to preserve confidences and secrets of a client.

In dealing with the crisis hotline the question arises as to the ethical obligation of confidentiality. The distinction between the professionals and the volunteers staffing the telephones may be the determining factor. The behavior of professionals falls within the ambit of professional disciplinary actions. Ethical obligations for professionals then clearly exist. As for volunteers, the confidential nature of the relationship is part of the training. This training, in turn, poses an ethical dilemma of its own. The private nature of telephonic communication is not guaranteed as one aspect of some training programs is the on-line monitoring of conversations between volunteers and callers.

Whether it is the professional or volunteer, confidentiality is often presumed in that the very nature of telephoning has been described as " 'interposed' private communication" (Aronson, 1986). It is rare to find a caller who specifically asks about the confidential nature of the conversation (Response Crisis Hot-Line, 1988). Privacy is an essential element of confidentiality. Privacy and confidentiality are not synonomous with anonymity and may exist in the absence of anonymity, as is the case in most face-to-face therapeutic communication. The telephone, however, offers the opportunity for an anonymity which fosters the sense of the exclusive sharing of intimacies with the counselor and reduces the sense of risk taking by the caller.

There are three situations in which disclosure of information in the area of therapeutic communication may be required: (a) compulsory reporting statutes, (b) duty to warn of dangerous potentials of counselees, and (c) compelled testimony versus testimonial privilege (Reisner, 1985).

COMPULSORY REPORTING STATUTES

Many states have enacted laws which require the reporting of information which might be considered confidential. Matters such as suspected child abuse (New York Social Services Law, Section 413), habitual use of narcotic drugs, and suspected gunshot wounds impose a duty of reporting on health authorities. Constitutional limits upon health reporting requirements have been addressed by the Supreme Court in *H.L. v. Matheson* (1981) which dealt with the constitutionality of requiring that parents be notified of minors seeking abortions. Some of the mandatory reporting statutes specify a wide variety of personnel responsible for reporting. For example, the child abuse reporting requirement of New York State states:

> The following persons and officials are required to report or cause a report to be made in accordance with this title when they have reasonable cause to suspect that a child coming before them in their professional or official capacity is an abused or maltreated child: any physician, surgeon, medical examiner, coroner, dentist, osteopath, optometrist, chiropractor, podiatrist, resident, intern, psychologist, registered nurse, hospital personnel engaged in the admission, examination, care or treatment of persons, a Christian Science practioner, school official, social services worker, day care worker or any other child care or foster care worker, mental health professional, peace officer, police officer or law enforcement official. Failure to report creates criminal liability as a class A misdemeanor and potential civil liability for dangers proximately caused by the failure to report. (New York Social Services Law, Section 420)

Crisis-line professionals such as psychologists and social workers are clearly within the mandated reporting requirements. Volunteers and the crisis counseling agency itself do not fall within the mandatory reporting requirements.

DUTY TO WARN OF DANGEROUS POTENTIAL OF COUNSELEES

A minority of states have adopted the obligation of a therapist to communicate to third parties the known dangerous propensities of a patient (Reisner, 1985). In *Tarasoff v. Regents of the University of California* (1976), an outpatient receiving psychotherapy at the hospital at the University of California at Berkely threatened to kill Tatiana Tarasoff. His therapist determined that his patient was, in fact, planning to kill but negligently failed to warn the victim. The Court ruled that the psychotherapist-patient relationship imposes on the therapist a duty to control the patient and a duty to protect the patient's potential victim. The therapist was found liable in a wrongful death action brought by the victim's parents. In dismissing the need for confidentiality the Court stated: "The protective privilege ends where the public peril begins" (Grossman, 1978). Although no such precedent to warn exists within the realm of telephone crisis counseling, there does appear to be a duty of care owed by professionals. The duty owed by volunteers has once again not been addressed by the courts.

COMPELLED TESTIMONY VERSUS TESTIMONIAL PRIVILEGE

Privilege is a legal issue. The law takes the position that there may be interests that outweigh the client's right to privacy and provides selected safeguards against the government's power to compel disclosure of privileged communication (Perr, 1982). Some of the traditional relationships provided this privileged status include attorney and client, clergyman and penitent, husband and wife, physician and patient. In recent years this privilege has been extended to professions including journalists, accountants, psychotherapists (Reisner, 1985). Mediators in dispute resolution programs have recently been added to this list in some states (Abrams, 1983). Wigmore (1961), the highly influential legal authority, has enunciated the limitations on privilege that provide the basis for the perspective of the legal system:

1. The communication must originate in a confidence that it will not be disclosed.
2. Confidentiality must be essential to the satisfactory maintenance of the relationship.
3. The relation must be one that the community believes should be fostered.
4. The injury to the relationship from disclosure of the communication must be greater than the benefit gained for the correct disposition of the litigation.

When dealing with privileged communication, judicial treatment in this area is clear, if limited. The sole case in point to date in the area of privileged communication and telephone crisis-line communication is State of Florida v. David Gregg decided in the Ninth Judicial Circuit in Florida (Kirkwood, 1983). Three volunteers at a suicide prevention center "We Care Inc." had conversations with Alisa Gregg in the weeks prior to her death. David Gregg, the decedent's husband, failed to take his wife to the hospital or call the police upon finding his wife unconscious from an apparent overdose of pills. He was then tried for manslaughter and was accused of "aiding a self-murder" ("Judge: Suicide Hot-Line," 1983). The state sent notice of taking depositions and attempted to take depositions of the three volunteer counselors from "We Care Inc." The volunteers interposed objections and asserted psychotherapist-patient privilege under Florida Statute 90.503. Judge Lawrence R. Kirkwood entered an order requiring that each volunteer respond to every question regarding any knowledge of this investigation or face contempt of court resulting in possible fine and/or imprisonment (Kirkwood, 1983). The court found that no privilege rested in a volunteer staff with no formal education or training in the field, a staff not authorized to practice medicine, a staff not licensed or certified as psychologists. Their activities did not raise them to any degree required by the privilege granting statute.

The reasoning behind the order entered in the State of Florida v. David Gregg sought to establish whether or not the volunteers qualified for legal privilege and inferred that if the witnesses were authorized to practice medicine or were licensed or certified as psychologists, the statutory requirements for asserting the privilege within the context of this mediated interaction would exist.

An area worthy of exploration in the future rests on precedent in which persons not within statutory privileged relationships themselves act on behalf and under the direction of those granted the privilege. In *United States v. Kovel* (1961), the United States Court of Appeals, Second Circuit addressed the issue of the application of the attorney-client privilege to a nonlawyer employed by a law firm. Kovel, an accountant advising the law firm's client on tax matters, was under the direct supervision of the law partners. He successfully asserted the attorney-client privilege upon receiving a supboena to appear before a grand jury. The opinion in this case clearly establishes that the privilege covers communications to nonlawyer employees with "a menial or ministerial responsibility that involves relating communications to an attorney." In addition, the privilege is granted if the communication is made in confidence for the purpose of obtaining legal advice from the lawyer. In the Gregg order, Judge Kirkwood sought to determine whether the activities of the staff were under the direction of a psychotherapist or psychologist providing diagnosis or treatment. In this case it was found that these professionals were merely administrators of the programs and training. If the organization of a crisis-line making use of volunteers does involve more direct reporting to or collaboration with the professional, these volunteers could be covered by privilege in the future.

The legislature rather than the judiciary may well be the appropriate forum in which to deal with the public policy question of extending testimonial privilege to crisis-line volunteers. An examination of relationships in which the law makes special provisions for confidentiality would suggest this extension. This assertion is further strengthened by an application of Wigmore's postulates with their emphasis on the essential nature of confidentiality in the relationship and the subsequent benefit to the community.

THERAPY ON THE AIR

On-the-air therapy is not new. Phone-in radio talk shows have enjoyed longstanding popularity and have expanded to the point where most markets have at least one station devoted entirely to talk with an emphasis on self-help programs (Snow, 1983). Television programmers are taking the idea further and moving the medium into modern psychiatry (Mirabella, 1987). There are a number of legal and ethical issues that can be raised within this type of programming, but as with the crisis hotline, these issues have not been crystallized by professional organizations or within legal decisions.

Once again, we must look at the nature of the relationship between the caller and the helper and the effect that the nature of the medium interposed will have on the relationship and on the rights and obligations of the parties involved. The expectation of privacy and confidentiality is defined by the public nature of phone-in radio and television programs. The intimacy of the therapeutic interaction is decreased despite some dyadic interaction between caller and helper. The radio talk show conversation is more a public performance than a private and interrelational act (Cathcart & Gumpert, 1983). Therefore, the ethical concerns for confidentiality and the legal concerns for privilege have been altered by the circumstances of the interaction.

In the traditional face-to-face therapeutic communication the patient discloses private information with the reasonable reliance that it will not be revealed. The patient reveals information that is not intended for public disclosure. Confidentiality even in group therapy has become an issue (Mellinger, 1984). Some groups now utilize contractual agreements among group members imposing breach of contract or tort liability against individual members found violating group confidentiality. It has been established that if a "casual third party" is present during privileged communications, the patient is presumed not to have intended that the information remain confidential (Reisner, 1985). When extending such reasoning to on-air therapeutic communication, the same presumption can be made. There is an alteration of the expectation of confidentiality and of privacy which in face-to-face situations would create ethical obligation and legal testimonial privilege. Dick Clark Productions which produces "Getting in Touch," a television program featuring psychiatrist Dr. David Viscott, has a phone screening of all callers who will be put through on the air. Such callers have to sign a mandatory release form before the program airs. This is express consent which not only serves the function served by all other television releases, but which also further removes the appearance of confidentiality.

The ethics of on-air therapy have been questioned (Mirabella, 1987). The American Psychological Association takes a position against on-air therapy and diagnosis. Principle 4k of the Ethical Principles of Psychologists of 1981 states that therapy and diagnosis are reserved for professional psychologist relationships. According to Dr. David Mills, director of Ethics of the American Psychological Association, it is important to make the distinction between on-air therapy and advice. The former is an ethical violation (Mills, 1988). There have been a few rare cases in which on-air therapy has been found to reach the level of an ethical violation by a licensed psychologist. The pivotal distinction is that advice by psychologists is permitted. Advice has been distinguished by its educational rather than prescriptive nature. Listing alternatives rather than solving problems and giving direction will not breach the ethics of this group of professionals.

In evaluating some of the ethical and legal obligations stemming from the relationship between the on-air helper and the caller, one must consider the nature of the media involved. Norma Romeo, operations supervisor of NBC Talk-Net in New York City, states, "The host is a psychiatrist, but that is not what he does on the air. There is no diagnosis, no prescription, no pretense of solving problems or drawing conclusions." On-air therapists talk to selected callers whose calls are screened. Since this is an entertainment medium, calls from the distraught, suicidal, and chronic depressives are not put on the air (Romeo, 1988). Critics note that such programs reduce serious problems into entertainment and, due to time constraints, offer only quick fixes (Mirabella, 1987). The policies set by the networks and production companies reflect the notion that what is being provided is entertainment rather than therapy. Legal departments and standards and practices departments have policies on ethics and legalities which evidence treatment of these programs as additional formats of radio or television programming rather than as vehicles for therapy. They do not acknowledge addressing the issue of confidentiality, of privacy, of mandated reporting. Internal regulations reflect an awareness of, rather than a preoccupation with, external liability.

REGULATION OF TELEPHONE SEX

Dial-a-porn or telephone sex has become big business. The name relates to two types of services; one is a dial-it service which is a prerecorded message without the intervention of a live operator. The second type of telephone sex service entails reaching a live operator who engages the caller in conversation. This type of mediated therapeutic interaction is a recent arrival on the call-in scene, with services launched in 1983. The crisis hotline and on-the-air therapy have been in service for a far longer period of time, yet ethical and legal considerations have been addressed for the most part by precedents in nonmediated situations. This may stem from the perception that these services are merely functional alternatives to, rather than departures from, existing therapeutic communication opportunities. However, in the case of telephone sex services there is a plethora of legislative, administrative, judicial, and private activity and debate concerning the ethical and legal issues involved. Those within the legal system and those involved in professional ethical procedures may perceive their activity as necessary when faced with a new service whose function is ambiguous. Telephone sex could be a means of self-fulfillment; it could be a means of free expression; it could be pure entertainment. What telephone sex is rarely thought to be is therapeutic.

The legal issues were joined early on. As soon as the first dial-a-porn number went into effect in New York City, sponsored by Car-Bon Publishers, Inc. and High Society Magazine, Inc., public concern was aroused by the availability of this service to minors (Cleary, 1985). In March 1983 a formal complaint was filed with the Federal Communications Commission charging that the New York Telephone Company was in violation of the Communications Act of 1934 (Section 223) which created criminal penalties for knowingly permitting a telephone under its control to be used for obscene, lewd, lascivious, filthy, or indecent calls (*In re Peter F. Cohalan and the County of Suffolk, New York,* 1983). The Federal Communications Commission referred this case to the Department of Justice which chose not to prosecute the New York Telephone Company and suggested the appropriate remedy should emanate from an administrative decision. The topic clearly raised sensitive First Amendment issues (Cleary, 1985).

Section 223, a 1968 amendment to the Federal Communications Act of 1934, was originally designed for "obscene, abusive, or harassing telephone calls" involuntarily received, rather than for sexually explicit communication solicited voluntarily (Public Law 90-299, Sec. 1, 82, 1968). In December 1983 a new version of Section 223 was signed into law in response to the dial-a-porn controversy. Now prohibited are (a) only "obscene or indecent" speech, (b) only transmissions to persons under 18 years of age, and (c) only speech made "for commercial purposes." Criminal, civil, administrative and injunctive sanctions may be used for enforcement (47 U.S.C.A. Section 223 (b) (1) (A)).

This amendment further requires that the Federal Communications Commission promulgate procedures by which potential defendants could screen underage callers (129 Cong. Rec. H 9356). The Federal Communications Commission response came in the form of regulations which confined dial-a-porn services to the hours of 9:00 P.M. to 8:00 A.M. Eastern Time.

In 1984 the Court of Appeals for the Second Circuit ruled that these Federal Communications Commission screening regulations were unconstitutional (*Carlin Communications, Inc. v. FCC,* 1984). The time restriction was interpreted as content- based regulation of speech. The regulation of message content is viewed with skepticism by courts reviewing free speech cases. "The FCC has failed adequately to demonstrate that the regulatory scheme is well tailored to its ends or that those ends could not be met by less drastic means" (*Carlin Communications, Inc. v. FCC*, 1984, p. 121).

In 1985, the Federal Communications Commission attempted to restrict children's access to "dial-a-porn" lines through the sanctioned use of access codes and/or credit cards for adults seeking such services (Second Report and Order, 1985). The Second Circuit set aside the access code regulations in a decision limited to a case involving areas served by the New York Telephone Company. The court said that the commission had not adequately considered blocking messages (Carlin Communications Inc. v. FCC, 1986).

The nature of the audience is the fundamental attribute of culpability under present law in the area of telephone sex. The emphasis on the audience is in marked contrast to the focus on the helper in evaluating culpability in crisis counseling and on-air therapy. Free speech and privacy rights of the telephone sex audience may conflict with current legislation. The problem is that the audience is nonsegregable. The rights of adults are distinguished from the rights of children but the telephonic audience is not readily distinguished into such discrete categories by the recipient of the call. Adults have a First Amendment right to free speech that exceeds that of minors. In *Stanley v. Georgia* (1969) the Supreme Court upheld an individual's right to private possession and enjoyment of obscenity in one's home.

Minors are presumed to have less capacity for individual choice, which is the presupposition for First Amendment guarantees (*Ginsberg v. N.Y.*, 1968). The authority to choose on behalf of a minor lies initially with the parent. The state may intervene either to lend support to parental choices or to protect the interests of the minor (Cleary, 1985). The Supreme Court has acknowledged that the minor has a right to privacy but the primary focus has been on the right to contraception and procreation rather than on obscenity issues (*Bellotti v. Baird*, 1979). For material that is not obscene as to minors, or indecent, the First Amendment protects minors against state efforts to limit access. However, to date, there is no authority supporting a right to privacy which would prevent parental or state interference with the access of minors to obscene or indecent material.

Section 223 may therefore raise constitutional problems. Further, the statutory language regulates both protected and unprotected communication. It also stands as a prohibition against the availability of "obscene" or "indecent" communication which extends to those under 18 years old who have parental consent. For these reasons, the statue may be on its face overbroad (Cleary, 1985).

Violations of Section 223 of the Federal Communications Act are distinguished between the sponsor of the dial-a-porn service who "knowingly" provides such service to persons under 18 years of age and those who "intentionally" provide such service (47 U.S.C.A. 223 (b)(1) & (b) (3). A "knowing" violation involves a sponsor aware that some callers are under 18 without being able to identify specific callers. A higher level of culpability emerges from the additional knowledge that a specific caller is under 18 years of age. This is an "intentional" violation which produces further penalty.

Section 223 of the Federal Communications Act was once again amended in April 1988. The current version removes the defense that the defendant restricted access to persons 18 years or older. The law's prohibitions apply to those who "knowingly" by means of telephone make or permit a telephone facility under such person's control to make (1) an "obscene or indecent" speech, and (2) "for commercial purposes" (Public Law 100-297, Section. 6101, 1988). Therefore, the scope of the law has been broadened to prohibit "dial-a-porn" services to consenting adults as well as children. The statute covers *interstate and foreign* telephone messages and local phone sex services that can be reached over long distance lines. (On June 23, 1989, the United States Supreme Court unanimously declared this law unconstitutional as only obscene but not indecent messages may be outlawed (Sable Communications of California Inc. v. FCC, 1989).)

Current interpretation of the statue prohibits "obscene" or "indecent" speech as these concepts were set forth by the United States Supreme Court. "Obscenity" has been defined in accordance with the three-legged test established in *Miller v. California* (1973). It is that which depicts or describes in a patently offensive way sexual conduct specifically defined by applicable state law so that an average person applying contemporary community standards would find that the work, taken as a whole, lacks serious literary, artistic, political, or scientific value. "Indecency," as articulated in *FCC v. Pacifica Foundation* (1978), is "language that describes in terms patently offensive as measured by contemporary community standards for the broadcast medium, sexual or excretory activities and organs, at times of the day when there is a reasonable risk children may be in the audience." To date, while the definition of "obscenity" has remained static, recent reinterpretations by the Federal Communications Commission of its indecency standard may result in changes in the application of this standard to section 223. An April 1987 ruling by the Commission stated that repetitive use of specific sexual or excretory words or phrases is not an absolute requirement for a finding of indecency in the broadcast context (Text of FCC, 1987). Might this revised standard be extended to telephonic communication?

There has been action in the private sector as well as in the public sector in the area of regulation of dial-a-porn services making use of "976" re-

corded dial-it information services. In the California Brian T. case two minor children, their parents, and two antipornography organizations
brought suit against Pacific Bell and some of its dial-a-porn information
providers. A California Superior Court Judge refused to issue an injunction
barring the distribution of dial-a-porn information. He based his decision
on First Amendment restrictions on prior restraint and ruled that the
proper forum for such a request was the California Public Utilities Commission ("No injunction," 1987).

A striking feature of the dial-a-porn issue is that even some ethical concerns of parties involved have taken on legal overtones. Telephone companies can refuse to grant or choose to rescind dial-a-porn exchanges. In
Carlin Communications Inc. v. Mountain States Telephone & Telegraph Co.
(1987), the Ninth U.S. Circuit Court of Appeals ruled that, while a state
may not censor telephone message content without a prior obscenity determination, a private party may. Mountain Bell, a telephone company
serving seven Western states, was deemed a private party despite its public
utility status. The telephone company sought to rescind the dial-a-porn
exchange under a threat of prosecution for allowing such service ("Phone
Company may ban," 1987). This supports a 1986 ruling in a similar case
involving Southern Bell Telephone & Telegraph (*Carlin Communications
Inc. v. Southern Bell Telephone & Telegraph Co.*, 1986).

In an effort to balance the legal rights and moral interests of callers and
dial-a-porn service sponsors, one solution has been to offer a "blocking"
service. The California Public Utilities Commission offers customers the opportunity to have an adjustment made which makes callers from a particular line unable to reach dial-it services ("No injunction," 1987).

CONCLUSION

Many legal and ethical questions remain unanswered with respect to mediated therapeutic communication. In delving into the unique issues raised
by these mediated interpersonal relationships, it becomes evident that the
traditional parameters of legal inquiry should be expanded. A comprehen-
sive evaluation of the rights, duties, and liabities produced by interaction
via contemporary electronic media requires an understanding of the relationship of the participants to the interposed medium.

The parameters for evaluation of reporting responsibilites, confidentiality, privacy, and free speech are currently defined by (a) the nature of the
professional relationship, (b) the nature of the disclosure, (c) the age of
participants, and (d) media differences.

The role played by the medium of communication involved has been
acknowledged. If the interposed medium is considered in telephone sex,

can it be ignored in on-air therapy and crisis-line counseling? If the medium interposed is ignored in one form of mediated therapeutic communication, should it be stressed in another? Future consideration of appropriate legal and ethical standards requires a more consistent recognition of the media variable.

REFERENCES

Abrams, R. (1983, December 30). Opn. No. F 83–17. Opinions of the Attorney General. New York State.

American Bar Association Code of Professional Responsibility With Amendments to February 17, 1976.

Aronson, S. (1986). The sociology of the telephone. In G. Gumpert & R. Cathcart (Eds.), *Intermedia: Interpersonal communication in a media world* (pp. 300–310). New York: Oxford University Press.

Barton, W., & Barton, G. (1984). *Ethics and law in mental health administration.* U.S.: Author.

Bellotti v. Baird, 443 U.S. 622 (1979).

California commission orders '976' blocking (1987, December 14). *Communications Week.*

Carlin Communications, Inc. v. FCC, 787 F.2d 846 (2d Cir. 1986).

Carlin Communications, Inc. v. FCC, 749 F.2d 113 (2d Cir. 1984).

Carlin Communications, Inc. v. Mountain States Telephone & Telegraph Co, 827 F.2d 1291 (9th Cir. 1987)

Carlin Communications, Inc. v. Southern Bell Telephone & Telegraph Co., 802 F.2d 1352 (11th Cir. 1986).

Cathcart, R., & Gumpert, G. (1983, August). Mediated interpersonal communication: Toward a new typology. *Quarterly Journal of Speech, 69,* 267–277.

Cleary, J. (1985). Telephone pornography: First amendment constraints on shielding children from dial-a-porn. *Harvard Journal on Legislation, 22:441,* 503–547.

Congressional Record 129, H 9356.

FCC v. Pacifica Foundation, 438 U.S. 726 (1978).

Ginsberg v. New York, 390 U.S. 629 (1968).

Grossman, M. (1978). Confidentiality: The right to privacy versus the right to know. In W. E. Barton & C. J. Sanborn (Eds.), *Law and the mental health professions: Friction & the interface* (pp. 137–181). New York: International Universities Press, Inc.

H. L. v. Matheson, 450 U.S. 398 (1981)

In re Peter F. Cohalan and the County of Suffolk, New York v. New York Telephone Company, FCC File No. E-83-14 (1983, March 31).

Judge: Suicide hot-line calls not privileged. (1983, March 10). *Associated Press.*

Kirkwood, L. R. (1983, February 17). Order granting state's motion to enforce state investigative subpoena in State of Florida v. David Glenn Gregg.

Kreps, G., & Thornton, B. C. (1984). *Health communication: Theory and practice.* New York: Longman.

Mellinger, J. (1984). Confidentiality in group therapy. In E. J. Hunter & D. B. Hunter (Eds.), *Professional ethics and law in the health sciences: Issues & dilemmas.* Malabar, FL: Robert E. Krieger.

Miller v. California, 413 U.S. 15 (1973).

Mills, D. (1988, January). Interview.

Mirabella, A. (1987, October 25). Here to help. *Daily News*, p. 15.

New York Social Services Law Section 413 & 420.

No injunction in dial-a-porn case. (1987, December 14). *Communications Week*, p. 6.

Perr, I. N. (1982). Privacy, privileged communications, and confidentiality. In R. Rosner (Ed.), *Critical issues in American psychiatry & the law* (pp. 263–288). Springfield, Ill.: Thomas.

Phone co. may ban dial-a-porn. (1987, September 28). *National Law Journal*, p. 33.

Principles of Medical Ethics With Annotations Especially Applicable to Psychiatry. (1973). Washington, DC: American Psychiatric Association.

Public Law 100-297-April 28, 1988, Part B-Prohibition of Dial-a-Porn, Sec. 6101. Amendment to the Communications Act of 1934.

Public Law 90-299 Sec. 1, 82 (1968, May 3). *Stat. 112.*

Reisner, R. (1985). *Law and the mental health system: Civil and criminal aspects.* St. Paul, MN: West.

Response Crisis Hot-Line. (1988, January 5). Interview.

Romeo, N. (1988, January). Interview.

Sable Communications of California Inc. v. FCC, No. 88–525 (June 23, 1989).

Second Report and Order, 50 Fed. Reg. 42, 699 (1985).

Snow, R., (1983). *Creating media culture.* Beverly Hills, CA: Sage.

Stanley v. Georgia, 349 U.S. 557 (1969).

Talan, J., (1985, March 10). New help in dealing with suicide. *The New York Times*, sec. 11, p. 14.

Tarasoff v. Regents of the University of California, 17 Cal. 3d 425 (1976).

Text of the FCC's radio indecency decision. (1987, May 4). *Electronic Media*, p. 36.

47 U.S.C.A. sec. 223.

United States v. Kovel, 296 F2d 918 (2d Cir. 1961).

Wigmore, J. H. (1961). *Evidence in trials at common law.* Boston: Little, Brown.

15

The Electronic Church as Therapeutic Community

Stewart M. Hoover

The last two chapters in this volume move beyond the interactive varieties of mediated therapeutic communication to analyze two other instances in which the medium of television plays a major therapeutic role. The first of these is an examination of televangelism. Here Hoover suggests that, beyond evangelism, delivering ''therapy'' or serving a therapeutic function is a central characteristic of the justification and appeal of religious broadcasting.

Recent decades have seen a remarkable increase in interest in personal, physical, and psychological development. Various therapies—Eastern mysticism, Rogerian psychoanalysis, Dianetics, Transactional Analysis, EST, and many others—have emerged, found currency, and in some cases, faded from view. Without passing judgment on either the efficacy or legitimacy of any of them, it is still possible to see in them a trend. After the social revolution of the 1960s has come the personal revolution of the 1980s. With it have come therapies to help the hurting and bring meaning to lives that for one reason or another lack it.

Some social theorists have seen these developments as the natural evolution of late-stage industrialization. The social consequences of industrial development—dissolution of the traditional, culturally-based social supports of family, community and church—have left a void where individuals traditionally found psychological, emotional, and moral support. Seen almost to be a "culture of therapy" by some (Lasch, 1979; Roof, 1982; Bellah et al., 1985), this movement may or may not be a "culture" but seems to have developed clear culture- and class-related ramifications. Simply put, such therapies are most actively sought out by the urban, professional classes. The stereotype of the now-discredited "yuppie culture" involves, among its package of dimensions, a healthy dose of therapy of both formal and informal kinds. To put the contrast in the world of representative types, Mike and Gloria Spivik would have been much more likely to undertake these therapies than would have Archie and Edith Bunker, and they would have found them more accessible in the first place, due to a variety of social and cultural factors. Admittedly, the professionalization of therapeutic training in the social services (social workers, mental health centers, the clergy) and the widespread interest in self-development, as well as the existence of such informal services as newspaper advice columns and radio call-in programs, has made therapy available to a wider clientele than could afford private psychotherapy. It can be argued that the class connection still holds, however.

There is another implication to the class bias of therapy, to the extent that that bias exists. That is the more cultural perception, common in the fundamentalist and evangelical Christian religious communities, that the therapeutic movement is a usurpation of the traditional role of religion in individual lives. The neo-evangelical critique of "secular humanism" which has grown more strident in the Reagan era carries with it a special condemnation of "self-help." Such individualism, this thinking goes, represents a rejection of the role of faith in the maintenance of mental health (Roof, 1982). Modern therapies cannot substitute and will ultimately fail to satisfy. This perspective on therapy has also helped widen the gulf between these neoconservative religious movements and the more mainstream and liberal Protestant, Catholic, and Jewish groups. The latter have tended to embrace the modern therapeutic movement, integrating its ideals into clergy training as well as educational and social programs. This has, in turn, been taken by the religious right as still further evidence of the bankruptcy of the American religious establishment.

As others have demonstrated, communication is the basis of therapy, and it could be argued that only therapeutic communication is authentic communication. Against the backdrop of the social and cultural meaning of the therapeutic movement, a particularly interesting communication phenomenon presents itself: modern, sophisticated "electronic church" religious broadcasting.

It is now common knowledge that the most prominent of these broadcasters are highly sophisticated (technologically) in their relations with their audiences. The production values of the programs are of commercial broadcast quality. They frequently introduce highly topical issues related to the dimensions of life of concern to therapy: family relations, success, stress, sexuality, frustration, financial difficulties. Probably most significantly, the largest of these ministries entail complex and sophisticated means of direct contact with their audiences. They have telephone banks which viewers can call to ask for prayer and to pledge donations. They maintain extensive direct-mail systems through which they circulate publications and secure funds. They all maintain "direct contact" ministries, including personal appearances by hosts and others, including personal contact with major donors using classic fundraising solicitation techniques (Hoover, 1988). In spite of their roots in conservative evangelicalism, some of them have even begun using the language of therapy. The "700 Club," for instance, calls its phone answerers "counselors." All of them stress that the phones are to be used for prayer and counseling as well as for pledging donations (Hadden & Swann, 1981; Horsfield, 1984).

The whole justification of these ministries is that needs are being met which are not addressed elsewhere (Armstrong, 1978). The mythology of the electronic church revolves around powerful anecdotes of individuals in need who have been "helped."If these individuals are well-known otherwise—celebrities—then the anecdotes carry added power by confirming that the claims of the electronic church's worldview are broad enough to effect even the secular establishment. An example is the following account of the salvation of Ephrem Zimbalist, Jr. by the "700 Club" as reported by a viewer of that program:

> I heard him speak, and he said he had everything in the world [but] that he had a real emptiness inside. So one night he just flipped the dial until he saw the "700 Club." . . . He couldn't sleep [and] he said he laughed his head off. He thought this was funny, these Christians and all. And he watched the next night and said "Just listen to this guy, I can't believe what he is saying!" and so became addicted and said he had to know more, and gradually he became aware that Pat Robertson was speaking to him. (Hoover, 1988)

This type of account, while relatively rare (compared with the total pool of celebrities available for salvation and with the total number of people who view these programs), helps undergird the image of broadcasting as a powerful tool not only of evangelism, but also of therapy. Common people are not immune, and their striking stories add to the perception. One viewer who had such an experience reports it this way:

> I was watching it [the program] on Christmas Eve and I had an experience, and then I just started watching it all the time. . . . I had seen it before, but I had never really followed it. My hand had just hit the [remote control] button and they were there saying the "sinner's prayer." It was a mistake, really, I hadn't planned on watching it, and suddenly I was on my knees, praying along with it. I must have passed out or something, because suddenly I was crying. I just sat there and cried for fifteen minutes, and then I found myself sitting there talking to them on the telephone. . . . I didn't even know what had happened. The lady on the phone . . . explained to me that I had given my life to Christ and that I was now a new person. I was healed of everything, in an instant. I was healed of smoking cigarettes, alcohol, drinking, in a matter of seconds, it went away, just like that. . . . (Hoover, 1988)

Far more common among viewers of these programs is an experience more consistent with conventional therapy or counseling. One viewer of the "700 Club" recalls that viewing of the program helped her through a

THE ELECTRONIC CHURCH 217

period of personal crisis brought on by the death of her son. She had been watching the program for some time when she was finally moved to action.

> I got down on my knees and prayed with Pat, the "sinner's prayer." And God must have known I needed to be prepared because a few months later our son died . . . committed suicide. . . . It makes me cry to talk about it even now. So in those six months I needed a strong faith badly. . . . If I hadn't had God, I wouldn't be here today. He pulls you through, and you just melt, you just can't get away from God, He pulls you through. There's really no way I'd be here today, if it weren't for God. (Hoover, 1988)

The idea that religious broadcasting serves therapeutic ends is thus basic to its most powerful metaphor, that of powerful, transcendent "breaking in" on individual lives, in a one-way, anonymous event. We have also seen that the structures of these institutions entail mechanisms whereby therapeutic communication of a more mundane sort (via mail, telephone, interpersonal contact) could take place.

We know, as a result of viewer accounts, that these programs are able to deliver therapy, of a kind, to at least some of their viewers, and that this function is an important, central characteristic of their justification and appeal. Does this therapeutic effect, though, form the core of their salience for all viewers? That is, do we explain their appeal by knowing that they can provide direct services of help and care to needy viewers? To answer this question, we must first consider who these viewers are, in general, their relationship to the programs they view, their reasons for viewing, and what gratifications, saliencies, and pleasures they might derive from viewing. In sum: Who is watching and how do these programs work for them? Only then can we understand how these ministries might or might not be therapeutic for their audiences at large.

A good deal of research has been devoted to charting the audience for these programs. The issue of the actual size of the audience for religion has been a matter of some controversy. Electronic Church broadcasters and their proponents have encouraged very large estimates of total audience (Armstrong, 1978; Clark & Virts, 1985). Critics have called for smaller estimates (Fore, 1975). Empirical studies have tended to support a smaller total audience size, usually based on ratings data (Hadden & Swann, 1981; Martin, 1981; Gerbner et al., 1984; Hoover, 1987). Perhaps surprisingly, reporting that one views religious television seems to be a socially desirable behavior for most Americans, who are, after all, rather religious when compared to citizens of the other developed democracies of the West (Hoover, 1987).

The demographic composition of the religious television audience is fairly well known. Viewers tend to be older, lower income, and less educated than their nonviewing cohorts. Women view in greater percentages than men, nonwhites are more likely than whites to view, people in the traditional "Bible Belt" areas view in somewhat greater numbers than those who live in the urban areas of the Northeast and far West (Johnstone, 1971; Buddenbaum, 1981; Gerbner et al., 1984).

In-depth studies have revealed the characteristics of the audiences of the most prominent of these programs which would speak to our central interests here (Bourgault, 1985; Hoover, 1985). Not all viewers of these programs fit the same profile, according to the quantitative studies above and a study of families who are members of the "700 Club" (Hoover, 1988). Most had always been evangelical or "born again" Christians, for instance, and were long past the point of striking commitment which befell Ephrem Zimbalist. A minority, to be sure, were not from evangelical or even Christian backgrounds (there are Jewish viewers, for instance), and many of these seemed to have been, in fact, drawn to the program out of severe personal crisis. The therapeutic aspects of these programs and their services are most obvious for the latter group, as we have seen. But what of the former, larger group, those who seem to be attracted to the programs out of their own basic evangelical or fundamentalist leanings?

The electronic church is part of a wider institutional framework. American evangelicalism has always been typified by an antiinstitutional, independent, antistructural organization based on a virulent critique of establishment religion (Marsden, 1984). The "neo-evangelicalism" of the late 1970s and early 1980s came to prominence through concerted efforts of a new network which brought together previously disparate groups into a new consensus intended to press its social agenda through sophisticated political organization and activity.

The network of evangelical church and parachurch organizations is more extensive than often recognized. Besides the denominations and independent congregations which ally themselves with the movement, there are a large number of parachurch agencies which pursue the same goals. There are record companies, publishing houses, service clubs, foreign mission projects, lobbying organizations, schools, colleges, and many commercial enterprises. What this means for the evangelical supporter of the electronic church is that religious broadcasting is only one among many ways, quite aside from formal involvement in church, that he or she might be religiously involved and through which he or she might seek guidance and help.

The evidence would suggest that for the majority of viewers of the electronic church who were evangelical before they became involved with these programs, their awareness of, and involvement in the evangelical parachurch serves their needs indirectly rather directly. In the "700 Club" study introduced earlier, some of them rarely, if ever, watched the program themselves (Hoover, 1988). For those who did, their analysis of it suggested that they evaluated it on the basis of how it may serve others—the "needy" ones like Ephrem Zimbalist. To put it bluntly, the primary salience for these people may well be in the sense that they are supporting religious broadcasting for "those out there who really need it," rather than for themselves.

This is important to them because it creates and reinforces the idea that the evangelical or fundamentalist faith once so marginal to society (as was the case in the popular repudiation following the Scopes trial early in this century) is now coming to a place of centrality for more and more people. The social and cultural significance of this belief in the broad appeal and penetration of evangelicalism is based in an important historical dimension of the Christian Fundamentalist world-view. It has, throughout the twentieth century, been a world-view confined to a distinct minority of the population. The pluralism brought on by successive waves of immigration, first from Europe and then from Asia, and now increasingly from Latin America and East Asia, has proven to be a profound challenge to fundamentalism and neo-evangelicalism, which have been rooted in the American native cultures of rural areas and the frontier.

As America has become diverse, the question facing this traditionalist subculture has been whether it is to resist the influences of a pluralistic society, or somehow accommodate to it, or even capture a share of it. For evangelical supporters of the electronic church, these ministries represent the use of a pluralistic, secularized medium (television) to project their world-view into the public sphere. Viewer descriptions of the program "700 Club" contain just this sort of consciousness (Hoover, 1988). This mythology (in the neutral sense of that term) is undoubtedly affirming, even therapeutic, for such viewers. For viewers who are drawn to the program out of direct need—loneliness, health crises, family crises, and so on—the therapy is more direct. For the evangelicals who support the programs merely for their own sake, the help offered to those truly in need justifies the expense and efforts involved.

Pluralism is, however, also an issue as the ministries carry out their direct service to the actually needy—those who may not be evangelical at the outset, but who find help through viewing the electronic church or call its prayer counselors to ask for help. Being on the public medium of television places specific, unique demands on ministries which are based in the particularistic world of evangelicalism or fundamentalism. In describing the training of prayer counselors for the "700 Club," one staff person reflected on the way in which particularism had to yield to pluralistic acceptance of the diversity of a broad, anonymous television audience. Volunteer phone counselors often come to the task with well set particularist, even idiosyncratic, beliefs.

> We are constantly having to say "don't do this" or "don't say that" to them. We don't want them to get on the phone and turn first-time callers off by preaching extreme beliefs to them. (Hoover, 1988)

Among the largely sectarian and particularist beliefs that have been encountered among counselors were that women should not cut their hair or wear makeup; that Christians shouldn't watch movies; that callers' problems are caused by demons; that ill callers are ill because they are "sinners"; that financial prosperity will follow salvation; that healing will always follow salvation; that Catholicism and/or Judaism are "sins"; that "speaking in tongues" is bad; and that immersion baptism is the only acceptable form of that sacrament. Some have been unable to deal with grief, the occult, or homosexuality (Hoover, 1988).

The technological sophistication of the "700 Club" organization's therapeutic ministries is impressive. Phone counselors use computer-coded forms to record the "prayer requests" of callers. Tailor-made letters can be drafted by the computer, based on these requests, with periodic follow-up correspondence. Through direct links with evangelical churches in many communities, phone counselors can arrange for visits by local pastors to callers who want direct, personal contact. Once in the database, callers can be contacted by telephone periodically and offered prayer.

For those who never call, but who just watch, the programs themselves are often structured so that hosts and guests speak directly to the camera, offering reassurance and help to viewers.

It is important to see that "therapy" and "help" are the point of these ministries not just because television, telephone, direct-mail links, and the networks of the parachurch can serve such ends. It is also the case that such therapeutic communication is an important avenue (perhaps the only available one) linking the particularism of the evangelical and fundamentalist community with the pluralism of the wider society. Everyone hurts: Jew, Gentile, black, white, rich, poor, powerful, powerless.

This reality received a penultimate statement in the midst of Pat Robertson's candidacy for the Republican Presidential nomination. In the fall of 1987, it surfaced that his first child had been conceived out of wedlock. This fact was thought by members of the press to be significant and potentially harmful to his standing with his natural constituency—the conservative and moralist evangelical community. Robertson turned the problem to his advantage, at least for his supporters, by calling up the claim that "hurting"—being in need of help—is the great leveler of modern, pluralistic America.

> We're proving that I am a human being, and I think the American people need to understand that I am a human being. The second thing the American

people need to understand that I have hurt just like they have hurt. If they are looking for a President who understands where they hurt inside and there are millions of hurting people in America. I am somebody who understands where they are coming from. . . . This won't be a problem for my supporters, they understand forgiveness" (*91 Report*, WHYY-FM, October 8, 1987).

We can stipulate that some caring, some therapy, some helpful communication takes place through the sophisticated systems of the modern electronic church. The significance of its therapies derive not only from its direct services, however. Therapy—helping the hurting—forms the basis of its justification to its viewers, to the broadcasting industry, and to the wider society. But its therapies also allow for a fusion of formerly disparate visions of public life.

The desire of modern evangelism to move into the mainstream places it in tension with its particularist roots. Modern means of communication allow it to project itself into the pluralistic, anonymous, public realm. The powerful idea that, in doing so, it brings help to the hurting provides an important gratification for its already-committed followers and supporters. It further allows a pluralistic society to be addressed on a common ground: the universal reality of individual, personal need for "help." How much can be built on that common ground before the competing claims within that society form a challenge to the world-view of the electronic church is the central question.

REFERENCES

Armstrong, B. (1978). *The electric church.* Nashville: Thomas Nelson.

Bellah, R., Madsen, R., Sullivan, W., Swidler, A., & Tipton, S. (1985). *Habits of the heart.* Berkeley: University of California Press.

Bourgault, L. (1985, Winter). The 'PTL Club' and protestant viewers: An ethnographic study. *Journal of Communication, 35*(1), 132–148.

Buddenbaum, J. (1981, Summer). Characteristics of the media-related needs of the audience for religious TV. *Journalism Quarterly, 58,* 266–272.

Clark, D., & Virts, P. (1985). *Religious television audience: A new development in measuring audience size.* Paper delivered to the Society for the Scientific Study of Religion, Savannah, GA.

Fore, W. F. (1975, September 17). Religion on the airwaves: In the public interest? *Christian Century, 92,* 32–38.

Gerbner, G., Gross, L., Hoover, S., Morgan, M., Signorielli, N., Wuthnow, R., & Cotugno, H. (1984). *Religion and television.* New York: Committee on Electronic Church Research.

Hadden, J., & Swann, C. (1981). *Prime-time preachers.* Reading, MA: Addison-Wesley.

Hoover, S. M. (1988). *Mass media religion: The social sources of the electronic church.* Newbury Park, CA: Sage.

Hoover, S. M. (1987). The religious television audience: A question of significance, or size? *Review of Religious Research, 29*(2), 135–151.

Hoover, S. M. (1985). *The 700 Club as Religion and as television: A study of reasons and effects.* PhD dissertation, Tho University of Pennsylvania.

Horsfield, P. (1984). *Religious television: The American experience.* Beverly Hills, CA: Sage.

Johnstone, R. (1971, Winter). Who listens to religious radio broadcasts anymore? *Journal of Broadcasting, 16*, 91–102.

Lasch, C. (1979). *The culture of narcissism.* New York: W. W. Norton.

Marsden, G. (1982). Preachers of paradox: The religious new right in historical perspective. In M. L. Douglas & S. Tipton (Eds.), *Religion and America* (pp. 150–168). Boston: Beacon Press.

Martin, W. (1981, June). The birth of a media myth. *Atlantic Monthly,* pp. 7–16.

Roof, W. C. (1982). America's voluntary establishment: Mainline religion in transition. In M. L. Douglas & S. Tipton (Eds.), *Religion and America* (pp. 130–149). Boston: Beacon Press.

16
Therapeutic Engagement in Mediated Sports

Lawrence A. Wenner

Further expanding the parameters of mediated therapeutic communication beyond the interactive one-to-one relationship, Wenner outlines the therapeutic values associated with mediated sports as well as the relationship between mediated sports and social control.

One might call the person at the receiving end of therapy a patient or client. In mediated sports, that person is called a fan. In therapy, the person controlling the communication is the therapist. In sports communication, that person might be a game announcer or sportswriter. To many, these are unusual parallels to draw. Certainly, other scholars in this volume have looked at settings apart from sport in examining the fundamental character of mediated therapeutic communication. As it is explored in this chapter, the case of mediated sports points to the range of communication activities that may be used to therapeutic ends.

While the therapeutic value of being a sports fan may not be readily apparent, it is apparent that engagement in mass-mediated sports is one of the most common leisure-time activities in the United States. Weekend activities in many households often revolve around the "big game" that will be televised. Reading the sports page is the most frequently cited reason for buying a newspaper (Greendorfer, 1983). These and other forms of mediated sports such as "sportstalk" radio call-in shows, the variant paraphernalia of sports unicommunication(caps, posters, pins, bumper stickers, etc.), and person-computer based sporting activities ranging from Pong to Rotisserie League Baseball point to the vibrancy of sports culture.

Sports culture has its own distinct customs, values, and communicative structures. Perhaps because watching a game on television or reading the sports page may be perceived as benign and frivolous "escapist" activities with little worldly significance, comparatively little research as been directed at its communicative import (cf. Wenner, 1989), let alone its therapeutic value.

There is little in such communication about sport that would be characterized by Watzlawick, Beavin, and Jackson (1967) as "pathological."

Rather communication regarding sport, particularly in its mediated forms, is about pleasure. As the psychologist and communication theorist William Stephenson (1967) would likely have put it, the consumption of mediated sport is linked to "communication-pleasure" not "communication-pain." When consuming mediated sport, one is not so much concerned with accomplishing matters of worldly import or in the garnering of utilitarian information, but rather in entering a world of ritualistic pleasures.

This mediated "sportsworld" (cf. Lipsyte, 1975) is an alternate but parallel world to the world of reality—one that holds the door open for the fan to be led on a guided tour of fantasies, dreams, and achievements in a context that is more orderly, glamourous, and eventful than everyday life. In communicative terms, sports communication is consummatory rather than instrumental (Dewey, 1925), more involved with the fruits of ritual rather than the transmission of information per se (Carey, 1975, 1977).

Similar to the way in which partaking in the rituals of religion function to help one find a sense of place in both the sacred and secular worlds, Novak (1976) has argued that sports produces meaning for today's sports fans. The rituals of fanship offer a "sense of place" in both the "sacred" mediated sportsworld and the "secular" world of reality in ways that undercut Meyrowitz' (1985) arguments that modern media tend to foster "no sense of place" (cf. Beiser, 1967; Edwards, 1973).

The sportsworld offers a place where the fan can be involved in a fantasized extension of self—the hometown team or a favorite local player—being covered in the media. As the fierce competition among emerging metropolitan centers for professional sports franchises demonstrates, sports teams are important to a place's psychic and economic identity. A town does not become "major league" until a major league team resides there. Lever (1983) argues that "sport is one institution that holds together the people in a metropolis and heightens their attachment to the locale" (p. 14). Because of this, teams work in their public relations efforts towards the perception of being "your team." To the degree to which an individual finds pleasure in such identification, some sense of place is found.

As a fan, you are one of many, yet part of an elite group. Such group membership has rewards, not the least of which is that it "legitimizes" an essential part of the ritual—the regular and continued consumption of sports media. The rituals of consumption, themselves pleasurable for the fan, and the information regarding sports ostensibly derived from it, form the basis of a shared sports culture.

Whether the underpinnings of this culture are "real," or "important," or "significant" in any objective sense is not the point. Much in sports communication involves conjecture, hyperbole, and downright wishful thinking—involving the kind of constructions that might be termed "fantasy." But even taken as fantasy, these "stories"of sports culture tend to "chain out" to a "fantasy group" in the audience, thereby becoming part of that group's reality (cf. Bormann, 1972). By sharing in this "vision" one places value in sports culture and finds a "sense of place" in its community.

One's sense of place as a fan serves as the basis for much communicative activity. It allows for a publicly viable partial definition of self that fuels finding one's counterparts in almost any social setting. A sports fan is not alone in this world, and one does not as often make enemies in disagreements about sports as one would with disagreements about politics or religion (cf. Zillmann, Bryant, & Sapolsky, 1979). Put simply, "sportstalk" is about getting along, and to no small end. Stone (1969) has found that people who talk frequently about sports are less alienated, more integrated into their neighborhoods, and have a stronger sense of belonging to the larger city than those who don't talk about sports.

Thus, as Gumpert (1987) suggests, having a place in a media community such as the one sports fans share entails much more than mere exposure. In explicit ways, mediated sports communication provides for what Webber (1964) has called a "community without propinquity"—or modern life's response to finding a little bit of Gemeinschaft in Gesellschaft. In this light, Guttman (1986) points to sports communication as "Geselligkeit," a form of communication that holds together a community's common ground. Lever (1983) contends that "sport promotes communication; it involves people jointly; it provides them with common symbols, a collective identity, and a reason for solidarity" (p. 14).

"Being part of something" can, in itself, be a therapeutic activity. Many therapeutic group activities, such as the ones Gumpert and Fish (see Introduction, this volume) point to, are outwardly aimed at "getting something done." However, their therapeutic value may be as much about "process" as "substance." Group therapy involves activities that promote empathy and understanding and use group processes as a mechanism to do so. Therapeutic engagement in mediated sports works with such "empathetic understandings" as its base. Because of this, it too, can often help to "facilitate communicators' development of personal insight or reorientation" and help "individuals to enhance their effectiveness and satisfaction with their future communication activities"—two characteristics fundamental to therapeutic communication (see Chapter 2).

The discussion that follows looks more carefully at the therapeutic values associated with the mediated communication of sport. The first section will focus on therapeutic values in the fundamental character of play, in communicative play, and in sports spectatorship. Second will be a consideration of the varied forms of mediated interpersonal sports communication and their therapeutic values. Lastly, there will be a discussion of the dialectical nature of therapeutic engagement in mediated sport that is symbolic of the larger dilemma of therapeutic mediated communication and social control.

PLAY, COMMUNICATIVE PLAY, AND SPORTS SPECTATORSHIP

Play is the central concept to understanding the therapeutic values of mediated sports. Often used as the basis of anthropological inquiry into culture (Huizinga, 1938), it has also guided much of the early research in the sociology of sport and leisure (Edwards, 1973). Interpretations of the term "play" vary, but most have linkages to the work of Huizinga (1938) and Callois (1961).

For Huizinga, play is "free," its activities set apart from the seriousness and materialism of day-to-day life, its boundaries clearly demarcated and accentuated by an alternate set of rules and conventions that guide behavior. Callois (1961) adds the view that play's lack of seriousness in real life terms is dictated by "make-believe" that contributes to its relatively unproductive and uncertain nature. These characteristics pertain to therapeutic communication, particularly in its mediated forms.

Play is free in the sense it is a voluntary activity. One may not be "forced" to play; once force is invoked, it takes on the character of work or punishment (Edwards, 1973). For example, the compulsory character that competing in professional sports takes on for the athlete is decidedly not play. Similarly, while one may be compelled (by court order or social pressure) to "go to therapy," once there one must voluntarily "open up" to reap the benefits of the therapeutic communication. Mediated therapeutic communication is always voluntary—one decides to tune in, call in, or log on. Similarly, therapeutic engagement in mediated sports must be voluntary, not compulsory, as the disinterested spouse of any armchair quarterback will gladly tell you.

The separateness of play refers to more than to where it occurs in time and space. Most significant is that the activities of play are taken on in a different "psychic place," and are "bracketed off from the realities with which the individual must contend in his daily life" (Edwards, 1973, p. 46). Consuming mass-mediated sports in a fashion such as in the ritualistic reading of the sports pages transports the fan to a "psychic place" that is decidedly different than consuming the worldly troubles on Page 1. Therapeutic communication—in its mediated and nonmediated forms—depends on getting to a "different place" to provide meaning that is significant for the individual seeking help (Rogers, 1961).

The separateness of play activities does not preclude "role playing" that might have practical "real life" value (Edwards, 1973). However, such "make-believe" role playing is not initially goal-directed on the part of the players even if it turns out later to have real-life applications. As well, in play, one can not "play" one's own real life role, for this transcends the separateness that distinguishes play. Thus, being that "armchair quarterback" allows one to take on a different role, one that may turn out to have applicability to later real life experiences. Role playing is central to therapeutic communication, and much of it entails putting yourself in "someone else's shoes" or "playing yourself"—but a "new yourself" that is guided by behavior modification strategies suggested by the therapist.

When ritualistic play of a specific kind spreads through a culture, the separate "psychic place" of that brand of play develops conventions and implicit rules that govern the activity (Shimanoff, 1980). As is the case with religion, when ritualistic play becomes more formal, so do its rules, and consequently the "seriousness" with which the activity is approached and the significances that are placed upon it. While play may be taken "seriously", it is done so within the confines of its own rules and quite apart from other aspects of daily life.

Therapy, as well, proceeds by an alternate set of rules, fashioned by the therapist but agreed upon by the patient. In mass-mediated sport, the rules are implicitly set by the sports press and agreed to by the fan. In one sense, these communicative rules (cf. Lull, 1980) merely "help" the fan to become a "better" fan. However, therapeutic value comes about because the individual fan is "helped" in developing greater communicative competence (Bostrom, 1984), with the net result of future communication activities becoming both more effective and satisfying (See Chapter 2). In the short run, the therapeutic value of mediated sports communication may be limited—helping the fan comprehend future communication about the sports world. However, because of the centrality of sports to American life, a "sport-competent" communicator—aided and abetted by sports media—is integrated more fully into the larger community over the long haul (Stone, 1969).

That such communicative play has social, as well as personal, value is central to Stephenson's (1967) reasoning in his play theory of mass communication. Even so, in his psychological approach, Stephenson embraces Callois' (1961) view that the aims of play are not in being productive, and as such, the outcomes of play tend to be uncertain. From Stephenson's perspective, the therapeutic value of communicative play grows out of, rather than in spite of, such unproductivity and uncertainty.

For Stephenson (1967), "communication-pleasure" reaches into the realm of fantasy and myth as a subjective explorative activity. This contrasts with a "worklike" orientation—"communication-pain"—that is characterized by a purposive information acquisition strategy that tends to defer gratification until an opinion is crystallized. In communication-pleasure, gratification is immediate and unconstrained by the normative press to accomplish something. In Stephenson's (1967) estimation, there is a "gain of self" that is characterized by a "heightened self-awareness," and "a greater receptivity in the person" (p. 35)—decidedly therapeutic outcomes.

In good part, the fan's experiences with mediated sports can be cast as "communication-pleasure." However, because of a tendency toward a "problem-orientation" (Roberts & Bachen, 1981), communication scientists have more often looked at potentially "troubling" outcomes of sports communication such as the increases in aggression that come out of viewing sports (Bryant & Zillmann, 1983), or the firming of certain political values (authoritarianism, dogmatism) in frequent sports viewers (Prisuta, 1979). However, even in the mainstream research literature, there is growing awareness of the benefits that sports spectatorship may yield.

For example, Zillmann et al. (1979) come to the defense of sport spectatorship, pointing out that "the typical sports fan manages his or her emotions admirably. He or she may yell and stomp the ground but, after the game, he or she usually will be no more vicious than after an exciting movie or stimulating concert" (p. 305). While there is little evidence that the viewing of aggressive sports can be a cathartic experience, aggression facilitation is most pronounced for viewers with hostile inclinations who perceive contests to be aggressive (Bryant & Zillmann, 1983). Because much engagement in the communication of sport takes place far away from the playing field (e.g., reading the sports pages, watching a pregame or half-time show or talking about a game or player), and the fact that not all sports involve hand-to-hand combat, the aggression issue tends to be subsumed under findings that paint a larger, more positive picture of how sports communication functions for the fan.

On a personal level, there is evidence that sports spectatorship can go beyond the mere relief of boredom to reduce tensions. The viewing of non-combatant competitive sports serves to dissipate annoyances and reduce hostile behavior (Bryant & Zillmann, 1983). It has been shown that sports spectatorship can develop the person along a number of fronts, branching out from the social learning of "fairness," (Bandura, 1969, 1971) to the control of what Zillmann et al. (1979) call "heterodox impulsive emotional behavior" (p. 307). Put more simply, we learn to cope in "pro-social" ways with the "agony of defeat." Since we cannot change the course of an ill-fated set of developments on the playing field, we learn to apply "passive inhibition" as we cope with a frustrating situation by waiting for it to change (Zillmann et al., 1979).

Research on sports spectatorship has also looked at the social dynamics of fanship. In being one of least threatening social lubricants, talk about sports promotes a salubrious bonding among fans. As sports is a "low risk topic" (Zillmann et al., 1979), people tend to approach talking about it honestly, while, at the same time "validating" what others may think (cf. Johnson, 1971; Stone, 1969). As well, empathy among fans builds on this honesty and validation as they share perceptions of the trials and tribulations of favored teams. As Kreps (see Chapter 2; Kreps & Thorton, 1984) has pointed out, empathy, honesty, and validation are central to therapeutic communication.

Fans identify not only with each other, but with athletes or teams. Harris (1973) contends that "much of the spectators' involvement can be explained by empathetic kinesthetic understanding they have for the performer and their ability to relate to the performer because of this understanding" (p. 179). In team sports, such "empathic understandings" are extended to the team, with fan becoming part of the "team group" (Sloan, 1979).

Interestingly enough, this identification is not unyielding, but rather is bounded by a fickle "defense mechanism." When teams win, fans "bask" in their "reflected glory;" fans tend to think "we won" while, when the team loses, "they lost" (Cialdini et al., 1976). What is so notable about this is that fans with recently damaged estimates of self-esteem are the most prone to "basking." Thus, "basking" can be a therapeutic strategy, aimed at a temporary bolstering of the public front that may serve until self-esteem has been repaired (Sloan, 1979).

The goodly portion of sports spectatorship takes place in a *mass*-mediated setting, and thus takes on the character of both play and communicative play. Quite clearly, the consumption of *mass*-mediated sports is "free," separated "psychically" from daily life, can involve "role-playing" and while guided by an implicit set of "rules," is not aimed at being productive or increasing the certainty of an outcome. Herein lie many of *mass*-mediated sports' therapeutic values. They tie together a gain of self with a sense of place; the byproduct being increased communicative utility and competence and the development of empathy, understanding, and fairness. The section that follows considers how therapeutic involvement may be characterized in a variety of mediated *interpersonal* sports communication settings.

MEDIATED INTERPERSONAL SPORTS COMMUNICATION

Cathcart and Gumpert (1983) have made a strong case that technology "mediates" a goodly portion of interpersonal communication encounters. In assessing such "mediated interpersonal communication," their larger point is that interpersonal encounters are changed structurally and substantively through mediation. These changes may add to or detract from the therapeutic value of communication between individuals. Following

Cathcart and Gumpert's (1983) typology, the therapeutic potential of four forms of mediated interpersonal sports communication will be considered.

INTERPERSONAL MEDIATED SPORTS COMMUNICATION

The first category in Cathcart and Gumpert's typology, interpersonal mediated communication, has close conceptual similarities to face-to-face communication. However, instead of being "face-to-face," the communication is a "person-to-person" transaction where a "technology is interposed between and is integral to the communicating parties" (Cathcart & Gumpert, 1983, p. 270). Thus, letters and postcards, electronic mail, computer-mediated games, conversations over the telephone and citizen's band or "ham" radio, audio and video cassettes, and even photographs are examples of interpersonal mediated communication. The "technologies" shape the communication because of variances in feedback time, limitations in channel capacity, the distances that may be traversed, and the "rules" that govern usage.

It's difficult to assess the frequency with which communication about sport is a topic in letter writing or conversations over the telephone or CB radio. One must assume that the topic of "sports" comes up occasionally in letter writing and that it is employed much as it is in conversation—as a bonding agent among those who have defined themselves previously as members of the "sports community." Letters traveling over long distances often get reflective writers thinking about distinctions in "sense of place," and thus it seems likely that much "sportswriting" of this type compares how "my team" is faring as opposed to yours. In such comparisons, sports provides a "neutral venue" for "validating communication" between individuals to occur.

The Media Sports Project[1] has collected open-ended interview data that shows that "mobile" fans in our society tend to follow more than one team (within a given sport)—the team in their geographical area and its counterpart located where the person may have grown up or previously spent considerable time. There is some evidence of a "no lose" strategy, one that parallels findings that fans "bask" in the reflected glory of "our" team winning, but limit involvement when "they" lose. Interview data shows that people shift their allegiances from a doomed "home town"

---

[1] The Media Sports Project data reported on here are based on qualitative interview data collected from 60 respondents in Summer 1987 as part of a Media, Sports, and Society seminar directed by the author. The author wishes to thank Frank Gjata, Edwina Lynch, and Mike Yoest for their research assistance and working papers. The interview schedule is available from the author.

team to a "second choice," one that generally heralds from the fan's old "home town." Occurring not only in professional sports team allegiances, such "functional" shifts in loyalties can be seen at the collegiate level as support for one's alma mater gives way to a successful local college team (or vice versa). In not putting "all of their eggs in one basket," sports fans "bias" their conversational patterns towards "communication-pleasure"—the characteristics of which are inherently therapeutic.

Similarly, in phone conversations, "sports" is used as a device through which people may nurture empathies, display honesty, and validate each other's perceptions. As families have been "fractionalized" by the larger trend of social mobility, they often tend to use a regimented pattern of long distance telephone conversations to "enforce" cohesiveness." With its "positive" bias, "sportstalk" may be therapeutic in two contradistinct communication situations. In conversations between family members with "healthy" communicative histories, "sportstalk" adds yet another pleasurable venue to promote empathy, honesty, and validation. In familial relations that have a "pathological" history, the neutrality of sportstalk can provide one of the few "pleasurable meeting places." That meeting place can serve to both limit further pathological damage (by avoiding "certain" topics, and hence, "certain" pathological communication patterns) and serve as a place to "therapeutically" rebuild the relationship.

In business settings, communication about sports is often used as an "ice-breaker" so that business associates may develop the "good will" that is essential to a "mutually-profitable" business relationship. Companies are well known to "wine and dine" clients with beer and hot dogs and seats at the 50-yard line. Similarly, because much business is done long-distance over the telephone, sports "chit-chat" can serve as a prelude to a successful business transaction by developing empathy and trust between business associates that may never or infrequently meet face-to-face. The "gender bias" of business "sportstalk" has tended to limit its therapeutic values only to business*men*. For women, its functionality has been dubious; to "play" on the "old boy's *team*," one must know the "groundrules" of sportstalk, and often one of the groundrules is that it is a male activity.

Computer bulletin boards serve some sports fans in the acquisition of "inside dope" that sets them apart from the "everyday" sports fan. Because "sports trivia" has been institutionalized in the form of "statistics" on the sports pages, anecdotes, and stories within magazines such as *Sports Illustrated,* and in specialized publications like *Basketball Digest,* "inside dope" has received "external validation" from the community of fans. Some fans add to this by crossing over into "fanatic" behavior, engaging in "insider trading" of sports news on bulletin boards. Here, "fan group" cohesiveness is actively increased as in-group values "validate" the activity they are engaged in. Bulletin board participants have an inherent empathy for each other's situation. They must come to trust each other and that the information "posted" on the board is honest and not intentionally deceptive.

Bulletin boards may be used to facilitate the playing of sports games between participants at different locales. For example, Rotisserie League baseball, a game that has recently fascinated die-hard baseball fans, is facilitated by bulletin board transactions (cf. Hirdt, 1986). In the Rotisserie League, individuals "play" manager on teams that are populated by major league players (in their statistical forms). Managers farm a team (having nothing to with the composition of major league teams) by "drafting" players by bulletin board. "Games" are "played" by "players" whose actions are governed by their performance in the "real" big leagues. "Managers" can communicate with other managers and make "deals" for players over the bulletin board as the season progresses.

Rotisserie League baseball, and other "sports" that are mediated in their playing by computer, offer participants a way to "act out" a pleasurable fantasy together. These are "competitive" fantasies, and the communication that takes place is structured around the "rules" of the game as they are shared by its participants. Many of the sports computer games on the market are aimed at children, who are further "socialized" into sports culture by "playing" the games, ostensibly with each other, but with the computer as a "mediator" that sets the "rules" and "game conditions" that they must agree on.

In such "playing"—and afterward—children validate the importance of each others behaviors, tend to be held to "honesty" in that "satisfying" play demands adherence to "rules" set by the computer, and develop empathies for the "dilemmas" one's opponent may be handed by the computer. Interpersonal *mediated* sports communication—whether it is mediated by computer, telephone, or some other technological means—shares with engagement in *mass*-mediated sports the fundamental characteristic of being communication-pleasure. It involves a pleasurable fantasy that may be played out honestly because of little fear of reprisal, and not only is there a gain of self, but because of the relative ease with which someone may grant validation of other people's perceptions regarding sports, it allows for the hurdling of dissimilarities and distances between people so that they may develop empathies that can be extended to other areas (e.g., business, familial relations, broader-based friendships, etc.).

MEDIA-SIMULATED INTERPERSONAL SPORTS COMMUNICATION

Cathcart and Gumpert (1983) distinguish between two forms of media-simulated interpersonal communication: (a) parasocial interactions, and (b) broadcast-teleparticipatory communication. The notion of parasocial interaction, first considered by Horton and Wohl (1956), has developed into a longstanding and integral part of media gratifications research (Wenner, 1985b). The concept shares much with Stephenson's (1967) play theory, and can be considered a well-articulated subset of it.

Para-social interaction hinges on the tendency for people in the audience to develop "quasi-personal" relationships with "people" they get "to know" over time through media exposure to them. The tendency accelerates in situations such as newscasts, sports play-by-play announcing, or stand-up comedy, where the media personality "faces the spectator, uses the mode of direct address, [and] talks as if he were conversing personally and privately" (Horton & Wohl, 1956, p. 215).

Over time, in getting to "know" these "personalities," people may come to think of them as friends. The "media friend" is dependable, always with cheery disposition, and poses no threats to one's shortcomings or self-esteem. Often times people "talk" to their "media friends," offering words of encouragement, joining in on an insider joke, cajoling with them, and even expressing disagreement with their assessments.

Such media-simulated interpersonal relationships develop easily for the fan viewing sports on television. Here, parasocial interaction tends to occur with two types of "media friends": (a) announcers, and (b) players and coaches. The announcer's style is aimed at cultivating the parasocial relationship, drawing even the tentative uninitiated fan into the group with gleeful "welcomes" to "all you fans out there." Even if you are sitting alone in your easy chair, and hadn't thought of yourself as part of a group, you'll be welcomed into it—personally—by the ringleader—your representative—who is both an expert and professional fan.

The Media Sports Project's interview data suggests that fans see their recurring experiences with commentary by game announcers or sportscasters appearing in other contexts (news shows, pregame shows and the like) as both the most liked and least liked aspects of sports programming. Parasocial relationships tend to develop with announcers that are perceived as straightforward, honest, competent, that make the fans feel like they are having a good time, and who tend to offer opinions that agree with those of the fan. Fans may identify with a physical attribute, such as liking John Madden, because "he's like a big teddy bear." The parasocial relationship may also grow because the fan comes to know of and identify with a personal aspect of an announcer's life. For example, one female fan found NBC's Ahmad Rashad her favorite announcer because "he's human," "I like his wife," and "he just had a baby."

Fans also seem to carry on long-term parasocial relationships with announcers they've grown to dislike, but put up with because of an overriding interest in a game or other bit of news. An announcer can become a parasocial "enemy" by being too egotistical or arrogant, attempting to be "cute" or "funny," "rooting" unfairly for one team, and offering either too many opinions or those that the fan disagrees with.

Fans are much more positive about their para-social relations with players. Many Media Sports Project fans look forward to getting "to know the players better as people, not players" and finding out "tidbits on the lives of the athletes." An "appealing personality" or "charisma" or just "seeming cool" may draw the fan to the athlete. Similarly, some fans key on specific attributes such as sportsmanship, "mental abilities," or "tenacity" in their parasocial relationships. There is some evidence mediated sport engender "parasexual relationships" as well. Some fans—primarily female—become "media friends" with players who are who are "physically attractive" or "cute" or who wear "skimpy clothing."

The Media Sports Project data suggests that players seem less likely to become parasocial "enemies" to the fan than announcers. However, this does not preclude the fan from "yelling" at players. Much yelling at players has to do with a "bad play" or "poor sportsmanship," but a goodly amount of fan discontent has to do with personal relationships that have developed with players. For example, while one fan yells at players for "spitting," another yells "at players if they were picked up for doing something stupid the night before."

Parasocial relations with coaches or referees is less personal, more directed at a role, rather than an individual. However, the data does suggest some fans make "media enemies" out of coaches, especially if the team is not doing well.

In total, parasocial involvement in mass-mediated sports is an important ingredient in acting out the ritual of sports consumption. Fans most like competent announcers who treat them with due respect, as equals in the sports community. This is often heard as announcers preface their remarks with "as you fans out there know," to show empathy and "validate" their relationship with the fan. In their television interviews, athletes uphold their part of the parasocial relationship by being sensitive to the "support of all you fans out there." The relationships between fans, and announcers, players, and coaches are fragile. However, the very existence of sport culture or a fan community depends on them being largely empathetic and trustful relationships, and ritualistically, fans, announcers, players, and coaches show that they care about the communicative needs of each other.

Ironically, even yelling at a referee or coach, or being "disgusted" with some "loudmouth, know-it-all" announcer is a pleasurable experience and has therapeutic value. It is an essential part of playing the game of "fan." The therapeutic benefits of the challenging the "media enemy" are residue of the structural attributes of the parasocial situation. The fan gets in the last word, "winning any argument" because the "media enemy" cannot respond to such direct challenges. The fan can bolster self-esteem in "winning" in a friendly rivalry against the media experts.

This dynamic—which plays off of the subcultural value that all sports fans are created equal—is altered in the sports version of "broadcast tele-participatory interaction" (Cathcart & Gumpert, 1983). "Sportstalk" radio call-in shows allow the fan to "act out" a parasocial relationship with the "host," who may be a team's game announcer, local news sportscaster, or unique expert. Frequently, players and coaches will appear as "guests" on these programs, and fans will get to talk with them as well. Thus, preexisting parasocial relationships underlie most radio sportstalk relationships and because of this, their therapeutic values are very much the same.

However, sports call-in shows change the nature of the para- social relationship because the therapeutic value of the "media enemy" relationship breaks down when a fan calls to disagree with a sportstalk host. As Avery and Ellis (1979) note, all parties are aware that the radio talk show host controls the flow and shape of this "ideal interpersonal performance" (Cathcart & Gumpert, 1983, p. 274). Because the conversation forms the basis for the "show," the host must interrupt or cut off a fan who is too persistent, irrational, or out of control.

As well, the "social reality" (cf. Avery & Ellis, 1979) of sportstalk radio may be misunderstood by some fans. In Los Angeles, many of the sports-talk programs are tied to the larger radio station image as the "Dodger station" or the "Laker station." Thus, "Dodger Talk," and "Laker Line" may be "masquerading" as "open sportstalk" while they aim to promote both the team and station. Often under the control of teams, these "closed sportstalk" programs often signal a break from the station's traditional format (e.g., easy-listening, country- western. etc.) rather than being a specialized part of "all-talk" format," a situation where the "social reality" may value "open sportstalk" as a communicative commodity.

Nonetheless, both "open" and "closed" sportstalk radio work are premised on a system of symbols shared with fans (Avery & Ellis, 1979). Calling a sportstalk radio program offers the fan a chance to actively participate in the "mediated sportsworld"—the big leagues of fanship. However, with this "chance" comes "risk." There is danger that host and fan will "mix it up" in pathological communication. However, it more likely that the communication will be therapeutic for the fan because the situation is merely a "stage" for showcasing the "empathetic" understandings that exist between the fan and the "superfan" media personality. Most sportstalk radio conversations are textbook cases of "validating communication" behaviors. Frequently, conversations end with the host thanking the fan for "good ideas" or "perceptive comments." In the main, sportstalk radio is a venue where social reality is shared and the values of the sports community are celebrated.

PERSON-COMPUTER INTERPERSONAL SPORTS COMMUNICATION

Cathcart and Gumpert (1983) make a distinction between "person-computer interpersonal communication" and "interpersonal mediated communication" where the "mediating technology" is a computer. Person-computer interpersonal communication has the person "communicating" with the computer itself rather than with a person at the "other end" of the computer. Of course, in a strict sense, this can never happen because "some person" must program the computer, and the computer merely serves as an extension of the programmer. Nonetheless, it is a form of communication that has become commonplace.

Even though a person may initiate communication, the communication situation is more formally controlled than in other forms of mediated interpersonal communication. Limitations within the computer program govern communicative structure and substance. Cathcart and Gumpert (1983) suggest that human beings compensate for this "loss of control" by anthropomorphizing the computer—giving it human qualities that make it our "computer friend." In person-computer sports communication, these human qualities extend to the computer becoming "athleticized."

Computer sports competition matches the fan with an "athleticized" opponent. In computer-simulated situations, the fan has a chance to "stuff one" over Dr. J, hit a home run against Sandy Koufax in his computer-constructed "best year," fight Jack Dempsey in his prime, or block a game winning field goal attempt against the New York Giants in next year's Super Bowl. All of these situations offer the fan an opportunity to "act out" fantasies of "greatness" by matching skills with a computer that is "acting out" the role of "anthropomorphized athlete" or coach. Of course, one may be called on to play different roles in "competing" in computer sports, but the computer is a fair player, taking on corresponding role so that play may continue.

Person–computer sports communication can be therapeutic in the same way that play in other contexts can be. As a voluntary activity, it is "free." Involving "rules" that govern "role-playing," the activity is separated "psychically" and physically from daily life. By definition, the computer must engage in play fairly and honestly, behave toward you "in a responsible and predictable manner" that indicates trust (see Chapter 2), and the shared communicative activity is premised on validation.

The experiences one has in playing computer-person sports has residual benefit if they are salient to later social communication. One learns of rules and strategies that may enrich other experiences with mediated sports and contribute to communicative competence and satisfaction with future face-to-face interactions. Friends who are "computer–players" will find pleasure in sharing experiences, and "conspire" against computer programs with new strategies. Part of the fun is in the human player learning to compete more successfully with an "idealized perfect opponent." That the computer's skill's will not improve provides an incidental yardstick. In taking pride in improving one's computer game skills one may receive a boost to self-esteem, and that may carry over into satisfying communicative activities apart from sport.

SPORTS UNI-COMMUNICATION

The fourth major category of mediated interpersonal communication, uni-communication (Gumpert, 1975), develops many of its typical characteristics from the sports setting. Uni-communication is "that communication mediated by objects of clothing, adornment, and personal possessions—houses, automobiles, furniture, etc.—which people select and display to communicate to others their status, affiliation, and self-esteem" (Cathcart & Gumpert, 1983, pp. 275–276).

The apparently endless variants of clothing that may be emblazoned with a team name or insignia—caps, T-shirts, jackets, sweatshirts, warm-up gear, "official" jerseys, even sox—are the most important to "sports marketing" because they are mobile billboards. Sports specialty shops such as "Scoreboard" trade exclusively in sports unicommunication. In addition to clothing, one is likely to find coffee cups, highball glasses, beer mugs, shot glasses, placemats, table settings, napkins, ice coolers, thermoses, trash cans, refrigerator magnets, pins, decals, bumper stickers, and most anything else you might think of—all stamped with official looking artwork that identifies it—and its owner—with a team.

Cialdini et al. (1976) suggest that the likelihood of using sports uni-communication is linked to the fate of the fan's team. They have found that when teams win a big game, fans pull their supportive sports uni-communication apparel out of the closet and put it on display—elevating their status by visibly "basking" in the reflected glory of their team's victory. Fans may use sport uni-communication to signify status in other ways. By wearing an expensive "official" team jacket or other piece of clothing, fans make a statement not only about their socio-economic status, but distinguish themselves within the fan group. Conspicuously consumed sports uni-communication makes a statement of commitment to the team that elevates "serious" fan over the casual one.

Uni-communication products "broadcast" an advertising message "sponsored" by a sports organization. As Cathcart and Gumpert (1983) point out, "the persons displaying these messages become part of the campaign as well as part of the transmission system" (p. 277). This point defines the essential nature of fanship, where "being part of something" is a defining issue, and central to the therapeutic value that may be derived. Fanship implicitly involves a never-ending campaign for a team or player. As being out on the campaign trail alone can be likened to banging one's head against the wall—a decidedly pathological act—fans "self-disclose" membership in fan groups to distinguish themselves to kindred souls in the larger community. Uni-communication helps in this regard as publicly displayed membership cards.

Toward this end, fans may distinguish themselves through the "defiant" use of sports uni-communication. A transplanted Bostonian living in Los Angeles may risk life and limb by showing up at a Laker game wearing a Boston Celtic T-shirt. In the "defiant" act, the fan may hold to an entrenched psychic "sense of place" that is physically at odds with his or her life situation. In this application, sports uni-communication is used as a mechanism to reach out to fans in similar straits.

Sports uni-communication signals both affiliation with the team-group and the fan-group, and indicates being part of the larger "team effort" of both. More importantly, to unacquainted individuals, sports uni-communication signals the increased likelihood that attempted communication would be therapeutic. With fanship as common ground, a larger relationship may build from the empathy, trust, honesty, and validation that tend to characterize the communication of sport. Because of this, and because it serves as a signpost of community, sports uni- communication is essential to finding a "sense of place" in today's world.

DISCUSSION

The arguments presented in this essay establish the fan's experiences with mediated sport as a therapeutic communication activity. The case that can be made for the therapeutic benefits of mediated sport point to the range of communicative activities that may hold therapeutic potential. The potent therapeutic attributes of mediated sports arise jointly out its fundamental character as play, and its larger role as social adhesive within American culture. The social communication of sport brings people together into a sports community where empathy, trust, honesty, validation, and ultimately caring, are communicative norms.

Certainly sports fans are not typically seeking help when entering the mediated sportsworld. They are not patients or clients, nor are announcers or sportswriters therapists. The therapeutic value arises largely out of structural conditions that add to the complex flavor of engagement. Here, mediated sports may have therapeutic value without being therapy, and it may offer nutrients without tasting bad. Engagement in mediated sports takes place amidst such apparent contradictions. A series of dialectically opposed tensions allow the fan to play in a cultural rose garden whose fragrances overwhelm the prickly scratches left by thorns. These tensions, some of which are briefly discussed below, raise questions about how "functional" private uses of mediated therapeutic communication may be juxtaposed next to and aid in social control.

RITUALISTIC AND PURPOSIVE BEHAVIOR

As viewed from outside, engagement in mediated sport may be seen as a purely ritualistic exercise. However, the fan may view the activity differently, and hold to justifying the activity as being purposive. After all, in the scope of what is valued in American culture, one *does* have to keep up with the latest sporting developments and keep an eye on how one's team fares in the "big game." An uneasy tension exists for the fan. The experience is pleasurable, yet at the same time, it calls out to be justified. And as justification may be difficult, the fan is fortunate that there is external validation for the activity within culture that allows for the activity to be thought of as "purposive." However, the larger "purpose" being served by therapeutic engagement in mediated sports is that there are greater understandings of the cultural ground rules, and those understandings "help" integrate one into the culture as it is presently constituted. That therapeutic engagement in mediated sport may be plagued by this "conservative bias" is consistently supported by research looking at the relationship of sport to political and cultural values (cf. Jhally, 1984; Hoch, 1972; Prisuta, 1979; Real, 1975).

DISENGAGEMENT AND AROUSAL

Related to the tension between ritualistic and purposive behavior is another between disengagement and arousal. Much has been made in the research literature about mediated sport serving as a stimulant for aggressive urges (Bryant & Zillmann, 1983). At the same time, much of the therapeutic value of mediated sport is derived from disengaging oneself from the realities of daily life. While catharsis may not come about, the pleasures of play leave therapeutic residue as they extend to social communication and make it more satisfying. Because pleasures associated with arousal and stimulation in engagement in mediated sports are later socially sanctified, disengaging from daily life toward those ends becomes more acceptable, and for some, desirable. Certainly, many of the theories of television viewing (Smith, 1986) suggest that "opponent processes" explain addictive behavior. In the case of the television sports addict, the social value of sport leads to a "functional addiction." However, culturally, addictions of any sort do not tamper with the social structure and those who wield power within it.

COMPETENCE AND CONSEQUENCE

Much of the therapeutic value of mediated sports is related to developing communicative competencies that may enrich future communication activities. In the course of developing these sports competencies, one invests in a "sense of place" that is dominated by sports values. Thus, any corresponding rise in self-esteem that allows for "therapeutic" integration into the sports community are tied to confirming these values. As Jhally (1984) points out: "Sports are an explicit celebration of the *idealized* structures of reality—a form of capitalist realism. They mediate a vital social dialectic, providing both an escape from the alienated conditions of everyday life and a *socialization* into these very same structures" (p. 51). Thus, the "consequences" of "therapeutically using" mediated sport to solve "problems" are that the "learned" competencies tend to reify those values from which "problems" tend to arise. Because of this dialectic, the private therapeutic functionality of sports competence has social control as its main cultural consequence.

OUTSIDE AND INSIDE

Mediated sports provides a way to mix with the outside world. Cozens and Stumpf (1953) have suggested that "rubbing elbows" with spectators in a stadium fosters "understandings across class lines." Watching a game on television allows for "social integration" of a different, more limited sort (cf. Wenner, 1989). Instead of encountering a wide range of classes, parasocial relationships are limited largely to those with sportscasters and players, both of which qualify as celebrities in American life. We may have brought the outside inside, and clearly we still cross class lines, but the empathies that develop are pleasurably restricted to a rather elite group of media personalities. The economic base of media tends to insure that those anointed with media fame pose little threat to social control. Parasocial experiences reinforce this. They may be therapeutic, but in the process of developing empathies with a limited "ruling" class, they also limit empathetic understandings with a wider range of classes not empowered by media.

MEN AND WOMEN

The empathies that develop are characterized by gender valuation as well. Mediated sport is a bastion of male culture. Thus, much of the "community" that builds around therapeutic engagement in mediated sport is male-dominated (cf. Morse, 1983). Not surprisingly, the relative exclusion of women from this culture, or their lack of interest in it, has fueled tensions between the sexes (Gantz, 1985; Morse, 1983). The heightened social valuation that sport receives signifies the values of male culture as dominant. For example, the sports pages provide a socially sanctioned gossip sheet for men in America, a place where a great deal of conjecture may be legitimately placed upon "heroes" and events of little worldly import. "Chit-chat" about sports is a legitimate prelude to a business transaction. However, when one looks closely at the character of content in the sports pages and in talk about sports, it has surprising parallels with the societally devalued "gossip" that appears on society pages and is heard in the beauty salon. The larger point here is that therapeutic values derived from a specific "genre" of mediated communication, such as sports is, may not be gender-neutral. Developing competencies in mediated sports communication may be therapeutic for men but compensatory pathological strategies for women to the degree to which sports culture perpetuates an extant cultural inequity.

CONCLUDING COMMENTS

The case of mediated sport as therapeutic communication serves to illustrate the fundamental dilemmas for the communication scholar making judgments about the "beneficial" outcomes of any form of therapeutic communication. Indeed therapeutic communication may be privately "functional." But herein lies a more perplexing problem, and one that media gratifications researchers who have become sensitive to the cultural consequences of media use are regularly confronted with (cf. McQuail, 1984, 1985; Wenner, 1985a, 1985b).

In assessing that there is a "need" for therapeutic communication, one makes an assumption about extant "dysfunctions." The goal becomes some sort of "equilibrium," and the "growth" that comes out of therapeutic engagement is perceived as having value only to the degree that It serves the individual in functioning within the confines of social and cultural norms. In other words, therapeutic communication is fraught with the same tautological dilemmas that tend to plague media gratifications research. If not viewed within a cultural perspective, therapeutic communication as an enterprise, and our evaluation of it as communication scientists, risks being held hostage by the status quo. If mediated therapeutic communication aims at a "healthy wholeness" at the individual level, we correspondingly need to answer questions about "healthiness" to whom, and how "wholeness" is culturally determined.

In the end it is therapists who evaluate whether "therapeutic" communication is taking place, and whether the outcome of therapy is "successful." Communication scientists looking at mediated therapeutic communication place themselves in a similar role. Culturally, that is a powerful position, and we must ask ourselves questions about whose power we may be implicitly endorsing and how we may be unwittingly contributing to maintaining that power. If broached in these terms, the questions we ask about "therapeutic" communication will be fruitful. If not, our answers most certainly will be doomed to perpetuating a view of "therapeutic" that is at one with the controlling interests in society. We will be doing our own little part in maintaining cultural hegemony.

REFERENCES

Avery, R. K., & Ellis, D. G. (1979). Talk radio as an interpersonal phenomenon. In G. Gumpert & R. Cathcart (Eds.), *Inter/media: Interpersonal communication in a media world* (pp. 108–116). New York: Oxford.

Bandura, A. (1969). *Principles of behavior modification.* New York: Holt, Rinehart, & Winston.

Bandura, A. (Ed.). (1971). *Psychological modeling: Conflicting theories.* Chicago: Aldine.

Beiser, A. R. (1967). *The madness in sports.* New York: Appleton-Century-Crofts.

Bormann, E. G. (1972). Fantasy and rhetorical vision: The rhetorical criticism of social reality. *Quarterly Journal of Speech, 58,* 396–407.

Bostrom, R. N. (Ed.). (1984). *Competence in communication.* Beverly Hills, CA: Sage.

Bryant, J., & Zillmann, D. (1983). Sports violence and the media. In J. H. Goldstein (Ed.), *Sports Violence* (pp. 195–211). New York: Springer-Verlag.

Callois, R. (1961). *Man, play, and games.* New York: Free Press.

Carey, J. W. (1975). A cultural approach to communication. *Communication, 2,* 1–22.

Carey, J. W. (1977). Mass communication research and cultural studies: An American view. In J. Curran, M. Gurevitch, & J. Woolacott (Eds.), *Mass communication and society* (pp. 409–425). Beverly Hills, CA: Sage.

Cathcart, R., & Gumpert, G. (1983). Mediated interpersonal communication: Toward a new typology. *Quarterly Journal of Speech, 69,* 267–277.

Cialdini, R. R., Borden, R. J., Thorne, A., Walker, M. R., Freeman, S., & Sloan, L. R. (1976). Basking in reflected glory: Three (football) field studies. *Journal of Personality and Social Psychology, 34(3),* 366–375.

Cozens, F., & Stumpf, F. (1953). *Sports in American life.* Chicago: University of Chicago Press.

Dewey, J. (1925). *Experience and nature.* Chicago: Open Court.

Edwards, H. (1973). *Sociology of sport.* Homewood, IL: Dorsey.

Gantz, W. (1985). Exploring the role of television in married life. *Journal of Broadcasting & Electronic Media, 29,* 65–78.

Greendorfer, S. L. (1983, July). Sport and the mass media: General overview. *Arena Review, 7,* 1–6.

Gumpert, G. (1987). *Talking tombstones and other tales of the media age.* New York: Oxford.

Gumpert, G. (1975). The rise of uni-comm. *Today's Speech, 23,* 34–38.

Guttmann, A. (1986). *Sports spectators.* New York: Columbia University Press.

Harris, D. V. (1973). *Involvement in sport: A somatopsychic rationale for physical activity.* Philadelphia: Lea & Febiger.

Hirdt, P. (1986, May). How to draft your dream team. *Sport, 77,* 79–80.

Hoch, P. (1972). *Rip off the old game.* New York: Doubleday.

Horton, D., & Wohl, R. R. (1956). Mass communication and para-social interaction. *Psychiatry, 19,* 215–229.

Huizinga, J. (1938). *Homo ludens.* Boston: Beacon Press.

Jhally, S. (1984). The spectacle of accumulation: Material and cultural factors in the evolution of the sports/media complex. *The Insurgent Sociologist, 12,* 41–57.

Johnson, W. O. (1971). *Super spectator and the electric Lilliputians.* Boston: Little, Brown.

Kreps, G., & Thornton, B. C. (1984). *Health communication: Theory and practice.* New York: Longman.

Lever, J. (1983). *Soccer madness.* Chicago: University of Chicago Press.

Lipsyte, R. (1975). *SportsWorld: An American dreamland.* New York: Quadrangle.

Lull, J. (1980). The social uses of television. *Human Communication Research, 6,* 197–209.

McQuail, D. (1985). Gratifications research and media theory: Many models or one? In K. E. Rosengren, L. A. Wenner, & P. Palmgreen (Eds.), *Media gratifications research: Current perspectives* (pp. 149–167). Beverly Hills, CA: Sage.

McQuail, D. (1984). With the benefit of hindsight: The uses and gratifications research tradition. *Critical Studies in Mass Communication, 1,* 177–193.

Meyrowitz, J. (1985). *No sense of place: The impact of electronic media on social behavior.* New York: Oxford.

Morse, M. (1983). Sport on television: Replay and display. In E. A. Kaplan (Ed.), *Regarding television: Critical approaches—an anthology* (pp. 44–66). Frederick, MD: University Publications of America.

Novak, M. (1976). *The joy of sports.* New York: Basic Books.

Prisuta, R. H. (1979). Televised sports and political values. *Journal of Communication, 29,* 94–102.

Real, M. R. (1975, Winter). Super Bowl: Mythic spectacle. *Journal of Communication, 25,* 31–43.

Roberts, D. L., & Bachen, C. M. (1981). Mass communication effects. *Annual Review of Psychology, 32,* 307–356.

Rogers, C. (1961). *On becoming a person.* Boston: Houghton Mifflin.

Rogers, C. (1957). The necessary and sufficient conditions of psychotherapeutic change. *Journal of Consulting Psychology, 21,* 95–103.

Shimanoff, S. B. (1980). *Communication rules: Theory and research.* Beverly Hills, CA: Sage.

Sloan, L. R. (1979). The function and impact of sports for fans: A review of theory and contemporary research. In J. H. Goldstein (Ed.), *Sports, games, and play: Social and psychological viewpoints* (pp. 219–262). Hillsdale, NJ: Erlbaum.

Smith, R. (1986). Television addiction. In J. Bryant & D. Zillmann (Eds.), *Perspectives on media effects* (pp. 109–128). Hillsdale, NJ: Erlbaum.

Stephenson, W. (1967). *The play theory of mass communication.* Chicago: University of Chicago Press.

Stone, G. P. (1969). American sports: Play and dis-play. In G. S. Kenyon (Ed.), *Aspects of contemporary sport sociology.* Chicago: Athletic Institute.

Watzlawick, P., Beavin, J., & Jackson, D. (1967). *Pragmatics of human communication.* New York: Norton.

Webber, M. M. (1964). *Explorations into urban structure.* Philadelphia: University of Pennsylvania Press.

Wenner, L. A. (1985a). Transaction and media gratifications research. In K. E. Rosengren, L. A. Wenner, & P. Palmgreen (Eds.), *Media gratifications research: Current perspectives* (pp. 73–94). Beverly Hills, CA: Sage.

Wenner, L. A. (1985b). The nature of news gratifications. In K. E. Rosengren, L. A. Wenner, & P. Palmgreen (Eds.), *Media gratifications research: Current perspectives* (pp. 171–193). Beverly Hills, CA: Sage.

Wenner, L. A. (Ed.). (1989). *Media, sport, and society: Research on the communication of sport.* Newbury Park, CA: Sage.

Zillmann, D., Bryant, J., & Sapolsky, B. S. (1979). The enjoyment of watching sports contests. In J. H. Goldstein (Ed.), *Sports, games, and play: Social and psychological viewpoints* (pp. 297–335). Hillsdale, NJ: Erlbaum.

Author Index

Subject Index

nonevaluative, 18
permissiveness, 18
therapist-patient compatibility, 21–22
dissimilarity, 21–22
genuine, 22
rapport, 22
similarity, 21–22
Therapy, 217, 221; *see also* Process, therapeutic
class bias of, 215
on-air, 205–207, 209, 211
Traditionalism, 219
Transactional analysis, 214
Trust, 33–34, 36, 38
Truth, 34
objective, 34
subjective, 34
Two-way radio, *see* Talk radio
Typology, 41, 52

U
Unconditional positive regard, 35
Uni-communication, 44, 49–51
defined, 49
sports, 237–238

V
Validation, 33, 35, 36, 38
Visual stimuli, 36
Volunteers, 201–205
Vulnerability, 35

W
Written communication, 44–45

Z
Zimbalist, Ephrem, 216